She-Calf

and Other Quechua Folk Tales

She-Calf

and Other Quechua Folk Tales

Compiled, Translated, and Edited by

Johnny Payne

UNIVERSITY OF NEW MEXICO PRESS

Albuquerque

Library of Congress Cataloging-in-Publication Data

She-calf and other Quechua folk tales / compiled,
translated, and edited by Johnny Payne.
    p. cm.
English and Quechua
ISBN 0-8263-2195-X (pbk.: alk. paper)
1. Quechua Indians—Folklore.   2. Tales—Peru.
3. Quechua language—Texts.   I. Payne, Johnny,
1958–

F3429.3.F6 S47 2000
398.2'089'98323085 21—dc21   99-043530

A Spanish/Quechua edition appeared as *Cuentos
Cusqueños* published by the Centro de estudios rurales
andinos "Bartolomé de las Casas" (Cusco, Peru 1984;
revised © 1999). The Quechua text from the revised
edition is reproduced in this book with the permission
and cooperation of the Centro de estudios rurales
andinos and its editor Sr. Andrés Chirinos.

Contents

An Interloper's Introduction

The fascination of the ethnographer, in some respects, is not unlike that of the indigenous dweller who sits listening to the story or oral history being told. In Quechua folk tales, the narrative act has its own special verb tense, -sqa, suggesting that this encounter grants freedoms beyond the everyday, and, at the same time, requires strict observance of injunctions and prohibitions. The listener exists in this sphere as something like that vulnerable young child who is bathed with scented soap, anointed with perfume, and placed in a spanking-new bed with candies and sweetmeats, to await the nocturnal visit of a magical calf. The child, attracted and fearful all at once, doesn't have any choice but to give himself over to what is about to happen. However keen his expectation and desire, there are specific limits on what he may or may not do or say. If he allows himself to believe that he is fully in control of his destiny, then he understands nothing about the world of magic. The act of initiation, the rite of passage, once it is embarked on, has little to do with one's own free will. The encounter between child and she-calf, told by Quechua storyteller Teodora Paliza, goes like this:

> At midnight, she heard the lament from the street corner, making its way toward the front door. "Aaaaaaahhh!" The she-calf opened the door slowly, and crept into the room. Beautiful candles were burning. She sniffed all that had been prepared, just a whiff. When she was done, she approached the boy's bed. And with a whoosh! she

slipped out of her calfskin. When she had slipped out of it, she climbed up on one corner of the bed.

It is not always easy to say precisely wherein the seduction lies, who is the agent, who the object. In this case, the child is enjoined to spend much of his young life pursuing the elusive object of his love as she metamorphoses. When he comes upon her at last, hidden inside the body of a goat, he cuts open the goat only to find a cat, and within the cat, a guinea pig, and within the guinea pig, a white dove. The notion that the traditional "objects of study" regularly assent to a passive, one-way correspondence is erroneous. They may steadily retreat before one, coyly or in earnest. A subset of society has its own motives for becoming permeable, and even when it consents, it may set precise limits on the integration and penetration it allows—this far and no further. A populace may have reasons, and not necessarily naive ones either, for not only consenting to, but even soliciting the presence of an outsider.

My first experience with the village of San Jerónimo came about when three of its prominent citizens invited me there, after happening upon me and asking me to translate into English a phone call to Los Angeles regarding the purchase of some buses for a transport cooperative they wished to inaugurate. In search of a greater autonomy, they availed themselves of the services of a *forastero*. That word, borrowed from Spanish, is a multivalent and ambiguous term used by Quechuas to refer to outsiders. It translates as "foreigner," outsider," "interloper," but also as "sojourner" and "pilgrim." It is difficult to predict, on any given occasion, its exact connotations. To thank me for my help, the San Jeronimians invited me to participate in a strenuous ritual hike around the borders of their community, where we drank cane liquor from a flute, and they piled stones along the boundaries of their lands to mark out what they owned, on account of past disputes with neighboring indigenous communities.

A few weeks later they confessed to me that on the day of the hike, they'd brought along a first-aid kit because they assumed I would pass out at some point during the walk. A certain form of machismo—the ability to tough it out—is highly regarded in the Southern Andes, and although I hadn't known about the first-aid kit, I realized at the very moment I was climbing those hills that I was being put to a test of manhood, egged on by men who had an amused and lively expectation of my failure. When I didn't succumb to exhaustion, they were nonetheless pleased, but now in a different way, one that seemed to ask for a continuation of our relationship.

Miguel Wamán, one of the peasant farmers who I would come to know extremely well, tells just such a story. The daughter of the hacienda owner, after her father dies, announces that she'll marry the man who accompanies her no matter where she goes. "Wherever I go, you must follow me…Whatever I eat, we'll eat together." Two rich suitors accept her offer, and she takes them one by one to the graveyard at the edge of town. When she's on the point of opening the gate to the graveyard, each of the suitors runs away screaming. Finally, the poor son of the hacienda caretaker takes her up on her dare, and stays beside her while she opens the gate with her key.

> Creeeak! It opened. He was at her side, and didn't let go of her. That little tiny key was right in her purse, that little bitty key was the key to the niche, just small. And with that, she opened the little iron gate covering the funerary niche.
>
> After she opened it, she pulled out a big platter of roast lamb. That's what she took out. Crack! She gave the young man a big old chunk of it, right into his hands. He took the whole thing right into his hands. The girl began to eat. The boy also ate his fill with gusto. Because, well, it was good meat, lamb. In the morning, they went back to the village. Right away, they married.

Miguel Wamán ends the tale by saying that through trials like those "That's how you find out about a man's weakness."

After the hike, the men invited my wife and me to eat succulent roast guinea pig, a delicacy in Andean cooking, along with corn on the cob, goat cheese, stuffed red hot chili peppers, bread, and potatoes in peanut sauce. As we sat among them at a long table, plates heaped with food and warm, spicy liqueurs, home brewed, being plentifully served, the liquor hummed in my head, freeing up a tongue that had gotten tied by the constant, abstract study of the Quechua language. I might, at that moment, if I'd known Miguel's tale, have nursed the ephemeral, drunken, and false feeling of being the boy who won the hacienda owner's daughter by dint of his perseverance. But I had yet to collect even my first folk tale.

Within a short time, I had moved into that village, San Jerónimo, to partake of a reality that turned out to be less heroic, and more monotonous than the kinds of intoxicated fantasies permitted within folk tales. I spent several weeks just hanging out. I helped some of the village's Indians dig wells and plant corn. I drank horrible, rancid *chicha*.

I paid black market prices to the crafty corner merchant to buy my daily newspaper-rolled packet of oatmeal, and most of all I waited, with obligatory patience, for circumstances to conspire so that I could collect on cassette tape my first folk tale, or even a measly riddle. Many people treated Miriam and me with courtesy, even with warmth, but the folkloristic occasion I awaited continued to evade me. I caught cold every two weeks from bathing in the freezing water of a garden hose, which made steam form around my shivering body like the numina that were supposed to leap from the mouths of those unlucky people who happened upon wandering condemned souls on mountain paths. I began to realize why the Quechua Indians divided their diseases into hot ones and cold ones. When I wasn't in bed with a cold, I accompanied the subsistence farmers out to their acreage, watched them, and once in a while joined in their labors. To tell the truth, I wasn't much real help during the sojourns in the fields, but they allowed me to offer those symbolic gestures as evidence of my ineptitude in questions of agriculture, and of my goodwill in questions of friendship.

They teased me ferociously, in a Quechua dialect that I still only halfway understood. They asked, when they saw me cooking and handwashing my clothes in a rented room, whether maybe I hadn't eaten too many sweets as a child. The women were just as intractable on this point as the men. When they found out that my wife and I didn't have children, they took to referring to her in half-serious jest as *mula*—a mule, that hybrid animal that can't produce offspring, and one of the gravest insults that can be laid upon a woman in Quechua culture. Rumors circulated that we were cocaine heads, the kind one always saw hanging out on Procuradores Street in Cusco, because after all, nobody could figure out where the money came from that we lived off of, and the words "grant" or "scholarship" didn't have any convincing meaning for them. The peasant farmers looked down on the so-called "international hippies" of Gringo Street with the strongest possible disdain, and just as I couldn't help clinging to vestiges of my preconceptions about them, they, for their part, couldn't give up completely the folklorisms in their attitude toward me. Several of them remained convinced that I possessed secret riches, and once, several of them visited me to propose a joint venture that had something to do with a metal detector. In that scheme, they had themselves marked out as the brains, and me marked out as the venture capitalist.

Even after the ritual hike, despite Miriam's and my warm reception, and despite general agreement among our dinner hosts that our liv-

4

ing in San Jerónimo would be a good thing, there had been no guarantee that we would be able to find an actual place to live within the town. Our limited resources precluded our having an entire house to ourselves, even if we could have found one, and families were not used to housing anyone besides their relatives within their walls. After some uncomfortable searching on our part, a mestizo named Braulio Rojas agreed to rent us an upstairs room in a house that he was in turn renting from an absentee landlord, with the provision that if the landlord showed up, we had to pretend to be visiting. He had already rented out another room, on similar terms, to an elderly widower who I'd seen in the courtyard pressing his clothes with an iron fueled by dry corn cobs, and he didn't want the landlord to know he was deriving income by subletting.

It is no accident that Braulio, who worked as a tour guide in Cusco, was the one to finally take us in. Though he spoke Quechua fluently, and was involved in the life of the village, he thought of himself as upwardly mobile and progressive, and was always hustling, hiring out the new car he owned as a taxi in Cusco, the one he guarded from theft at night by having his housegirl sleep in it every night. Braulio left nothing to chance, and he managed to derive both income and prestige from our presence in his house. When the end of September came, he turned out, appropriately, to be one of the dancers during the celebration of the village's patron saint, in the spectacular folk dance Los Majeños, decked out in leather boots with spurs, riding breeches, colored long-sleeved shirt, leather jacket, wide leather belt, straw hat, scarves, and a grotesque mask with a long nose and an exaggerated mole.

The dance Los Majeños had been reintroduced into the village repertoire only two years before my arrival there, after a hiatus of more than twenty years. The fact that San Jerónimo was located within a transitional zone that had started to become urban during that period because of its proximity to Cusco, had much to do with the reprise of the dance, and with the particular quality of my acceptance within the town. Los Majeños is a dance favored and introduced by the mestizos, who hold more economic power and influence and are higher in the social hierarchy than the peasant farmers. The dance is seen by them as more elegant than more traditional village dances such as the *diablada* or devil-dance, and is a hybrid representation of the mule-drivers and hacienda owners from republican times, with more modern innovations such as the costly leather jacket. Zoila Mendoza Walker, in her study of the majeños dance in San Jerónimo, surmises that

The persons who revived the dance *krewe Los Majeños* during the seventies found in the personification of the mule-driver of Majes and the hacienda owner, figures out of an immediate past, a way of defining their own identity in a context in which social and ethnic categories were passing through an accelerated moment of redefinition. Within the dance the dancers define dichotomies such as White/Indian, master/servant, and concepts such as masculinity, economic power and social prestige, trying to delineate their own identity. Ever since the new groups decided to reinstitute the *majeño* dance, their members have begun to select and idealize certain characteristics of those characters from another time and place, combining them with some of their own, in an effort to define themselves as being as similar as possible—in their time and in their village—to those idealized characters.*

The same outside presences who are frequently pilloried and mercilessly satirized in folk tales, jokes, and certain other of the folk dances, are also objects of emulation, who, through stylization and selective innovation, serve to lend a borrowed prestige to those who are somewhat tenuous about their own recently acquired "superior" status within the community. Braulio's motives in housing us were decidedly not self-effacing or naive, and our sojourn in the village immediately became part of the ongoing cultural negotiation of the San Jeronimians as they struggled with the dialectic of tradition and innovation, going so far as to reinvent traditions that had been abandoned.

Our acceptance by townspeople such as Braulio, by the socialist mayor's administrative assistant (himself an outsider from the jungle town of Quillabamba), and by the entrepreneurial, politically active "progressives" who had first invited us there, in some ways made my acceptance by the campesinos more difficult, because of my guilt by association with the *arrivistes*. But at last, the man who would become one of my most prolific and genial storytellers, Miguel Wamán, a campesino, invited me to his house for a meal. That night we drank a lot of beer and aguardiente, and with his wife and ten-year-old daughter tucked beneath the covers, and me seated at the foot of the bed, Miguel began to tell me riddles, one after another. He spoke to me of his parents, who had died a long time ago, and began to sing in his perma-

*Zoila Mendoza-Walker, "La comparsa *los majeños:* poder, prestigio y masculinidad," *Música, danzas, y máscaras en los Andes*, Ed. Raul R. Romero (Lima: Instituto Riva-Agüero, 1993), 111.

nently hoarse voice a song about an orphan: *Noqa pobreqa, mana tay-tayoq, wakchaschallay, mana piniyoq, wakchaschallay.*

The words mean: I'm a poor wayfarer, I don't have a father or mother, I'm a poor soul, I don't have anyone. The figure of the orphan crops up with frequency in Quechua songs, perhaps for good reason. The fact that Miguel became sentimental, especially when he'd been drinking, doesn't negate the truth of his self-representation. In spite of the fifty years difference in Miguel's age and mine, and even more pronounced differences in culture and class between us, we became close within a short time. The other peasant farmers sometimes jeered at him when they saw us walking in the street together every day. The general feeling was that Miguel was allowing too much leeway to the forastero, beyond the tacit limits agreed upon within the campesino community. The implication, on the part of certain members of a sub-sistence population that had an understandable propensity for being suspicious, was that Miguel was somehow about to be made a dupe. The fact that my presence became an issue of dispute was evidence of the fissures and tensions that already existed within San Jerónimo and its adjacent cooperative, Chimpawaylla.

Miguel had worked hard through the years—first as a bricklayer, later as a worker in the Cusco Brewery, and finally as a subsistence farmer, after Velasco's agrarian reform. He was in his seventies, and took an earthy, slightly swaggering pride in the fact that he had fathered a child in his sixties. "We have a strong seed," he once told me. At the time, I chuckled to myself at his macho boastfulness. But given the course of political events during the eighties and nineties, the genocidal cam-paign that both Shining Path and the governmental counterinsurgency became engaged in, killing or dislocating thousands of Quechua In-dians, I've since thought more than once about that remark about pro-creation in a different light.

Despite his ambitions and his pride, Miguel definitely wasn't what is referred to in the Southern Andes as *ambicioso* or "avaricious"—another strongly pejorative and normative term in the Southern Andean social context, as damning in its own way as *mula*. As is the case in most An-dean communities, one of the highest honors one can achieve is ac-cepting the crushing burden of becoming the patron or sponsor of the village's religious feast days, a responsibility that can easily put one into debt for life. And those who succeed financially in the world are ex-pected to selectively share that wealth if they are to maintain their standing within the community. Miguel, though, for all his traditionalism, didn't worry too much about how others saw him, and he didn't care about gossip. He was at an age where he more or less did as he pleased. A skeptic in religious matters who liked to tell dirty jokes about priests and nuns, freely mixing his spoken Quechua and Spanish, and capable of adapting to the demands of new situations with a surprising lack of resistance, he all the same felt very secure in his identity as a Quechua Indian, didn't need to have it ratified at every turn, and thus was amused and slightly annoyed at the caution of his neighbors.

If I say that he was content with his lot, I don't mean to suggest he accepted the position of being socially cast aside that he'd inherited. But he didn't foster illusions either, and he didn't have a stingy disposition. He was building a second adobe house—of sorts—brick by brick, in his spare time, and sometimes he woke me before daybreak to go make adobes with him. At the same time, he was in the habit of working in *ayni*—helping others build their houses in exchange for their help on his, something like the concept of a barn-raising. The peasant farmers had divvied up among themselves, in private parcels, the majority of the rocky, miserable, sloping lands they'd been handed over during the agrarian reform, and Miguel, like the rest, spent most of his time tending his own parcel. But he also worked in the so-called cooperative farmland—the parcel down in the valley that was held in common. He farmed it with good cheer, and ungrudgingly, but also without participating in the dubious fantasy that the modest, supposedly anti-capitalist cooperative was the first step toward some kind of Quechua, socialist, neo-Incan empire. If they had a good crop, he might make a little extra money at market. That was the most he expected.

In certain important regards, Miguel lived strictly by the precepts set down by the folklore of the Southern Andes. As I say, he wasn't avaricious. When I think of him, I always think of the woodsman in the folk tale "The River-Siren," a story told to me by Miguel. A poor woodsman, who supports his family by cutting wood, possesses nothing in the world except his small axe. One day the axe falls into the Vilcanota River, and when he begins to lament its loss, a river-siren comes up out of the water. She shows him two axes, one made of silver and one of gold, but he answers that neither of them is his. She retreats once more into the water, and returns holding aloft the woodcutter's own little axe. "Is this your axe?" she asks him. At that moment, says Miguel,

Ay, tususpa yaqaraq wañurun! "*Hachachaymi, hachachaymi mamita!*"
"Kayqa respondesuyki, mana ambisiosuchu kasqanki. Respon-

desuyki kay qori hachachapuwan, kay qolqe hachapuwan, kay hachachaykipuwan."

In English, we'd say:

Oh, the wood-cutter almost fell down dead dancing for joy! "My little axe, my little axe, river-siren!"
"This is your reward for not being avaricious. I'm giving you this gold axe, this silver axe, and your own axe."

But this tale of sudden riches doesn't permit too many illusions either. It ends by telling how the woodcutter's relatives, who covet his fortune, serve him dog meat to annoy him. One day, when I'd returned to San Jerónimo after having travelled to Bolivia for a week, Miguel informed me that the various participants in the cooperative Chimpawaylla had had a terrible fight on account of some complaints about how the private parcels had been divided up. He hadn't participated in that fight, but he related with sadness and bitterness how his fellow peasant farmers had begun throwing stones at each other, and several people had ended up wounded.

In spite of his temperamental sweetness, Miguel nonetheless had the spark of sly mischief and hard teasing that is part of the essential makeup of the Quechua psyche. That's why one day he too decided, when I least expected it, to pull the gringo interloper's leg. When we went to visit the grave site of his mother, Miguel offered me, as refreshment, a bottle of the salty holy water that the Catholic church sells on the Day of the Dead. Without knowing what it was, I took a long drink, and when I made a horrible face and spat a mouthful of the salty water onto the ground where his mother had been laid to rest, Miguel burst out laughing, and shouted "Priest piss!"

Not long after this practical joke, another form of participation in the collective life of the village presented itself. A couple in San Jerónimo who were going to be married, although they were no older than us, invited my wife and me to be the godparents at their wedding. The wedding ceremony was read by an ancient, monotonous, serious priest even skinnier than the Jesus he served. At the end of the wedding ceremony, the newlywed couple baptized their baby in the fountain of the chapel, because everyone around those parts knows what can happen to the fruit of sexual relations that haven't been consecrated. Teodora Paliza tells the story of an infant born as the result of incest, after a young girl is raped by her father. The mother, without knowing the seriousness of the sin, tries a remedy that is orthodox in religious terms, but it turns out to be too little too late to compensate for the violation of the incest taboo.

"What am I going to do with this little slut? Who is the father? Tell me." The mother questioned her and gave her hard slaps. But the girl didn't talk.

The baby was crying horribly. "Anh, anh, anh, anh, anh."

"What is he crying about? Oh, he needs to be baptized. Let's run and get him baptized," said the mother. The girl's mother bundled him up in diapers, a hat, put a shirt on him and carried him off. The baby was crying. They were crossing the threshold of the church.

Right then, the baby died.

Fortunately, nothing of the kind happened during the happy ritual Miriam and I participated in. The beautiful, placid child was held over the baptismal font, and we hurried on to the house of the bride's parents, where we partook in a bacchanal of food, drink, and music, which lasted for two solid days without stopping. The plates were heaped with boiled yucca, roast guinea pig and lamb, toasted corn, and goat cheese that we, as godparents, were served and expected to eat. The two newlyweds danced first, as a slightly disreputable and off-key band played. Then I danced with the bride, and Miriam danced with the groom. Then she danced with the bride's father, and I with the bride's mother. And so on. There was no roof over the yard where we enjoyed ourselves beneath the stars. It had rained buckets during the day, turning the entire yard into one big mud slick, and while we danced *waynos* and *rompetablas*, and while the local peasant women, seizing hold of their dance handkerchiefs, did their best to throw me to the ground, the deep mud flew everywhere from beneath our heels, covering saints and sinners alike with slime and indignity.

If this really were a folk tale, instead of a reckoning, I'd gladly leave myself there beneath the stars, splattering the earth of San Jerónimo over my own body and those of the human beings surrounding me. I would at last be integrated into the Andean world, united with the earth, the cosmos, and the underworld, the *ukhu pacha*, the *kay pacha*, and the *hanaq pacha*. In fact, Quechua folk tales often end with a wedding, and the narrator winks slyly at the listener, saying "I was there at the wedding myself, and I was going to bring you a plateful of delicious leftover lamb. But some mean stray dogs followed me, and took it away." I was, and am, however, a forastero, and was never allowed to forget that fact for long.

Indeed, it must be said that one of the reasons the groom, Reiser Arévalo, had sought us out as godparents is because he himself had not been born in the area, and had met his wife-to-be, Dora, by coming to the experimental agricultural station K'ayra, just outside San Jerónimo, to work on a forestry project. Like myself, though to a much lesser extent, and in a much more restricted sense, Reiser too was a forastero. When I went home to sleep for a few hours, and returned to the house of the bride's parents during the second day of the party, he had been forced by his wife's relatives to drink liquor far beyond his tolerance, and I found him hunched in the corner weeping copiously over the fact that he was so far away from his family, and that none of them had been on hand for his wedding day.

I, the inadequate but indispensable stand-in, did my best to console him. Though in the weeks to follow, Miriam and I adhered to such rituals as bringing the baby a *t'anta wawa*, a whimsical figure baked out of bread, on the specified day, it was evident that the fact of Reiser's own marginal status lessened the symbolic meaning of the act, and after a time it became clear that we were expected as godparents to do very little. By lending Reiser a temporary whiff of the mild exoticism we retained as the foreigners in town, we had gotten him out of a tight spot by allowing him to feel that, even in the absence of his own kin, he had added something to the wedding preparations.

Toward the end of my stay, I moved back into Cusco, and had the good fortune to take a room in the house occupied by a sixty-nine-year-old widow, her daughter, and her grandaughter. The widow, Teodora Paliza, who told me the story about the boy and the maiden calf-human girl who becomes his lover, turned out to be one of the most formidable storytellers I ever met, in that culture or any other. She and I spent long hours sitting in her dark dry-goods store, speaking Quechua, a language that I was finally beginning to handle with a certain amount of ease. Even when she and I spoke together in Spanish, if someone entered the shop to buy something, she would make me switch suddenly into Quechua, just so she could relish the looks of shock on her customers' faces when they saw a rail-thin, bearded gringo drinking an Inka Kola, and holding his own in Quechua, also known as *runasimi*— the language of real people. When they walked out of the shop with their mouths still hanging open, Teodora would go into fits of laughter. That fleeting moment was probably the closest I ever came, in Andean eyes, to becoming a real person, rather than an exotic foreigner with a tape recorder and no visible means of support.

But such moments are rare, and deceptive if they don't acknowledge that when it comes to ethnography, no one is altruistic, and everyone has an agenda. Two stories that were told to me by Miguel Wamán capture the paradox of my stay in San Jerónimo. One is called "The Stupid Gringo," and the other "What the Gringo Ate." These were two stories that he had obviously held back, given their theme, until a moment when we knew one another very well, so that I wouldn't take offense at their content. Just like the joke about priest piss that he played on me at his mother's grave, these jokes were at the same time a way of making fun of me, and a way of confiding in me. They marked out, in the same breath, both the profound intimacy that I had achieved with him, and the insurmountable and necessary limits between natives and interlopers, boundaries set up by a fierce history between antagonistic cultures. He told me the story "What the Gringo Ate" one evening after having invited me to a dinner of boiled corn and broad beans heaped steaming on a blanket, while we relaxed in the candlelight of his half-constructed house and rubbed our bellies. The story goes thus:

This gringo was coming along on horseback. A woman was selling breaded frog legs, served up nice and hot. The gringo ate two or three platefuls, all he could eat. "Man, is this delicious!" He got a bellyful! After he'd eaten, he went off on his horse. While he was going along the path, he saw a whole mess of toads heaped up on each other along the riverbanks. The gringo gathered up enough of them to fill his knapsack. Then he arrived at his lodging.

He lit up his camp-stove, breaded the toads with flour. He fried them up and ate them. But after eating them, in the middle of the night, he fell seriously ill. The gringo was in bad shape. When he was at the point of death, he called out to the landlady of the lodging. "Help me ma'am, I'm a goner!"

The landlady said to herself, "Ah, let him leave if he wants to! As long as he covers his lodging bill. He's crazy if he thinks I'm getting out of this bed. I could care less whether he leaves or not."

The gringo called out again. "Help me ma'am, I'm a goner!"

"Who the devil cares? What am I supposed to do about it? I don't care whether he pays me or not."

He called out to her a final time. "Help me ma'am, I'm a goner!"

"Well, then get going, will you?" In the morning, the landlady got out of bed. When she looked outside, the gringo's horse was still there. It turns out that the gringo was dead. The landlady got to keep all his money. She even kept his horse, and there wasn't anybody to claim it for the gringo.

Miguel offered me this story without any additional commentary. He simply let out a belly laugh, and flashed me the smile of a good pal, beneath his lightly ironic eyes. That night, it was his turn to be the ethnographer, and I the dupe. He showed me, in a few words, that the Quechua native, far from being the passive object of outsiders' researches, has for a long time been working out his own analysis of the contact between cultures.

Johnny Payne
Florida Atlantic University
August 1999

The Eagles Who Raised a Child

I was introduced to the grandmotherly but sly Teodora Paliza by a linguist named Joan who had become exasperated with this "informant" who claimed that she didn't know any folk tales to speak of. When I came into the picture, I was only looking for a short-term room to rent in Cusco proper for a couple of months while I transcribed the stories I had already compiled up to that time. Widowed Teodora and her widowed daughter Juana Rosa Callo (see her stories, also in this volume) had a spare room to let in their little house in Barrio Magisterio. Apart from the spiders who crept down into my room at night from a crack in the ceiling, the place was pleasant, and both women had engaging personalities. When Teodora discovered that I was transcribing folk tales, she offered to tell me, unbidden, some stories and riddles in Quechua. When I expressed my utter surprise that she knew any, since I had pointedly been told by Joan that Teodora was fresh out, she laughed and said sure, she knew lots, only she didn't want to tell them to a dictionary. Joan's chief interest, as she had explained honestly to Teodora, was in looking for variants and possible new definitions of Quechua-language words, and she had exhausted all the available dictionaries. Extracting individual words was the seed, and Joan, well within her professional rights, would afterward cast off the hull, which was the story itself. But Teodora seemed to have a need to tell the story as a story, not as glossary. That's why she had played dumb at first. In this case, the fact that I was "just" looking for a folk tale, without a theoretical motive, was a piece of sheer luck that worked to my advantage. Her response reminded me that for most "informants," as they are often drily called, the story, whatever its other significance, never fails to be an artistic expression. She wanted to entertain me. Teodora's manner of storytelling was quite expressive, punctuated often by laughter, betraying her own clear enjoyment of her onomatopoeic animal noises and her imitations of different types of human voices. The mewing of a crying baby left in a bramble-thicket, or the slapping "ch'aqlan!" of an eagle's wing on an erring adopted child's face are sounds that bring us squarely into the special power of oral tradition. The tales are not only glosses on cultural meaning, but little incantations.

The Eagles Who Raised a Child

Told by Teodora Paliza

There once was a mail carrier. He carried letters, you know, to different villages. Letters to different villages, here and there. One day, as he was going along, along his way, the calf on one leg started to hang heavy. His calf began to grow and grow. So he said "I wonder what's happening to my leg? What's going on here?" Well, even so he kept walking, walking, walking. By now, his calf was really hanging down toward the ground. "What in the heck could this be, by God. It's barely letting me walk." After trying to walk, he finally sat down. Sitting down, he said "What in the heck could this thing here be?" As he started to cut it out with a knife, he said "Could it be pus, or just what is it I have here?" He cut it open. And when he cut it open, there was a baby. "This is disgusting. This is the reason my leg felt so heavy." And he threw the baby out. There was a bramble-thicket. That's right where he threw it. He went off on his way, pounding the path with his feet like crazy. He just kept right on walking along the path. Meanwhile, there was the baby, crying out "Aaahhh, aaahhh, aaahhh." In the middle of the bramble thicket.

An eagle and a she-eagle happened to be flying in circles around that place. They spied the little baby. When they saw the baby, they said "Whatever could it be doing here?"

"Come on, let's carry it off," said the she-eagle.

The eagle answered back, "Let's carry it off." And then, "But however are we going to bring up this baby?"

Wayna Uywaq Aguilakuna

Huk correos kasqa, runa. Hinaspas chay cartata apaq riki llaqtakunaman; chay llaqtakunaman apaq. Hina cartata, sapankaman. Chaypiñataqsi viajasqanpi viajasqanpi hina, ch´upanqa llasayapusqa. Wiñapuchkasqa ch´upan. Hinaspa nin: "¿Imanantaq kay chakitari?" nispa. "¿Imanawantaqri?" nispas nin runaqa riki. Bueno, hinalllas purichkan, purichkan, purichkan. Astawannñas warkukacha-kapuchkan ch´upaqa ankayman, hinata riki. Chaysi nin: "¿Imapunitaq kaypiri kanmanri, carambas? Manaña puriqtawanpas dejapuwanchu", nispas nin. Huk caminasqanpiqa tiyarun riki; tiyaruspas: "¿Imapunitaq kayri kanmanri?" Cuchilluchata urqurakamuspa riki, ñachu, "q´iyachu kaypi kanman; imachu kanmanpas?" Kuchurusqa riki. Kuchuruqtinsi, riki, wawacha. Hinaqtinsi, "kay porqueriallataqmi, kaypaqmi khaynata llasawasqa", nispas, urqurapusqa riki. T´ankar kasqa. Chayman wikch´uyatamun, iq. Chayqa locupaq chakinta churarukuspa, siguipullan. Caminuntaqa purichkan, purichkan. Wawachaqa chaypi: "Iñaw iñaw iñaw" waqakuchkan riki. T´ankar kiskapi.

Hinaspas chayman warmi-qhari aguilakunaqa muyukamuchkasqaku. Chaysi rikurusqaku riki wawachataqa. Wawata rikuspankus "¿Imachataq kayri kanman?" nispas ninku. "Haku apakusunchik", nispas warmiqa nin.

Chaysi riki "Apakusunchik" nispas nin, nin aguilaqa. Hinaspas, "¡Ah!, ¿imanchikwantaq uywasunmanri kay wawatari?" nispas nin.

"Mana. Imaynatapas uywakusunchikpuni. Kay munaychatáq kasqa-

"It's all right. We'll figure out some way to bring it up. It's so beautiful."

So they carried it off. And made her a niche in the cliff. And the niche, you know, was really big. That's where they took the little baby. But the more she grew and grew, the deeper and deeper they had to make the niche. They brought all kinds of things for the child to eat. And so they raised her. The child was doing just fine, getting bigger. Soon enough she learned to walk, and was getting along fine. She was becoming a little lady, a young woman.

The eagles flew all around together getting food to bring to her. They gathered together every kind of food. They really worked hard trying to bring her up. So there she was, getting bigger and bigger, becoming a young woman. As time passed, they brought a little parrot for a playmate. They brought a kitten and other kinds of animals for her to play with. And they made a gate at the entrance so she wouldn't fall down into the river. There inside, their woman-child was getting on, getting on, getting on. The eagles brought the child up with love. On one side her hair was gold. On the other side it was silver. And very carefully they combed it with their beaks, and counted each hair. One by one, they counted and accounted for every single hair.

By this time, the girl had become a young woman. She looked out, and saw the river flowing below her. But there was no way for her to get down. It so happened that the son of a king went there often to that place to bathe. So there he was bathing, you know. And to wash his face, he had to bring the water up close to it, in his cupped hands. When he looked into it, he saw a pretty little face. "What? Can this be my face?" He touched it, like so. It didn't belong to him, though. It wasn't his. It was another's. "Whatever can this be?" he said. He never thought to look high above him.

The next day he went back. He returned to the same place to bathe. And while he was bathing, he saw the same face again. He washed himself, and said to himself, "She's so pretty, so pretty," looking at her face. At last, he looked up above him, and there he saw the girl's pretty face. "Oh, it can't be. I wonder how I can climb up and reach her? I have to find a way to marry her, to marry that girl. How did she get there? Was she enchanted, or what? How did she climb up there?" The ravine was deep. And she was too high up to hear him. She was so high up, she just couldn't hear him.

So he sent to have a folding ladder made, one that would reach that high. And he took the ladder there, and climbed up. There, he asked her, "When is your mother here?"

pas", nispa nin. Aparakapun riki. Hinaspas, t´uqusqanku; hatunchá riki t´uqu karan. Chaypis riki chayman apayun wawachataqa. Pero astawan astawan avanzanku t´uqutaqa, según wawap wiñasqanman hina. Imaymanata apaqku wawapaqqa riki. Hinaspa uywakusqaku. Chayqa ñas wawachaqa allinchaña, allinchaña kachkan. Chayqa ñas puriychatapas yachapunña; ña allinchapuniña wawachaqa riki. Señurachaqa kapuchkan, warmicha.

Hinaspas naq, aguilaqa, iskayninkus pasapuqku riki, mikhunata apaqku. Huñuyamuqkus intirumanta mikhunataqa. Chayqa paykunallachá aknata naspanku, uywaranku imaynata uywarankupas riki. Chaypis riki ñas señorachaña kapuchkan, hatunchaña, hatunchaña. Chaymanñataqsi apamun nachata luruchata pukllakunanpaq. Michichata ima apamun pukllakunanpaq. Chaypi, chaypis riki rejachata hina ruwanku riki, mana mayuman urmayapunanpaq riki. Chay ukupi wawaqa, señorachaqa kachkan allinña, allinchaña, allinchaña. Munasqata uywachkanku nataq wawataqa. Chaysi kay laduchansi quri kasqa; kay laduchantaqsi qullqi. Chayta sumaqta yupaspanku, ñakch´aqku, picunkuwanchá riki. Ch´ulla ch´ullamantas sumaqta yupaspa saqiqku.

Chayqa ña allin jovenña kapun. Qhawarinanpaqsi, mayu pasachkan. Ni imaynata urayunanpaqpas kanchu. Hinaspa chaypiñataqsi, huk reypa wawanqa bañakuq risqa, chay sitiuta. Hinaspas, bañakuchkasqa riki. Bañakunanpaqsi, aknatas unuta. Qhawayuqtinsi chaypi munayllaña uyataqa rikun, ih. "¿Nuqaq uyaychu, imaynataq?" nispas; hinata llamiyukun. Manas hinakachansi. Manas paychu; huksi. "¿Imataq kanmanri?" nispa. Manataqqa altutaqa qawarikunchu.

Hinaspas paqarisnintinqa ripun riki; kaq kutillantaq chay sitiuta bañakuq. Chaysi bañakuqtinqa, kasqallantataq uyataqa rikullantaq. Ñan kikillantaq bañakuchkan. "Munaycha, munaychapuni kayqa", nispa, qhawakachakunsi . . . qhawarusqa. Chaymantas hinata qhawamuchkasqa señorachaqa, bonitallaña. "¡Ay manan! Imayna mudupipas urqusaqpuni, casarakusaqpuni, casarakusaqpuni kay señoritawanqa. ¿Imapitaq chaypiri encantakunchu, imanantaqri?" nispayá nin. "¿Maynintataq wicharanri?" nispayá. Altu qaqapisyari. Chayqa nasi (paldos) manas uyarinchu riki. Altumantataq riki, manasyá uyarinchu. Chaysi nata, escalerata doblanata ruwachimun, hasta chayman aypanankama. Hinaspas na apan escalerataqa. chaysi nin: "¿imay horasta chaypin mamitayki?" nispa nin.

"Tal horata lluqsinku", nispas nin. "Hamunki tal horasta", nispas nin. Chayni chicuqa riki escalerantin wichan riki. Ña pasapusqanku qi-

"They go out at such-and-such a time. You come at such-and-such a time." At that time, the boy climbed up the ladder, you see. They went inside, to the back of the little cave. There, they talked. And the girl was just so pretty. "How did you get here?" he asked her.

"I don't even know who my real parents might be. I never knew my mother or my father. Those eagles are my parents, but they're evil and ugly to me," she said. "They're evil. My father is evil."

"Poor girl," he said.

So they played together, and while they were playing by the window, well, he plucked out a strand of her hair. "Climb down! Get out of here! My parents are coming!" He climbed down as fast as he could, folding up the ladder behind him. And he hid the ladder in the heart of the bramble-thicket, so that he could come back the next day.

Another day came, and there they were again, talking on and on together. The boy took away another strand of her hair. When the eagles counted, another one was missing. Then they said: "Where's your strand of hair? Who took it out?"

"The wind carried it off into the river," she said.

Well, anyway, the very next day, the same thing happened again. The boy took away a strand from the other side, a silver one this time. And of course, in the morning, the eagles were combing with their beaks, combing through. That's how they discovered another hair missing. "Where is this other one of your hairs?" they asked.

"I was playing with my kitten," she said. They pushed the kitten off the cliff. That killed it; them throwing it off, you know. Now there was nobody left to accuse, I mean, if the boy climbed up and stole another strand of hair. So the girl said, "What will I do now?" Then she thought, "I know. We'll get married. I'm going to get all my bridal clothes together. And early in the morning, I'll sneak off."

The boy set the wedding day with his parents. They said "Our child is marrying well. A prince is marrying a beautiful girl." They got everything ready in style. Cleaned up the whole village, decorated it with flowers. They sent the best band out to receive her. "Here comes the bride!" everyone said. All the village heard the news. "The groom's father is doing everything up right!" They travelled way, way out into the countryside. Everyone was saying "Where is she? Has anybody seen her? Where is she? Has anybody seen her?" They had rolled a carpet all the way into town for her to enter in. The carpet was decorated with flowers and baskets all alongside. But the bride hadn't shown up.

Just as the bride and groom were about to arrive at the village, the

pataña. Chaypis parlanku riki. Munaychata, bonitallañas chicaqa. "¿Imaynapitaq kaypiri kankiri?" nispas nin.

Hinaspas, "¿Imaynapichá mamitay papay uywakuwaranpas?" nispa. "Manan mama-taytayta riqsikunichu", nispas. "Paykunallan mamay taytay, pero millay malvadullañan kanku", nispas nin. "Malvadun kanku", nispas nin. "Papayqa malvadu".

"¡Ay!", nispas nin.

Chaysi pukllanku, pukllaspanku chay ventanamantas riki, huk chukchachanta t´iraratamun. Hinaspas "Urayarapuy. ¡Pasapullayña. Hamurunqañan papay-mamitay!" nispas. Loculla urayaramuspa, doblarusqa riki. Sach´a-sach´a sunqullaman escalerata pakatamun riki.

Chaysi hina parlachkanku, parlachkanku, huk p´unchawqa. Huk lado chukchachantañataqsi aparullantaq, anchaypi. Yupaqtin mana kapusqachu huk. Chaysi nin: ¿"Maymi chukchachayki? ¿Pin urqurasunki?" nispas nin.

Pukllachkaykun; hinaspan luruschaymi k´uturuwan" nispas nin. Luruchantas wañurachipunku.

"Wañuchipunchik."

"¿Chaypaqchu nuqa qayna sumaqta uywaykiman? ¿Kay luruqa chukchachayki k´utunanpaq?" nispas nin. "¿Maymi chay chukchachari?"

Wayra apayurun mayu ukuman", nispa.

Chaysi, bueno hinas, paqarisnintinqa, kasqallantaqsi. Huk lado chukchachantañataq aparullantaq, qullqi kaqchatañataqsi. Hinaqtinsi chaypiqa paqarisnintinqa kasqantas ñakch´allantaq; picunwanchá ñakch´an. Chaysi mana kapullantaqchu chukchachanqa. "¿Maymi huk kaq chukchachayki?" nispas nin.

"Michichawanmi pukllachkani" nispas. Michichanman tanqayun riki. Chaysi, wañurachipun; wikch´upun riki. Chaysi nin, manaña imamanpas tunpanan kanñachu, riki, nanta chicup wichasqanta apasqanta ima riki. "¿Imanasaqtaqri?" nispas nin. Hinaspa, "Mana, casarakusunmi. Alistachkaniña novia ropata lluytaña. Tempranuta paqarinqa lluqsiruqtiy hinallan", nispas riki nin. Ña casamiento p´unchawsi papanpaman mamitanmanqa.

Chaysi riki mamintan, papanqa "Sumaqta wawaymi casarakunqa. Huk lindawan, huk reywanmi casarakunqa". Chaysi sumaqtas allchaychin riki. Nataq llaqtantinsi, sumaqta pichayunku, t´ikawansi. Hinaspas banda sumaq riki, hamuyuchkan, tarpayamuchkan. "Yaqaña hamunqa novia" nispa. Lluy llaqtantin novedadmanqa riki, "Ñaraq lindataq, chaytaq, chhaynaniraqri papan alistan", nispasyá. Richkanku,

eagle appeared. "Ohhhh! So this is what I raised you for?" Whap! He hit her and turned one side of her face to a donkey's. Whap! The other side turned to a horse's face. There wasn't a single hair left on her head. One side was a horse's face, the other side a donkey's.

The young man led her like that into town. When everyone saw, they said "Oh, gross! This is what we turned out for? With so much eager- ness, and so much pomp? You, the king's son, are going to get married to something like this? We can't believe our own king's son is getting married to this—this donkey face." Everyone was insulting them. And the poor girl was crying. Her tears were falling like hailstones. When the boy tried to bring her in, his father threw them out. "Look at the shame you've brought on me, by trying to marry this thing! What would the other kings say to me? What would I say to my friends to introduce them to this?"

Oh! Once they were thrown out, they set up house in a shack in a little corner of the town. And that's where they were living. They slept there in a miserable little bed. They bought one little stew-pot, and that's about it. She didn't know how to cook or anything. The boy had to bring food to the house. He had to work as a day-laborer, because his parents had thrown him out of the house with nothing but the clothes on his back.

The wives of his older brothers, on the other hand, were—wow!— elegant, I mean elegant. And the birthday of their father-in-law was com- ing up. So they said: "Hey, let's go. Let's go to donkey face's house. Hey, I just wonder what she's making for our father-in-law. We, of course, are making beautiful shirts. And hey, I just ask myself what gift she'll give." They entered the little shack. "Sister, sister, here we are. Sister. So, anyway, what are you preparing for our father's birthday?"

"It's nothing. I'm only sewing this little rough cloth shirt by hand. I don't have a sewing machine. Sewing by hand, that's all, to offer it to him. Will he accept it, or won't he accept it? But I doubt he will," she said. She was sewing a little rough cloth shirt.

When the women went out of her house, they said to each other, "Oh, gross! Now can you imagine our father-in-law putting that thing on? How gross! I'll bet he's going to throw that rough shirt right back in her face." So they went off. That's how things stood, when the birthday came the next day. Oh, yes! They sprinkled perfume and stuff on the shirts and sent them off on a tray. They were trying to one-up each other.

The poor couple had a boy, a helper. They said, "Take this. Give it

richkanku karu panpataraq riki. "¿Maytaq, rikhurimunchuri? ¿Maytaq, rikhurimunchuri?" nispas, lluy. Chaymansi alfumbrawan mast´asqa naman, llaqta ukuman, yaykunanpaqqa riki. Alfumbrawan t´ika-t´ikantinsi, canasta-canastapi kayuchkanku . . . Chayqa mana rikhurinchu. Hinaspa ña llaqtaman chayarunanku kachkaqtinña, aguila rikhurirapun. "¡Ayyyy! ¿Kaypaqchu nuqa uywarayki?" nispas. ¡Ch´aqlan! Asnu uyaman tukurapun. ¡Huk ladontas ch´aqlan! caballu uyaman tukurapun. Mana ni chukchachanpas ni imapas kapunchu. Huk lado caballu, huk ladotaqsi asnu uya.

Hinatas jovenqa riki pusachkan riki, pusan riki. Hinaspas rikuruspanku hina, "¡tataw! Kayllamantaqchus tarpachimanki, chaynaniraq afan, qaynaniraq nawan pompallawanña." Ña kaywanñataqchu casarakunki, reyninchikpa wawan, nispa. "Reywanñataqchu casarakunki; reyninchikpa wawanñataqchu kaywan, kay asnu uyawan", nispa Lluy k´amiyuchkanku. Niñataqsi waqayuchkan riki; chikchi-chikchimantaraq waqayuchkan riki. Chaqa . . . apayuqtinqa, papan qarqun. "Ima p´inqaymanmi churawanki, kaywanchus casarakuwaq", nispa "¡Ima nispataq Rey masiykunatapas niymanri. Ima nispa amiguykunaman presentayman kayta!" nispas.

¡Ay! chaysi qarqunpuqtin riki llaqtap esquinachallanta ch´ukllachata ruwayukun. Hinaspas chayllapi riki tiyachkanku riki. adefecio puñunachallapis nayun, hinas chayllapi. Mankachatas rantimun, chaychallapis. Nisyá wayk´uyta, ni imatapas yachanchu riki. Chayqa naqa chicuqa lluyta riki apayamuchkan. Llamk´apayakamuchkan ima chicuqa riki; mama-taytan cuerponpi ropachallantin qarqumuqtin.

Nas ñas hinaspaykis kuraq kaq wawqinqa warminkunataqsi, ¡uuyyy! elegante, elegante riki. Chaysi nankuq suegrunkup fiestan kanan kasqa. Hinaqtinsi: "Hakuchu; chay asnu uyaqta rirusunchik. Imatachá ruwachkan a ver, suegrunchispaq. Nuqanchikqa camisata sumaqta ruwachimuchkanchik. Imallatachá obsequianqa a ver", nispas. Yaykun Ch´ukllallataqa. "Hermana, hermana hanpuchkayki". "Hermana", nispas nin. "¿Chayri papanchik fiestanpaq, imata qamri preparachkanki?" nispas.

Mana; nuqaqa kay tocuyullamanta makillapi sirachkani, Mana maquinaypas kanchu. Makillapi sirakuchkani, kay chaskispaqqa. Chaskiswanqachus, mana chaskiwanqa, chayqa manachá", nispas. Tocuyuta sirakuchkan camisachata.

Hinaspas lluqsiramuspataq "¡Tataw!"; thuqapakuspankus. "¡Tataw! kaywanñataqchus kunan suegronchik churakunman kaywan. ¡Tataw!

to the king." The shirt was folded up in a little matchbox. "Give him this," they said.

The king put on the other shirts. "What in the heck?" None of them fit him. He put on still another one. It was way too big; it didn't fit. And when he put on yet another one, he said, "These fishwives don't even know how to sew! And what do you want?" he said to the helper-boy.

"Pardon me, sir. My mistress sent me with this for you. My mistress, my little donkey-face mistress sent me with this."

"Oh, great. He's probably brought some piece of junk. Let's see, bring it over." He handed him the matchbox. And in it was a beautiful shirt. Folded up, the size of a thumbnail. Wow! It was really handsome. He put it on. The collar, the sleeves, the body, all fit him perfectly. He put it on.

At the hut, the couple were talking. "Let's invite my folks here."

"Well, if you want to," she said.

The young man, her husband, said "Come on, let's go to them."

"No. I don't want to bring any more shame on your parents. I'll never go there."

"Come on, let's just go see. We'll ask them to forgive us. Your parents, I mean." The two of them set out for that place on foot, arm in arm. There was the eagle, circling above them. There, in tears, the girl begged to be forgiven.

"Oh, I see. So this is what you want? So this is what I raised you for? This is why I rescued you from the bramble-thicket? I suffered and raised you just so you could do something like this. All right, I forgive you." Whickety-whap! The eagle slapped her hard, and she turned back into a beautiful girl. Her hair shone brightly, gold on one side, silver on the other. Both sides shone.

She said, "Ohhh!" Her clothes were elegant too. You know, she put on the bridal clothes that she had made. And she had another dress made for the dance.

After she was changed, the boy said, "Father, could I bring my fiancé?"

"Yuck! You'd bring that donkey-face here?"

"No, father. She already asked her parents to forgive her. Couldn't she come in?"

"Oh, bring her in, I guess!" And so he did bring her in. Whew! The girl was just pretty.

Oh, my! His sisters-in-law almost died of envy. "Oh, no! What's wrong with our shirts? Why doesn't he put them on? Look at him wearing her shirt. And ours are tossed in a corner."

Uyanmanraqchá laq´ayamunqa kay tocuyu camisataqa", nispas. Pasanpunku riki. Chaymannñataqsi hinalla kachkan, paqarisnintin fiestanpaq. ¡Ayy! Paykunas sumaqta charolapi apayachinku perfumiwan, imaymanawan. Nasqataraq gana-ganaraq.

Chaysi huk chicuchanku kasqa chay naqpaqqa riki, maqt´achankuchá riki. "Kaytan apanki. Wiraquchaman intrigamunki", nispas nin. Nachallapis nachata, fusfuru cajachallapis doblasqachata. "Kayta intrigamunki", nispas. Hukkaq camisawanqa churarukunsi. "¡Akakaráy!" cuerpunpas mana chaypaqchu. Hukkaqwannñataqsi churarukun. Chayqa p´istunñataqsi, manas cabinchu. Chayllapiñataqsi hukkaqpaqqa: "¡Kay wankhikuna yachallankupaschu sirayta" nispas nin.

"¿Imata munanki qamri?," nispas nin chicuchata.

"Papáy, kaytan mamitay apachimuwachkan. Señorachay asnu uya señorachaymi apachimuwachkan", nispas nin.

"¡Ahhhh! adefesiutachá apamuchkan. ¡Apamuy, a ver!" nispas. Chaskirun fusfuru cajachataqa. Chaypis riki lindallaña camisa riki. Uñachaman doblasqacha. ¡Ayyy, sumaqllaña riki! Chaywansi churakun. K´apaq cuellunpas, mangasninpas, cuerpunpas. Chaywan churakusqa riki.

Chaysi riki naqa. "Invitasunchikyá."

"Munaqtiykiqa", nispa nin.

Qusanqa riki, chay jovenqa nin. "Hakuyá, risunchik." "Mana. Imaynatas p´inqayman churamuyman mamitay-papaykita. Manapunin riymanchu", nispas nin.

"Hakuyá pursiancaso. Perdunta mañakamusun", nispas nin. Mamitayki-papaykimanta", nispas nin. Chay sitiota richkaranku riki, chakillapi iskayninku riki, de brazo hinas. Chiqaqta muyumuchkasqa aguilaqa. Chaypis perdunta mañakun waqayuspa.

"¡Hola! ¿kaytachu munaranki? ¿Kaypaqchu nuqa uywarayki, hakay t´ankar patamanta urquspay? Nuqaqa hina sufrimientuwan uywarayki chhaynata ruwawanaykipaq", nispas riki. "Kayqa perdunasayki", nispas riki. ¡Ch´itiq! ¡Ch´aqlan! Kallpawan kasqanta linda tukurapun. ¡Huk laduwansi ch´aqlan! Lo mismo, linda niña. Chukchachanpas llipipichkaq, qurimanta, qullqimantas. Iskaynin lado llipipichkan.

Hinaqtinsi nin: "¡Ayyy!" Ropanpas sumaqsiyá kachkan. Novia ropan ruwachipusqan riki; hinas kachkan. Chaysi, huk vestiduta bailipaq ruwachipusqa riki.

Chaysi cambiasqata riki: "Papá, ¿pusamuymanchu nayta noviayta?" nispa nin.

"¡Aaqqq! Chay asnu uyatachus pusamuwaq . . .

Then the boy's father said, "All right, now you two will get married."
And as soon as the birthday party was over, they started getting the girl
ready for the wedding. Again they sent out invitations. Again they sent
out for a brand new wedding dress. Oh, yes, and first there was a dance.
So while everybody was dancing, pearls were spilling from the bride-
to-be. The sisters-in-law scrambled on hands and knees to pick them
up off the ground. "How can this be?" they said. Then they took the
helper-boy off to the kitchen to ask him.

"Hey! Hey there! What sort of lotion does your mistress use?"

"My mistress doesn't use anything. Except…she snatches a handful
of potato peelings, and sticks them on her throat. She stuffs them in
her cleavage."

Naturally, they did just what he said. They all gathered up potato
peelings and stuffed them into their dresses. And while they danced,
potato peelings started to spill out, you know.

Their husbands said, "What in the heck have they done now?" They
yanked them outside. "Now what have you gone and done?"

"I didn't put anything on."

"And this? And this? What's this, then? What is it?" They gave each
one of them a smack. In the next room, there was the the girl, beautiful as ever.

At last, when that was over, the preparations for the ceremony were
done. Everybody was there for the wedding. Everyone who was invited
came. They brought in the best priest, everything. And finally, they
married.

At the wedding, I was also hanging out there, helping out. And I was
going to bring you something from the feast. But the dog took it away
from me.

"Mamá, papá", nispa nin. "Ñan mamitan-papanmanta perdunta mañakapunña", nispa. "Chay waqamuwaqmá nantá tayta-mamantaqa, nispas nin. "Manan atinmanchu yaykumuyta nispas nin. "¡Pusamuyá!" nispas nin. Chaysi riki pusayurun. ¡Whiiihh! Lindallaña chicaqa.

¡Ayyy! nankunas, qhachunmasinkunas invidiapi wañurunkuraq riki. "¡Ayyy! ¿Waqtantachu kay churakunan, imaynan karan kay?" nispa. "A ver, paypa apachimusqanwantaq camisawanpas churarukun. Nuqanchikpataq haqayna wikch´ulayachkan", nispas ninku.

Chayqa riki papanqa nin: "Bueno, kunanqa casarakunkichikchá", riki. Chayqa chay fiestan tukuytaqa casamientunpaq nataqsi chicapaq preparapunku riki. Yapamanta invitasiun kaykun. Novio ropakunatas huk-hukta ruwayachinku. ¡Ah! Tusuchkasqakus. Hinaspas riki, tusuchkaqtinku nakuna perlaskuna t´akarikuchkan riki . . . perlaskuna t´akakachayukuchkan riki.

Qhachunmasinkunataq pallakuchkan riki pampamanta. "¿Imaynatataq kayri?" nispa. Hinaqtinsi naqa chay chicuchankunataqa riki cocinaman pusayuruspa tapun: "¡Yaw yaw! ¿Ima hawiyllatan churakamun señorachayki?" nispa.

Señorachayqa mana imatapas churakunchu sino", nispa. "Papa qaratan llapch´aruspan, kunkanpi churarukun", nispas nin. "Uqllayninman churarukun", nispas nin. Chaysi riki paykunapas lo mismo; papa qarakunata riki, lluyta kaykunaman churakunku riki. Hinas tusuqtinkuqa papa qaraqa t´akarikapun riki.

Chayqa qusankunaqa riki, "¿Imatataq kaykuna ruwamunkuri?" nispayá. "¡Táq!" niruspa hawaman pusaruspa riki. "¿Imatataq kay cuentuta ruwankichik?" nispa. "Mana imatapas churakunichu", nispas, "¿Kayri? ¿Kayri? ¿Imataq kayri? ¿Imataq?" nispas. Maqayapunku riki, sapankata. Huk kaqtaqsi chaypi lindallaña kayuchkan riki.

Por fin, chay tukuytaqa alistapunku casamientunkupaq. Chaysi riki karan casarakunanku, lluyta. Invitadukunallaraq hamuyun. Nakunachá padreta mejorninta pusachimunku, lluyta. por fin casarakapusqaku.

Casarapuqtinku nuqapas chaypi muyuchkarani, yanapakuspa riki. Hinaspa apamuchkarayki lonche, puchukunata. Hinaspa allqu qichuruwan.

The Woman Who Tended Ducks

Though strictly speaking these folk tales are all "collective creations," in some cases, a story can act as a mask or persona for the teller's own life-issues. During the short weeks I knew her, the 69–year-old Teodora had a hospital stay for pneumonia, which impeded her ability to tell me as many stories as she had wanted. When I visited her on a ward in the public hospital, I remember how fragile she looked, and how she clasped my hand ever so tightly, not wanting me to leave when it was time for my visit to be over. She did return home within a few days, while I was still living in her house, and we broke bread together several more times before I departed. But there was a self-consciousness on Teodora's part that she was close to death, and she did indeed die less than three months after my departure. She was, in part, speaking her legacy, the more so given that her grand-daughter Iliana was not much disposed to learning her grandmother's stories. As such, the telling of "The Woman Who Tended Ducks" seems singularly appropriate, with its theme of a beautiful maiden trapped in the body of a disparaged old hag. When I listened to the tape recording of her version, months later, I was struck by the parts of the story in which Teodora, on the cusp of seventy years, assumes the speaking voice of an adolescent disguised as an "old woman." Her crone-like timbre is comical, but also touching, in its staging of a persona: age acting as youth acting as age. When Teodora reverts to her normal voice to resume the account of the prince's love-sickness for the duck-tender, after he has seen her "unclothed" and nubile at the river, she somehow professes her own relative youth through this mimicry—she has had to make a special effort to "sound old." As poor health overtook Teodora, she enacted her own drama of self-renewal in the theater of symbolic action that the oral tradition can provide.

The Woman Who Tended Ducks

Told by Teodora Paliza

Once there was a king. And he had a single child, a daughter. It happened that his wife fell sick, she got sick. When she was about to die, she said to her husband, "Whoever this ring fits, you must marry that person." That was the request she left him. So anyway, the girl grabbed the ring off of her father's night table. She grabbed the ring. And because the girl was playing around, she put on the ring, the wedding band. Then, she couldn't take it off. She tried and tried, but couldn't remove it. So she hid her hand behind her back.

When her father realized it was missing, he said, "I thought it was right there."

The girl was hiding her hand, and said to herself, "How will I explain this to Daddy? Am I supposed to marry him? How can I marry my own father? What do I do? What do I do now?" She was really scared. She went to the place of an old witch-woman. And she asked her for advice, you know. "How can I get rid of this thing here? What do I do? How can I marry my own father? I was playing around, and ended up putting on my mother's ring, her wedding band. Now it won't come off."

The old woman said "My little miss. My little miss. I'll fashion you a wooden doll. That's how you can save yourself from this."

The girl went around feeling really scared. She couldn't even eat, and didn't touch anything. At last, the doll was ready. Somehow, the old witch-woman put her inside of it. Casting a spell, she put everything

Patera Payacha

Huk reysis kasqa. Hinaspas ch´ullalla wawanku kasqa, ususin. Chayñataqsi warminqa unquqyasqa, unqupusqa. Hinaspa riki wañunanpaq nisqa qusantaqa "Pimanchá kay aroy cabinqa, chaywanmi casarakunki", nispa, encargaspa saqisqa. Hinaspas nanqa, chicap papanqa riki mesa de nochen patallapi hap´iq anilluta hap´iq. Chayñataqsi chicaqa riki, traviesa kaymanta anilluwan churarukusqa riki, arowan. Hinaspa mana lluqsipuyta atisqachu. Chaysi mana imaynata ch´ustikuyta atinchu. Hinalla pakasqalla kachkan riki.

Chayqa papan watukuqtinpas nin: "Chaypichá riki kachkan", riki nispalla.

Makintaqa pakachkallan riki hinallapi; "¿Imaynataq kunan papaywanri? nuqari casarakuymanri?" nispas nin riki. "¿Imaynataq casarakuyman papaywanri?" nispas nin. "¿Imanasaqtaqri?" "¿Imanasaqtaq kunanqa?" nispas nin. Mancharisqa kachkan riki. Chaysi naqa kuk layqa mamakuqa yaykusqa chayta. Hinaspa, paywan consultakusqa riki. "¿Imayna modupin kayta nayman chinkaymanchu? ¿Imaynan kayta? ¿Imaynataq kunanri papaywanri casarakuymanri? Khaynata traviesa, kaymanta anillunwan mantaypawan churarukurani aronwan. Hinaspa mana lluqsinchu", nispa. Chaysis chaysi riki: "Señoracháy señoracháy. Nuqaña k´ullu muñicata ruwaranchinpusayki. Hinaspayki chaypi, chay modupi kaymanta nanki salvakunki", nispa.

Chaysi naqa chicaqa riki manchasqalla, hinalla kachkan. Manas ni mikhuypis, ni imapis hasp´inchu riki. Chayqa, por fin ruwachinpusqa

inside, the girl's clothes, and every last thing she had inside. The girl went inside, and the woman closed it up. All arranged inside, holding a guitar, the girl set out.

A soldier who saw her said, "Where did that rheum-eyed old woman come from? I wonder who that rheum-eyed old woman is? Go on, get out of here! What do you want here?" he said. And the soldiers chased her away. She kept walking along the path. Kept on walking. Poor thing! That little old woman had to walk a long way, rheum-eyed, leaning on her cane.

Around about sunset, she came to some distant town. There, the sun was just about to set. She approached a house, and knocked on the door. "Ma'am, ma'am," she called out.

"Who is it? What do you want?"

"Ma'am, could you put me up here?"

A servant went to the mistress of the house and said, "A broken-down old woman has come, asking for lodging. We have a lot of ducks to be tended. I think she'd be really good for tending and feeding the ducks."

They let her in. She came in, trembling, and said "Good woman. Good woman, couldn't you use me, use a poor little old woman just as your duck-tender? Couldn't I just feed the little ducks? What do you say? You won't hear a peep out of me," she said, weeping.

So the mistress said, "All right, let her stay. Give her that tiny room underneath the stairs. That's good enough for her to sleep in." There, the old woman settled in as best she could. They gave her a little bed. That's where the old woman lived. The next morning, she started tending the ducks. She herded them down to the river. There was a river nearby. There they foraged. Two or three days went by, and each day she'd coax them, coax them down there and let them eat.

One time the youngest son went down to the river. Meanwhile, the girl had said to herself, "I'd like to bathe in the open air." She took a good look up, down, all around, and came out of the wooden doll. After she had a nice bath, she took out her little guitar. Sitting down on top of a boulder, she played a pretty little song. She sang, and she played.

The young man was walking by there. "What's this?" he said. "Is it her, or not? Who is that young girl? Has somebody cast a spell, or what?" He kept looking at her, blinking his eyes again and again. Because the girl was really pretty. Then he said to himself, "I wonder where she'll go? Let's see, I'll keep my eyes peeled. Where on earth could she be from?" he said, looking out from his hiding place. Well, when she had

riki. Hinaspa imaynapichá riki chay ukuman apayruran mamakuqa riki. Layqaqa chay ukuman riki lluyta, ropachakunata, lluyta q´alata cosaschakunata chay ukuman naspa riki. Chicaqa riki yaykurapun; wisq´arakapun riki. Chaypis munayta guitarrachanpis, chaypis chaynintin lluqsinpun.

Hinaspas nakunaqa soldadukunaqa riki nin: "¿Maynintataq kay ch´uqñi payari yaykururanri? ¿Pitaq chay ch´uqñi payari? ¡Fuera, pasay! ¿Imatan munanki kaypi?" nispas qarqumunku riki nakunaqa, sodadokunaqa. Ñan puririnpunsi, puririnpunsi. ¡Ay! karutañas purichkan payachaqa, ch´uqñi bastunchantin riki. Ña inti yaykuy hinataña, huk karu llaqtaman hinaña chayan. Chaysis riki ña inti yaykuyña kachkan chaypis riki. Huk wasitaqa yaykun. Hinaspas takayun. "Señoráy" señoray", nispa.

"Hay. ¿Imatan munanki?"

"¿Manachu señoráy alojaywankiman?"

Chaypis riki patronanmanqa nin: Unquq payachan hamusqa", nispa 'Alojaway' nispa. Askhatataq patuta uywayku. Chayqa patu uywananpaq michimunanpaq kusayá riki kanman", nispas nin.

Chaysi, yaykun, "Mamitáy" nispas; chukchuspa riki yaykuchkan. "¿Mamitáy manachu paterallapaqpis munawankiman, kay pobre payachaykita? ¿Patullataq michimuymanri? ¿Imata niwaqtiykichispas? Kayllapiqa ankhaynallaqa kayman", nispas waqaspa.

Chaysi riki señoraqa nin: "Quidakuchunyari, qumuyá chay gradas sikipi cuartuchata. Chaypiyá puñumuchun", nispas. Chaypis riki payachaqa acomodakun. Hinaspa camachata qun. Chaychallapis payachaqa kakuchkan riki. Paqaristinmantaqa patukunata qatiyta qallaripun riki; mayup patanta riki. Mayus kasqa chaypi. Chaypis michiyamuchkanña, ña iskay kimsa p´unchaw imaña michiq qatichkan, qatichkan chaypiñataqsi.

Huk kutinpiqa nasqa sullk´a kaq wawanqa risqa. Bueno chicaqa riki "Campopi bañarukusaq", nispa riki. Wichayta, urayta qhawakacharukuspa nanmantaqa lluqsirun riki, k´ullu muñicamantaqa. Chaypis riki sumaq bañananmanta urqurun guitarrachanta. Chaypis rumi patapi tiyaruspanmi lindullataña tukayun riki. Takiyuntaq, tucayuntaq.

Hinaspa chaypi purichkasqa riki, "¡Imayna!" nipas riki. "¿Paychu manachu? Imataq hakay niñacha. ¿ima encantuchu, imataqri?" nispansi riki, ñawinta picha-picharikusparaq qhawachkan riki. Lindallañasyá chicaqa riki. Bueno, hinaqtinsi: "¿Maytachá rinqa? A ver, qhawasaq qhawasaqpuni, ¿Maymantataq kanmanri?" nispas riki, pakayukuspalla

finished playing her guitar, she slipped back in to bathe. She washed all over. She got freshened up and everything. She folded her towels up, they were all dry, folded, and she put them away. Back she went into the wooden doll. And then locked it shut. Shut inside, she saw that the sun was starting to go down, and led the ducks home. The young man, watching this, said, "I can't believe my eyes! I'll come back tomorrow and see."

Well, the young man hurried home. He got there before she did, and said to the hired girls, "I want you to take a good dinner to that poor old duck-tender woman, and breakfast. Poor old woman. Poor old woman." He had fallen in love.

So then the hired girls said to each other, "He's fallen for a rheum-eyed old woman. He even makes us take her stuff!"

"Oh, thank you little girl, thank you little girl. All this for me?" the old woman said, taking the food and eating it.

The next day, she went and led the ducks back to the river. The young man said, "I can't believe this is true. What's going on?" But it was true. She looked up, down, all around. Not a soul anywhere. She hopped right out, hopped out and played her guitar, you know, sweetly, sitting on top of the boulder. The young man said to himself "Whatever am I going to do about this? I don't care. One way or another, we're getting married. We're getting married. But there's no way my parents are going to let me marry her. Still, no matter what else happens, I'm going to marry her," said the boy. The girl had enchanted him. Well, he saw the same thing again. Two or three times the boy took pastries and chocolates to the old woman.

Then, trembling, she'd say, "Little boy, little boy, you brought this for me? For a rheum-eyed old woman? I'm a bother to you."

"It's okay. Just eat. Enjoy it." Then one day, the young man got sick. He got deathly ill; completely lovesick over her. Running a high fever, in a delirium over the old duck-tender. The hired girls said "Yuck! I can't believe he's so sick over that old woman, for that old woman. Over a rheum-eyed old woman, over somebody like that." They said lots of insulting things.

And he was crying out, "Ohhh, send up the duck-tender, send up the duck-tender!"

So they called for the doctor. "Look how bad he is," they said. The doctor gave him a thorough examination. He shooed everybody else out. He alone gave him a thorough examination.

The young man told him what was wrong. "But don't say anything

qhawachkan. Chayqa chaymanta guitarranta tucayta tukuruspa, bañakuqsi yaykurapun. Bañarukun lluyta. Sumaqta arreglarukun, lluytas. Doblarun toallankunata, lluy ch´akirachispa, doblaruspa, kasqanta churarapun. Yaykurapun k´ullu muñicanmanqa. Chayqa hinaspa wisq´arakapun. Wisq´akapuqtinqa, chaymantaqa hinatas intita qhawarispaqa, patukunata qatipun riki. Chayqa jovenqa ña rikurunña: "¡Ay, manan creenichu! A ver, paqarintawan qhawamusaq", nispas nin.

Bueno, ripunsi, pasapun jovenqa riki. Antestaraq Chayarusqa chayta ninsi, "Chay patera payachamanqa allinchata almorsayta apayachinki, desayunuta. Pobre viejita, pobre viejita", nispas, munakuchkanña.

Chayqa hinas warmakunapas nin, Ch´uqñi payata munakuchkan preferensiyawanraq apayachiwachkanchik", nispas warmakunaqa riki.

"Chay gracias niñacháy, gracias niñacháy, nuqapaqraqtaq", chakiyukuspa mikhukuchkan riki hina.

Paqarisnintinpas qatillantaqsi riki; paqarisnintinpas rillantaqsi. "Manan kayqa chiqaqchu, imaynan kanman", nispas. Chiqaytas riki. Wichayta urayta qhawakacharukun. Manas pipas kanchu Ch´in. Faciltas lluqsiramun, lluqsiramuspaqa tucayun guitarrantaqa riki, sumaqta, rumi patapi tiyaruspa. "¿Ay imaynatan kaytaqa ruwasaq? ¡Manan Casarakusaqpunin, maski imapas kachun", nispas chicuqa riki, encantasqa chicamantaqa . Bueno, iskay kimsa kutitaña chay naqsi apayuq chicuqa riki, sumaqta pastelkunata, chocolatilluskunata ima apayuq.

Hinaspa "Niñucháy niñucháy nuqapaq kay ch´uqñi payapaqri." Hinaspas khatatayuspa "molestakuchkanki".

"Manan, mikhukuy. Ch´unqaykuy", nispas. Chayqa chaymantaqa unquyapun jovenqa riki. Gravetas unquyuchkan; khuyay munasqankuraqtaqsi riki. Calentura fuegos, musphayuchkan paterallawan riki. "¿Tataw chay payawanchu chay payamantachu kayhinataraq unqun?" nispas riki warmakuna. "Kay ch´uqñi payamanta, kaymantachus." K´amiyuchkankus riki. "¡Ayy, pateralla wicharamuchun, pateralla wicharamuchun!"

Chayqa medikutas riki waqachimunku, "Khayna malmi kachkan", nispa. Chasis lluyta examinaramun. Hinaspas hatiranpun; pay sapallanpi riki lluyta examinayun.

Chayqa ninsi, willakunsiyá ; "Pero ama mamitayman, papayman willankiraqchu", nispas riki willakun.

"Arí khaynatan rikuni, kay patera payachata."

"Paywanmi casarakuyta munani", nispa. "Paywanmi casarakusaq. Mana chayqa wañusaqmi", nispas riki.

Chaysis riki (naqa doctor, medikuqa mamataytantaqa) hawapi

about it to my parents, okay? I saw her turn into someone else, that old duck-tender. I want to marry her. Whatever it takes, I'll marry her. If I can't, then I'll die," he said.

Meanwhile, they were waiting outside for the doctor, to ask what was going on. "What could it be? What could be wrong?"

And he told them, "If you don't let your son marry the person he wants, your son will die. Whether you agree or don't agree. The person he loves, that's who he has to marry. That's how you can save your child," he told them.

"Who, who, who, whoever is it we should marry him to? Whoever he wants, fine." So his mother and father went in to ask him. "Son, who do you want to marry? Whoever your heart is leading you to, we'll marry you to her, we'll marry you to her. But just get well. Just get well."

"Send up the duck-tender. The duck-tender woman."

"Oh, yuck! Her? What should we do? I guess we'll have to tell her to come up." They called the old duck-tender. "The child is sick, trembling all over because of you. You have to go up and speak to him. That's the only way he'll get better."

"What's this? The child loves me, this rheum-eyed old woman, in that way? He's making my walking-cane dance too much." The old woman climbed the stairs one by one, creaking along. Then she went in.

When she entered, he said, "Come closer." Then, "Reach your hand out. Give me your hand." She gave him her hand. He said, "I don't care. We two have to get married. If that can't be, then I can't live. I'm in love with you."

"Oh, little boy! Don't speak of such things. How could you marry me? Could you marry this ugly, broken-down old woman, this snot-faced old woman? I don't think so. I don't think so."

His mother and father said, "The child is in love with you. You'll marry him."

"But how could he marry someone like me?"

Of course they hated the old woman. "With her, with her," they said to themselves. They couldn't stand the old woman. "Well, then. We'll just marry them right here. What else can we do? What would our relatives in town be saying? 'They made him marry an ugly old woman,' that's what they'd say." So they had her put on some cheap old mestizo clothes. The only ones in attendance were the siblings, the parents, and the priest. To marry them, they just sent for the priest to come to their house. And then, what did the young man do? He bought pretty

suyayuchkan medikutaqa riki, tapunankupaq riki. "Imawanchá, imamantachá", nispa.

Chaysi nin: "Sichus mana casarachinkichik wawaykichikta pin munasqanwan, wañurunqan wawayki. Munankichik, mana munankichik; pichá munakun, chaywanmi casarakunqa. Chaywanmi salvankichik wawaykichikta", nispa, nispa nin.

"¿Pitaqri, pitaqri, pitaq, piwantaq casarachisaqkupasri?" nispas. "¿Pitachá munanpas riki", nispas. Chayqa yaykunsis mamitan riki, papanqa tapuq. "Hijito, ¿piwanmi casarakuyta? Pimanmi sunquyki aysakun, casarachisaykikun, casarachisaykikun; contalquella qhaliyaykuy, qhaliyaykuy".

"Patera payachallan wicharamuchun. Patera payachalla", nispa.

"¿Tataw kaywanri? ¿Imanasunkitaqri? Hinatachá nisunchik wichamunanpaq", nispas riki. Patera payachataqa ninku riki."Khatatataspa niñuchan unquchkan qammanta. Rinkipunis, rimayamunkis; chayqa qhaliyananpaq", nispas nin.

"¿Imatataq? ¿Nuqatari niñuchari munakun, kay paya ch´uqñita, khaynaniraqta?" Astawan tusuyachichkan bastuntaqa, riki. Wichansis, wichansis ñak´ayllataña payachaqa riki. Hinaqtinsi yaykun.

Yaykuqtinqa nin: "Achhuyamuy". Hinaspa, "Llamiyllapis llamiwayyari", nispas riki. Makinta nan llamiyuchkan. "¡Ay, manan! Qamwanpunin casarasunchik. Manan mana, chayqa manan kawsayniy kanchu. Qammanta enamorakuni", nispa riki.

"¡Ay niñucháy! Amayá chaytaqa rimariychu. ¿Imaynataq nuqawanri casarakuwaq? ¿Kay millay thultu payawan, kay ch´uqñi payawan, kay qhuña sapa payawanchu casarakunki? Manapunin, manapunin", nispas "Mana", nispas nin.

Mamitan papanpis riki nankuq, "Niñuchaqa qamta munasunki. Casarakunki", nispa.

"¿Imatataq nuqawanri casarakuwaqri?" nispayá.

Chiqniyukuwachkanku riki payawan. "Kaywan, kaywan", nispa aborresiyukuchkanku ima payachataqa. Chayqa mamitanpapan: "Bueno, pues. Kayllapiñayari nasunchik, casarachisunchik.

¿Imanasuntaq? ¿imanispataq famillanchispas, llaqtapis ninqari? 'Kay millay payawan casarachin', niwanqakuchá riki", nispasyá. Chaysi naqa mistisa ropata corrientillata riki, ropatapas ruwachinpun. Chaypi padrinupas paykunalla kanan karan riki, mama-taytalla. Chaysi riki naqa, casarakunapaq riki, señor curaqa waqachinku wasinkullaman. ¿Chaypis jovenqa riki, imatas ruwan? Sumaq t´ikata hinas riki nata

flowers and bridal clothes, the best, the best. And the others saw this, of course.

His brothers and sisters said, "Oh, gross! With that old woman, gross! Our brother is going to marry that worn-out woman, that ugly old woman? The ugly one, the ugly one."

At that moment, she entered in, the way she really was. She came in, changed back into her pretty self. The girl looked really good, really fine. The two of them stepped up to the altar. It was about eight in the evening that they took their vows. They stepped up there, the girl looking just so good, beautiful, you can't imagine! His mother and father didn't know what to say. His brothers were full of envy.

The fiancés stopped the wedding. They postponed it, postponed it, you know. "No," they said. "We'll get married in a few days. Why should we do it this way? If we do, what will our family say? 'They married them in secret,' that's what they'll say." They made preparations to wed on another day. And everybody, every last person, was invited. So they got married, on that day. And they were very happy about it. His brothers were saying, "How did he see that in her, how did he figure it out?" Because, well, she didn't turn out to be an old duck-tender after all.

(ropa) novia ropata riki ruwachimun, sumaqta, sumaqta riki. Claro rikuchkantaq chaykunapis riki.

Chayqa nansi wawqinñataqsi; "¡Tataw! Kay payawan, ¡tataw! ¿Kay paya-sunqu, kay millay payawanchu casarakunqa wawqinchik?" nispas. "Millaywanchu, kay millaywanchu", nispas riki. Chayqa pay kikinsi yaykun riki. Yaykuspaqa, sumaqta cambiyamun riki. Sumaq, sumaqllataña chicataqa riki. Chayqa chaypisyá wichanku riki. Las ocho tutatachus hina casarankunanku karan, *no sé*. Chayqa wichanku, linda riki chicaqa riki, hermosa, ¡aayyy! . . . Chayqa mamitan papanqa aknarakapusqa riki. Wawqinkunapas envidiapis.

Manas casarapusqachu. Tatipusqa riki, tatipusqa riki, nisqa riki, "Mana", riki. "Huk p´unchawña casarakunkichik, ¿Imaynataq khaynañapiri, ima nispataq niwankunman famillanchikkunapasri? 'Pakallapi casarachin' niwasunmanchá", nispas. Huk diapaq alistayapunku riki casamientuta. Chayqa lluysis invitadukuna, lluy. Chayqa casarakapunku riki, p´unchawpi. Chaypiñasyari cuntintu riki. Wawqinkunañataq: "¿Imaynapin kay naran, qhawaran, catiyaran?" nispas riki. Chayqa manaña patera paya kapunchu.

The She-Calf

The title-story is, quite simply, one of the most beautiful I've had the pleasure of hearing. Quechua-speakers are known for their earthy humor, but in this narrative, delicacy and tenderness prevail. The erotic undertones are subtly presented, when the mother borrows the neighbor boy for the evening to offer to the she-calf, first bathing him ritualistically with perfumed soap, and surrounding him with "virgin" wine and bread. We expect significant archetypes in folklore, presented in bold strokes. And while archetypes are present here, there is also as much depth of human psychology in "The She-Calf" as one might expect to find in a modern short story. At the same time it does, like most folk expressions, contain motifs borrowed piecemeal from elsewhere and grafted on, since originality in itself is not a paramount virtue. The innocent boy's search for the disappeared maiden hearkens back to a motif found at least as early as the circa-1600 Huarochiri Manuscript. When the trickster god Cuni Raya Viracocha goes in hot pursuit of the fleeing Caui Llaca, he rewards and damns various animals depending on whether or not they confess to having recently seen the disappearing object of his desire. Likewise, the young pretender in "The She-Calf" passes through a similar gauntlet of pursuit. But because the young man isn't a god, it is he, and not those he questions, who is put to the test, when the carnivorous condors ask him to divide up their ritual offering to the mountain god, before offering the young man, in turn, concrete aid. In the Huarochiri story of Caui Llaca, the god tricks her into having "relations" and bearing his child by putting his semen into a lucuma fruit so that she will unwittingly swallow it. Interestingly, in "The She-Calf," there comes the moment when the boy first gazes on the maiden's real face in the darkness, by the light of a candle. A drop of something warm falls onto her face, awakens her, despoils her anonymity, and causes her to flee. On the cassette tape, Teodora clearly appears to say esperma (sperm). She then corrects herself, as if she were merely stuttering, and says the Spanish word cera (wax), which makes much more obvious sense in context, as the boy is holding a lit candle over her. In translating, I opted for her corrected choice, "wax," since the sexual association of a drop of warm liquid wax falling onto the maiden still manages to suggest itself.

The She-Calf

Told by Teodora Paliza

Once there was a newlywed woman, and she lived with her new husband. She always said, "How cute! I wish my child could be like that.
Oh, I wish my child would be just like my cat and dog." The woman
played with the cat and the dog. She spent a lot of time gazing on the
faces of the cat and the dog. She loved them to a fault. The woman became pregnant. Time went by, until she was in the last months of her
pregnancy. She was in about the seventh month, well along. Even so,
she let the cat and the dog nestle on her stomach, and said, "Oh, I wish
my baby could be like them! I wish my baby could be like them." She
was ready to give birth.

The labor pains began. Her parents were there when the pains
started, and her mother served as the midwife. The woman suffered a
lot, but finally she gave birth. When she birthed, a she-calf came out.
The parents said nothing about what had happened. They put the calf
off to one side, with a pacifier, and didn't say a word about what had
happened. At last, she called out, "Where's my child? Give it to me.
Bring it to me. I want to nurse it. My breasts are really full. I have to
nurse it. "

"All right, but don't be afraid. Here it is. Why were you so crazy about
animals? Look what it did to your child. Now you won't be able to show
her to our relatives, or to anybody. They'll say about you, 'She gave birth
to an animal.'" Even so, the mother adored her baby.

But her husband said, "Don't get the idea we're going to raise that

Wakacha

Huk señoras kasqa. Hinaspas recién casado. Hinaqtinsi chay señoraqa riki recién casado hina tiyakuchkanku. Hinaspas nin, "Michichan, allquchan." Hinaqtinsi nisqa, "¡Ay hinachá waway kapuwanman! ¡Ay munaycha, hinachapuni kanman wawayqa!", *diciendo*. Pukllakuq michichawanqa, allquchawan ima riki, señoraqa riki. Hinaspas khuyayta qhawapayan uyanta, michiptapas, allquptapas riki. Munakuq kapasta. Chaysi unquq riki kachkan señoraqa naqa. Huk kuti, ña altutaña apachkanña, altutaña. Ña qanchis killapiña, hinapiñachá altutaña. Siguichkallan napis wiksanpatallapis michichatapis allquchatapas uywaq riki. Chaysis, "¡Ay khayna waway kapuwanman!", nispa. Chayñataqsi ña unqunan cercaña riki.

Hinaspas riki dolur hap´ipun. Dolur hap´iqtinqa ña mamitan papanqa chaypi. Mamitanqa riki atienden, atienden. Hinaspa ñak´arin riki khuyayta. Hinaspas riki wachakapun. Wachakapuqtin, uña wakachata wachakun, uña wakachata. Mana unquqmanqa willankuraqchu riki. Huk ladullapis riki mamaderawan uywachkanku riki uña wakachataqa. Mana willankuraqchu. Chaysi nin, "¿Maytaq wawayri? Qumuwayari. Apamuy; ñuñuyusaq. Ñuñuymi khayna k´iqniwachkan, ñuñuyusaqyari", nispa, nispa riki, willan riki. "Pero maman mancharikunkichu. ¿Khaynan, imapaqmi animalkunata munanki? Kay kayqa khaynan wawayki", nispas riki nin. "Imaynatataq kunan presentankichik famillanchikmanpis, pimanpas. 'Animalta wachan', nispachá riki nisunkiku", nispas nin. Manan, hinata munakun riki khuyayta.

43

animal. No, instead we're going to send her up to the grazing lands with Marianito. We'll send the she-calf up there." The name of their house-servant was Marianito.

She called him to her. "I want you to take this calf, this little girl. Leave her by the side of the boulder that's up there."

"Yes, ma'am. Yes, ma'am. I'll take my little friend up there." He tied her up in a poncho, and putting her on his back, he carried her off. He carried her a long way, until they arrived at the high mountain plateau. And, as the woman had said, there was a boulder there, flat and circular, like a pestle-stone. He took the she-calf's face between his hands, and kissed her. "My lady, I'm going to come visit you every Sunday. I won't forget you. Don't cry, my little lady," said the boy, and he left the she-calf there. He went to gather firewood. He collected firewood from right around where he was, bundled it up in the poncho, and carried it back to the house. Arriving at the house, he spoke with the woman.

"Did you leave her?"

"Yes, I left her. I left her. Then I gathered firewood, and came back. And she said to me, 'You must come every Sunday.' I'll go every week to see my lady." How slowly the week passed! The boy was apathetic, waiting for the time to go by. When Sunday came, the boy went running to see her. The she-calf was there, waiting patiently. "My little lady!" I've come to see how you are, my lady." The boy kissed her on the cheeks. Afterward, he stood a long time gazing on the she-calf, caressing her. As the sun was beginning to set, the boy suddenly said, "My lady, I have to go now. Our mistress is going to be angry with us." Gathering the firewood together, he put it in a bundle and hurried back to the house.

The boy fell into the custom of going to visit her every Sunday. The she-calf was starting to grow up and grow up. One Sunday, as he was arriving, he called out to her, "My lady! My lady! Here I am!"

"Ah, Marianito," the she-calf said to him.

Later, he gathered together the firewood. "I have to go, my lady. Our mother will be angry with me."

"Today I'm going to give you a message for our mistress. Tell my mother, without anyone else hearing what you say to her, that she has to order an ovenload of bread. It has to be taken from the first loaves of bread to come out of the oven. She also must leave out for me the first cup of wine from the bottle. After that, flowers, and holy water. She has to leave an innocent boy waiting for me. Then, a pretty bed, spanking new, that no one has slept in, in a room made up perfectly,

Hinaspas qusanqa nin, "¿Imaynataq khaynatari uywasunmanri? Mas bienyari nawan, chicuwan, wikchuchimusunchik", nispas nin. "Uñata", nispas nin; uñacha riki. Chayqa chaysi chicuchaqa Marianucha sutin kasqa.

Chaysi, "Yaw Marianitu. Qamyá apanki kay wawachataqa, kay señorachata. Hinaspa sumaq rumi (p´araqcha) rumi pastalla saqiyamunki", nispas nin.

"Bueno mamitáy. Bueno mamitáy. Señorachaytaqa apasaqyari", nispas riki. Apan riki. Q´ipiyukun. Q´ipiyuspa apapun riki, karuta riki, muntiq kasqankama. Chay muntipis riki, chiqaqta rumi hatun, maran hina, p´alta riki. Chay patapis saqiyapun riki uñachataqa. Hinaspas uyachanmanta hap´iruspansi, uñachataqa much´apayan. "Señacháy, sapa dumingunmi hamusaq. Manan qunqamusaykichu. Señoracháy, ama waqankichu", nispas chicuchaqa riki uña wakataqa saqiyanpun. Chaysi llant´arukun. Ladunkunamantas llant´arukuspansi, chayta q´ipiyukuspa hanpun. Wasitaqa chayanpun. Chaysi willan riki.

"¿Saqimurankichu?" nispa

"Arí, saqimunin. Saqiyamunin. Llant´arukuspa hinan pasanpuni. Hinaspa, 'Sapa dumingunmi hamunki', niwanmi", nispas nin. "Risaqmi sapa dumingun señorachaymanqa", nispas. ¡Kharay! Semanaqa chirillañas chicuchaqa suyan riki.

Chaysis dumingutaqa tutamantaqa tira siqayun qhawaq riki. Ch´usaqllapiñas allinta, allinta wakachaqa kachkan riki chaypi. "Señoracháy hamuchkaykin, hamuchkayki señoracháy". Hinaspa much´arqarin uyankunapi, much´arqarin riki. Chaysi chaymantaqa hinas chaypi kachkan, qhawapayaspa, uñachatas qhawapayaspa hina, llamipayaspa hina. Chaymantaqa kasqantas ña inti yaykunanpaq hinaña kaqtinqa, lucupaqsi, "Señoracháy pasapusaqñachá riki. Mantanchikchá phiñakuwanman", nispansi, "nawan". Llant´ata llant´arukuspa, llant´antin hanpullantaq riki.

Chaysi paypa oficionqa kasqa riki, sapa dumingun riy. Ñas uñaqa hatunña kachkan, hatunña kachkan. Chaypiñataqsi huk dumingu riyninpiqa, "Ña señoracháy, señoracháy hamuchkanin", nispas riki.

"¡Ay, Marianitu!", nispas rimarirun wakachaqa.

Hinaspas llant´arukunsi. Pasapullasaqña, señoracháy. Mantanchik phiñakuwanqa", nispa.

"Kunanmi encargasayki mamitanchikman, Mamitanchikta ninki; ama piqpapas uyarisqallan ninki, hornadanpin t´antata ruwachinqa. Hinaspa chaymanta ñawinllanta, vinuta ñawinninta. Chaymanta nata t´ikata, agua benditata. Huk inocente chichuchatawan suyachiwanqa,

that no one has entered. Make sure she leaves a young boy waiting for me, an innocent boy."

The boy drew near. "Whatever you wish, my lady, my lady. I'll tell our mother," he promised, and kissed her. Oh, he caressed her little hooves, and returned to the house, content. He told the woman what had happened. "Ma'am, I have something to tell you. But don't talk about it to anyone else. No one can hear any of this. It's a message from the she-calf. She told me to deliver it."

"What? What did she send you to say? Tell me, tell me."

"Oh, mistress! You have to prepare an ovenload of bread. You have to put the first loaves you take out on the table, along with lovely flowers, holy water, the first cup of wine, all together, and leave waiting an innocent boy, ma'am. Also a bed just bought from the store. She said to me, 'She has to do all of this herself. No one else may touch it.'"

"Is that everything she told you?"

"Yes. She's going to come, I don't know whether she said Saturday night, or Sunday night. But she said she'd come at midnight, that much I know."

The she-calf's mother prepared everything with care. Then she asked herself, "Now for the boy. Who will I get?" Well, she had a neighbor woman, and that neighbor had a son, an innocent boy. She paid her a visit, and said, "Missus, my husband is away on a trip, and I'm all by myself. I don't have anyone to stay with me. Would you mind loaning me your son to sleep in my house with me? I'll take good care of him," she said, and gave money to the boy's mother.

The woman said, "Well, he can go, but just for tonight." She accepted.

That evening, the boy bathed all over with soap. The woman cleansed his whole body with hot water. She put beautiful, clean clothes on him, she splashed perfume on him, and prepared everything. Bedtime came. "Let's sleep right here. Tonight I'll stay and sleep by your side. We'll sleep like this, because I'm all alone." So the boy spoke to the woman about this and that, and she didn't answer, until at last the boy began to feel sleepy. At last, he fell asleep. The woman crept out of the room, but she couldn't fall asleep in her own room. "Will my daughter come in this door, or the other one? I want to see her."

At midnight, she heard the lament from the street corner, making its way toward the front door. "Aaaaaaahhh!" The she-calf opened the door slowly, and crept into the room. Beautiful candles were burning. She sniffed all that had been prepared, just a whiff. When she was done,

suyachiwanqa. Hinaspas na camata sumaq, ama piqpa puñusqanta musuqchallata. Hinaspa chaypi suyachiwanqa chicuchata, huk inucinti chicuchata", nispas nin.

Chaysis chicuchaqa riki yaykumun. "Estaría bueno señoracháy, señoracháy", nispa. "Nisaq mantanchiktaqa", nispansi much´arqarin. ¡Ay makichankunapis, lluyta llamiyuspa pasanpun cuntintu wasitaqa riki! Chaysi naqa nin, "Mamitáy, mamitáy. Pero ama pimanpis rimarinkichu. Aman pipas uyarinqachu imatapas. Uñachaymi encargakamuwachkan", nispas. "Señoracháy encargamuwachkan".

"¿Imata? ¿Imata encargamusunki? Willawayari, willaway", nispas nin.

"¡Ay, señorachaymi! Chhaynata hornadanpis t´antata masanki. Hinaspas chaymanta ñawillanta urquspayki mesapi; sumaqta t´ikantinta, agua benditantinta, vinuntinta ima hunt´aqata mama suyachinki huk inucinti chicuchatawan. Camantapas sumaq mamanta urqusqallata, comerciomanta urqusqallata. Pay kikillan lluyta nanqa.

Aman pipas llamiyunqachu", nispas.

"¿Chayllatachu nimurasunki?"

"Arí. Hamunqas nata, sábado tutata ni dumingu tutatachus nisqanchus hina. Pero 'doce tutatan hamusaq' nisqa riki".

Mamitanqa sumaqtas riki preparayun. Hinaspas, "Chicuchataqa riki. ¿Pitataq consiguisaqri? ¿Pitataq Consiguisaqri? nispas riki. ¿Pitas consiguisaqri? Nispa. ¡Ay, chaysi vecinunqa kasqa, huk wawachayuq, huk inucinti chicucha! ¡Chaypis riki rimapayaq yaykun riki! Chaysi, "Señora, khaynatan qusay viajan. Hinaspan sapachallay kachkani. Manan pipas acompañaqniy kanchu... ¿Manachu nawankiman, mañaywankiman, puñuyraysimuwananpaq? Manan imanpas faltanqachu", nispas qullqita ima quyun riki mantanmanqa.

Chayqa, "Bueno richunyari tutallapaqqa", nispansi nin. Aceptayun.

Hinaspas chicuchaqa tardentaqa sumaqta jabuncilluwan, sumaqta bañarun. Q´uñi unuwan lluyta bañarun chicuchataqa. Ropachantapas sumaqta; limpio ropawan cambiarun, perfumikunawan sumaqta, lluyta alistaspa. Chaypis riki tardeña kapun riki. "Sunk´ischapi puñukuchkan. Kunallan nuqapis puñuq yaykumusaq laduykipi. Puñukusunchik khayna; sapallaymi kani", nispa. Chaysi chicuchaqa riki parlapayachkan; señorataqa niyuchkan. Mana payqa parlapayunchu, puñuy aysanankama. Chayqa por fin puñurapusqa chicuqa. Chayqa allillamanta lluqsiranpun riki señoraqa. Chaysi riki, manas cuartunpiqa puñunchu riki. "Kayñachu, chayñachu yaykuramunqa wawayqa, qhawayunaypaq", nispas.

Kuska tutatas, ay esquinamantaqa, "¡a a a a a!", nispa waqan.

she approached the boy's bed. And with a whoosh! she slipped out of her calfskin. When she had slipped out of it, she climbed up on one corner of the bed.

The young lady drew close to the boy. She slid to his side to sleep next to him. The boy was asleep. He woke up, and when he turned over, she was sleeping by his side. He softly touched the maiden who was at his side. Softly he touched her. "Who could this be? Is it the mistress's face?" Her face was soft to the touch as silk. He stroked her hair, which was also like silk, and her head. After a while, the boy fell asleep again. While he slept, the she-calf vanished. He didn't see her go.

In the morning, the woman asked him, "Did you sleep well?" The woman gave the boy breakfast; cookies, and all the best of what she had. She didn't ask him anything more, or bother him in any way. Afterward, she offered him all manner of toys to play with there.

That afternoon, the boy said "I have to go back to my mother."

"Sure, go ahead, and take these things with you for your mother." She sent along cookies, sugar, and other things with the boy. His mother accepted all of it.

"Mommy, mommy," said the boy. "I'll go over again tonight to sleep at her house. She has to sleep by herself." And within himself, the boy was thinking, "I'll take along some matches and a candle. Who can it be? At least I can get a glimpse of her face." He took them with him that afternoon. He and the woman chatted about lots of things, while she lay in the pretty bed. I'll get in there too, mistress," he said. He talked and talked for a long time, just as before. Then the boy pretended to fall asleep, and the woman went out.

Again, at midnight, the lament of the she-calf could be heard at the street corner. "Aaaaah." The boy was awake, hidden beneath the covers.

"What is it, and why is it coming here?" He took a peek. The boy had been astute, and stayed awake. The she-calf entered, stood on her two hind legs. She savored the aroma of everything the mistress had left out, but she didn't touch anything. When she was done, she blew out all the candles. After they were out, she drew close to one corner of the bed. The boy heard a whoosh! and she slipped out of her calfskin— whoosh! and laid it in a heap for the next morning.

During the night the girl slept soundly, but the boy didn't sleep. Without making any noise, he slowly took out the matches and the candle from beneath the pillow. He lit the candle, and contemplated her face.

"¡Ay chayqa hamuchkanña!", nispasyá.

Yapamanta achhuyamuchkanña, achhuyamuchkanña callipunkupis, "¡a a a a a!", nispa uñachaqa waqarun. K´irr nispas, kicharukun punkutaqa. Hinaspas pasayapun chay cuartutaqa. Allichallamanta yaykun. Chaypis riki sumaq velakuna yawrachkan riki. Lluy, lluytas muskhirqarin riki q´alata, saburllanta. Mana tupayunpaschu; saburllantas lluyta muskhirun. Hinaspa chaymantataqsi riki, chichuchap ladunman achhuyun. Hinaspas qarachantaqa chhuwww niqllata ch´ustirakapun. Ch´ustirakapuqtinqa munturun napi, riki catrep esquinallanpi.

Hinaspas chaymantaqa riki, señorachaqa achhuyapun riki. Achhuyapun, achhuyun puñunanpaqyari. Chaysi puñuyuchkan riki chicuchaqa riki. Rikch´arimuspaqa riki t´ikrarikamun. Hinaspas ladunpi puñusqa. Chaysi wawataqa ladunpi mullkhuyun uyantaqa. Hinatas mullkhuyun, hinata. "¿Imataq kaypiri?" nispa. "Señorap uyanchá", riki nispayá. Paypa sunqullanpi riman. Hinaspas sumaqchallaña, sedachallañas uyanqa. Chukchachantas llamiyun, sedallañas; umachanpas. Chayqa bueno chaymantaqa puñurapusqa riki. Puñurunankama pasapusqa uña wakachaqa. Mana rikupusqachu.

Chayqa kasqantas, riki paqarisnintinpas, "¿Allinchu puñuranki?" nispas riki. Señoraqa desayununta, sumaqta nakunayuqta, gallitasninkunayuqta, lo mejorta riki chicuchataqa riki. Manas tapunchu, ni imananpaschu riki, Hinaspas chaypi, pukllakunanpaq, lliwta, juguetekuñata ima invitachkan riki. Hinaspas nin, tardintaqa nin, "Mamitaypata rirusaq", nispa.

"Riruyá. kay, kayta apanki, kaykunata. Apay mamitaykiman", nispas riki. Nakunata, galletaskunata, azucarta, lliwta apachin riki. Chaysi mamitanqa chaskiyun.

"Mamá, mamá. Kunantawan puñuysimusaq señorata. Sapallanmi puñukuq kasqa", nispa nispas riki. Chicuchaqa riki yuyayninman riki, "Apakusaq fusfurutawan, velatawan", nispa. "¿Imapuni? Qhawayusaqpuni uyachanta", nispas riki. Hinaqtinsi apakun tardentaqa riki. Q´alas parlachkanku señorawanqa; pay kikin riki sumaq camachapiqa. "Nuqapas mamitáy hamusaq", nispas. Yapamanta parlapayan, parlapayan. Hinaspataq puñuq tukurapun. Pasapun señoraqa.

Yapamantas kuska tutataqa riki uñachaqa riki "¡a a a a a!", esquinamanta waqamullantaq. Chicuchaqa manas puñunchu riki. Frazada ukuchallamanta riki pakachallamanta. "¿Imapunitaq kanman, yaykumunanpaqri?" nispa. Chayqa qhawachkan riki. Mana puñuyunchu riki; astutu chicuchaqa. ¿Chaysi riki yaykumun ih? uñaqa, waka uñacha. Hinaspa iskay chaki sayan. Hinaspas sumaqta muskhirqarin, lliwta

49

Ah, the girl was gorgeous! Even her hair shone. The boy, gazing on her, said to himself, "Oh, how beautiful she is!" When he was about to blow out the candle, a drop of wax fell on her face.

Oh, the boy didn't know what to do! The girl vanished, she simply disappeared. At that same instant, he lit the candle and began to stitch together sandals, as fast as he could, seven pairs, just as she had said for him to do. In the morning, he lit out after her. He walked along, asking and asking everyone he met about her. He arrived at the outskirts of a village. There he asked, "Ma'am, you didn't happen to see a young lady who passed through here?"

"Yes, she came through this morning," she said.

"She already came through?"

"Yes, already."

He kept on after her. He walked and walked along the path. He arrived at another village. By now, he was a young man. He had worn out two of the pairs of sandals. "Oh, now what will I do?" He arrived at another village, and there he said "Ma'am, ma'am, I want to ask you. A young lady didn't happen to pass through here, did she?"

"Yes, she passed through. She came already, just a little while ago."

"Maybe I can catch up with her." He kept walking, faithful. So he went through one village and another, asking one person and another. At last, he came to a village, and said "It looks like the villages are running out."

A woman there told him "There aren't any more. From here on, it gets tropical." By now, the young man was headed toward the jungle. "There are no more towns," she told him. "Where are you going to go?"

"But ma'am, did she pass through here?"

"Yes, she did pass through here. The young lady was headed toward the tropics."

"Oh! Then maybe I can catch up with her," he said, and kept on walking. He only had two pairs of sandals left. He was getting near the end of them. He pressed on into the heart of the jungle, and was surrounded by plants. All the same, he kept on ahead, further into the jungle.

He reached a place where some condors had killed a cow. But they didn't have any way to divide it up. Seeing the young man, they said to him, "Stop! Where are you going? What do you want here? You shouldn't be walking in this place."

"No, sir. No, sir. But a sorrow is driving me on. I'm walking because my heart is sleepwalking."

"What?"

chaypi churasqankutapis. Lliwta muskhirparispa, mana tupayunchu. Hinaspas chaymanta ichaqa phukurapun tukuy velakunata. Phukurapuspas, achhuyun catrep esquinantaqa. Hinaspas chaypi shuuq uyarichkansi. Shuuq, qarachanta ch´ustirukun. Hinaspa munturun riki, chayqa tutamantapaqqa.

Tutataqa riki, chicaqa riki. Secota puñurapusqa. Chicuchataqsi mana puñunchu Ni t´ik nirillanpaschu. Fusfuruta allichallamantas almadun sikimanta urqurun; velatapas. Hinaspas hap´irachispansi, hinata uyachantayá lliwta qhawayuchkasqa riki. ¡Ay! munaychallañas señorachaqa riki. Hinas chukchachanpas brillachkaq. "¡Ay ñañaw!", nispansi riki qhawayuchkan. Phukuyurunan kachkaqtin...uyanman sut´uyurusqa.

Rikch´arun riki. "¿Imapaqmi qhawawachkaranki? Napaq, Kunanmi isu sí mana tariwankiñachu. Kay imaymana qanchis paris husut´ata ruwakunki, chaypis manan chaypa tukukunankamapas tariwankiñachu", ¿nispa ih?

¡Ay manas imanakuyta atinchu chicuchaqa riki! Pasapun. Ch´usaqman kapunchu chicaqa. ¡Ay, kasqan ratus velata hap´iyuchispa riki!, Husut´ata chanin, mana chaninchu ruwayukun cuchilluwan riki husut´achata, nisqan hina, qanchis parta. Hinaspas tutamantaqa cohete qipanta siqayun riki. Tapu-tapurikuspas, taputapuriyukuspas puriyuchkan. ¡Ay, llaqtap esquinanmansi chayarun! Chaypis tapuyukun, "¿Señoráy, paqta huk señorachata rikuwaq karan; kaynin pasaruqta?" nispa.

"Arí. Naqha tutamantaraqmi pasachkaran" nispas nin.

"¿Pasaranchu?"

"Arí, pasarunmi."

Yapamantas qatiyuchkallantaq. Caminutaqa, puriyuchkan puriyuchkan. Huk llaqtamansi chayan. Ña waynaña riki kapuchkan riki. Ñas ikay paris husut´a hinaña thantayukuchkan, "¡Ay! ¿Imanasaqtaq kunanqa?" Huk llaqtamansi chayayullantaq. Chaypis tapuyukullantaq riki. "Señoráy, señoráy, tapuyukusayki. Paqta kayninta huk señoracha pasarunman karan", nispas.

"Arí, pasarunmi. Naqha-naqhachallamá pasarunqa", nispas nin.

"Icha ayparuymanchu", nispas riki puriyachkan, chiqaqta riki. Bueno, chaymantataqsi riki, ña achka llaqtataña riki pasachkan riki, khayna taputapuyukuspa. Por fin huk llaqtaman chayasqa. Chayqa nisqa, "Kaypimá huk llaqtaqa tukukapun", nispa.

"Manan kannachu, kaymantaqa ch´ura-ch´urallanñamá." Naman, muntiman ripuchkan. "Manan kannachu", nispa. "¿Maytataq riwaqri?" nispas nin.

"¿Pero señoráy, pasaruran?"

"This is how it is, sir." And he told his story. "And she passed through here just a little while ago."

"Well, all right. If you want me to let you pass, divide up the meat of this cow in equal parts. Because first we give an offering to our mountain god." They gave an offering of meat to the principal mountain, their chief deity. He ate of the meat, the heart, the eyes, the tongue, all of that. That god ate until he was satisfied, and then the others afterward. So the young man butchered the whole cow into equal parts, and divided it up among the condors.

They gobbled up the beef while the young man waited. "Oh, life! Have I done all this in vain? Are they going to eat me too?" he said to himself, trembling, while he waited.

At last, the condor said to him "All right. Now one of us will carry you to the lake. On the bank of the lake, a goat is frolicking and eating. Capture it, and cut open its little stomach. Inside the stomach there will be a cat. Cut open the cat's stomach. Inside the cat's stomach there will be a guinea pig. Cut into the guinea pig's stomach. Inside will be a white dove. You have to capture that white dove."

"Come here," one of the condors told him. "Come here, and grab hold tight." He held fast to the condor's body, as hard as he could, even with his legs, and the condor flew, carrying him up high. Oh, the boy shut his eyes as tight as possible. When he looked down, the trees were tiny, miniature. "Keep holding tight, eh? Make sure you don't fall. I won't be responsible." The condor swooped down a ravine. He left the young man by the side of a lake, and departed.

Just as they had told him, there was a goat grazing by the bank of the lake. The young man said "Oh, and now? How will I capture it? How will I capture it?" He started out after the goat, but it wouldn't let itself be caught. Oh, he pursued it for a long time, from one spot to another, from one spot to another. The goat always got away. At last, he caught it. When he'd captured it, he cut open its stomach with care. And he found the cat inside. He cut open the cat's stomach, and inside the cat's stomach, there was a guinea pig. He cut open the guinea pig's stomach, with his little knife, with such care, and inside he found the white dove. In a wingbeat the white dove escaped. "Oh, oh," the boy moaned. "Now what will I do? Oh, what will become of my life? Oh, what will I do? Oh!" The poor boy was crying.

An eagle was flying in circles around there, and the boy said "Oh, little eagle, little eagle! Couldn't you do me the kindness of knocking down that dove with your wing?" The eagle did as he was asked. He

"Arí, kaychantan pasarun. Kay ch´ura-ch´uranta pasarun chay señorachaqa", nispan nin.

"¡Ay! anchachus ayparuyman", nispas riki puriyuchkan. Manañas, huk parchallañas husut´apas kachkan riki. Tukuyukuchkannas. Chaysi riki karutañas muntañata riki puriyuchkan, sach´akuna ukuta. Muntañatapuni puriyuchkan riki.

Chaypis riki naqa kunturkunaqa, wakata wañurachisqaku.

Hinaspas mana mayninmanta partinakuyta atichkasqakuchu riki. Hinaspas nin, "¡Yaw! ¿Maytan hamunki?" nispa. "¿Imamanmi hamunki? Kayta manan qampaqqa purinaykichu", nispas nin.

"Manan, papáy, manan papáy. Huk llakin qatiriwan chaymi khaynata purimuchkani, sunquy musphasqa", nispan nin.

"¿Ima?" nispas nin.

"Khaynatan papáy karan", nispa. Tukuytasyá q´alata willan riki. "Hinaspanmi kunan pasamun."

Hinaspa, "¡Ah! Chayqa, bueno. Munanki chayman saqichimunayta, chayqa igualchankalla, aychata partiruway; kay wakantinta", nispas nin. "Primirutaraq apuchunninkuman", nispas nin. Jefenkuman aychata riki, corazunninta, ñawinta, qallunta, lliwta mikhun. Chaymantari yapamanta hasta saksanankama apuchunninkuqa mikhurun riki. Llipinku chaymantañas.

Ichaqa lliwta partichin, sapankaman. Igualchankalla partiyun riki, wakantinta.

Chaypis mikhuychkanku; suq´uychkanku wakataqa, aychata riki. Paytaqsi chaykama suyayuchkan riki. "¿Yanqapaqchu? ¡Ay vida! ¿Nuqatawanchu mikhuruwanqakupas?" nispasyá, khatatasparaq suyayuchkan.

(Bueno chaysi riki chaysi riki, na) "Bueno khunanmi saqimusunki. Huk quchan kachkan. Qucha patanpiña cabra phawakachachkan, mikhuchkan. Anchay cabrata hap´irunki, chay cabrata.

Hap´irunki, wiksachallanta kuchurunki. Chay wiksachanpin kanqa michi. Chay michip wiksachanta kuchurunki. Chay michip wiksachanpin kanqa na quwi. Chay quwip wiksanta kuchurunki. Yuraq palumacha kanqa. Chayta hap´irunki", nispas nin, nispasyá.

"Hamuyá kayman kaymanta qaqata hap´ipakuwanki", nispayá kunturqa nin riki. Kaymanta qaqata ch´ipayukuchkan chakinkunawanraq riki. Ch´ipakun. Huktas vulayachin, altuta riki. Ay, ñawintas qaqallataña wisqayun riki. Qhawariyunsi, ñas na hinallañas mallkikunapas, huch´uychallaña alayriyuchkan.

"¡Allinta hap`ipakuwanki, ah! Paqtataq urmayuwaq. Manan nuqaqa respondisaykichu", nispas. Bajadaman urayapun naqa riki. Por fin

knocked down the dove with his wing, and made her fall to the earth. The boy captured her, and at that moment she was changed into a young girl. She had been enchanted.

She said to him, "Oh, it's true that you love me. I had said about you, 'I don't think he loves me.' I've suffered a lot."

"How did you come to be that way?"

"I was enchanted."

"Oh, now can we be married?"

"Is that what you sought me out for?"

"Yes," he answered. "Yes, we'll marry."

In an instant they were transported to the edge of their village. One minute nothing was there, and the next they appeared there. They decided to build a beautiful home, like a palace, in that place. And in an instant, in the middle of the night, it appeared there, with servants, butlers, everything one could want inside. All the neighbors were astonished. "What's happening here? Just yesterday it was an open field. And now look, a beautiful palace has appeared. Is this place enchanted, or what is it? How can a house be raised in a single night?" Everyone was astonished.

Finally, the two were married. They called the priest, and were married with great pomp. I was there too, hanging around, and I was going to bring you a plateful of the wedding food, canapés and all. But there at the streetcorner a dog snatched it out of my hands.

quchap kantunpi . . . Nan riki, pasapun. Kunturqa pasapun, saqiyuspa riki. Chicuta saqiyuspa pasapun. Chaysi chiqaqta riki, naqpa marpa patanpi, cabraqa mikhuyuchkasqa pastuta. Chaypi hinaspas riki nin, "¡Ay!, ¿Imaynatataq kunanri hap´isaqri? ¿Imaynatataq hap´isaqri?" nispas, qatikachayun cabrataqa riki. Manas hap´ichikunchu riki. ¡Ay! qaqayniraqtas qatikachayun chay laduman, kay laduman, chay laduman. Cabraqa riki ayqikachayuchkan. Por fin hap´isqa.

Hap´iruspaqa, (nisqa) hinansi wiksanta kuchurun riki. Allichayllamantas kuchurun wiksanta. Chiqaqtas chaypi michi. Chay michip wiksantas kuchurullantaq. Chay michip wiksanpis quwi.

Quwichap wiksachantas munaychallata cuchilluchawan riki kuchurullantaq. Chaypis chiqaqta riki yuraq paluma. ¡Pharr! ¿Pasapun? "Ay, ay! ¿Khunanri imanasaqtaq? ¡Ay! ¿Imataq nuqaq vidayqa? ¡Ay!, ¿Imanasaqtaqri?" nispas nin. "¡Ay!" Waqayuchkanraq riki pobreqa.

Chaypi hinaspas riki naqa, aguilaqa muyumusqa. "¡Ay! aguilitáy, aguilitáy kunanchá munayman; chay palumachata ch´aqllayramuwanaykita karan" nispas nin. Chayqa chiqaqtas palumataqa ch´aqlayun aguilaqa riki, pampakama chaypis hap´irusqa. Chaypi niñaman tukurapusqa riki; encantatarakapusqa. Chaypis riki, "¡Ay! munaykuwasqankimá. Nuqaqa manachá munakuwanchu; nirayki". Hinaspa, "Khaynaniraqtan sufrini."

"¿Imaynatatq chayamuranki kaymanri!" nispas ih?

"Nuqaqa encantasqan kaypi karani", nispa.

"¡Ay, kunanqa casarakusunchá!", riki nispas riki.

"Chay condicionwanchá maskhamuwarankiqa", nispas riki nin.

"Chay condicionwanchá maskhamuwarankiqa nispas nin.

"Arí", nispas nin. "Arí, casarakusunchikmi", nispa.

Chaysi ratuchalla llatap esquinanpi rikhurirapunku. Manañapas . . . . imapas kanchu. Ratuchalla chaypi rikhurirunku.

Hinaspas chaypi riki, sumaqta riki na, palaciuta hina ruwayachin riki, wasita ratulla tutap sunqullanpi rikhurirun. Lliw runakunas, sunqunantin, lliw sirvintikuna, lliw q´ala, warmakuna lindo. Chayqa chapis riki napusqaku admirakapusqaku. "¿Imataq sucidinri kunan? Qayninpunchawllataq pampa kachkan. Kunanqa khayna niraq sumaq palacio rikhurin. ¿Ima, encantuchu? ¿Imataq kanman? ¿Huk tutallapi wasiq sayarinanpaqri?" Lliw admirakunku riki.

Chayqa chaypi por fin casarapusqaku riki. Padreta waqhasqaku. Sumaqta pompasionllañas riki casarayukunku. Chaypi nuqapas muyuchkarani. Hinaspa apamuchkarayki chay lonche, puchukunata, lliwta. Hinaspa chay esquinapi allqu qichurapuwan.

The Condor

This brief, mythic account of a kidnapped shepherd girl bears a strong resemblance to "The Man-Bear." A child's game turns serious and results in a "marriage" based on forced captivity. The elusive hummingbird serves as the messenger of a supernaturally trapped girl's deliverance, as well as playing the part of a mischievous co-conspirator in punishing the interloper who disrupts her relation to her kin. Hummingbirds, frequently seen in the Andean countryside sipping nectar, are still more pervasive in lovelorn songs, poetry, and stories. The teller, Gloria Tamayo, was one of my Quechua teachers.

The Condor

Told by Gloria Tamayo

In a village, a man lived with his daughter. This daughter tended the sheep, llamas, and other animals. Every day a young man dressed in fine clothes would come looking for this young woman. A good dresser, with a black suit of clothes and a white muffler, and a hat too. And every day he went to see her. In time, he and the young woman came to be good friends. They got in the habit of playing together. And one day they were playing. "You carry me on your back, then I'll carry you on mine." They kept playing like that, like that, and he was lifting up the girl, tossing her around. One time, when he'd lifted her, the girl suddenly realized they were flying.

He took her up to a cliff, and put the young woman inside a niche. Then and there, the young man turned into a condor. Anyway, he kept the young woman there like that for a month, then two months. He fed her meat and all kinds of things; gave her roasted meat, boiled meat. So, when they'd been there a year or so, the girl became a woman. The girl gave birth to a little baby. And the girl cried night and day for her father. "How is my father getting along all alone? Who is keeping an eye on my father? Who is keeping an eye on my little sheep? Take me back to the place you brought me from. Take me back there," she begged the condor. But the condor didn't pay her any mind.

One day a hummingbird appeared. And she said to the hummingbird, "Oh, little hummingbird, hummingbird. There's no one else like you. You have wings. But there's no way on earth I can climb down from

Kuntur

Huk comunidadpis, huk runa tiyasqa ususinwan. Kay ususinsi uvijata michiq, llamakunata ima. Chaysi, kay warmichamanta sapa punchaw riq watukuq huk wayna, allin k´achalasqa. Sumaq p´achayuq, yana p´achayuq, yuraq chalinayuq, sombriruyuq ima. Chaysi, sapa punchaw ripayaq. Hinaspansi, warmichawanqa na allintaña amistadta ruwasqaku; pukllakuqku, imas. Hinaspansi, huk punchaw pukllasqaku. "Qam uqariwanki; nuqa uqarisayki", Chaynata. Chaysi, hinapi hinapi pukllasqankupis, warmichataqa uqarirparin. Ña altutaña uqarichkaqtinsi chayraq warmichaqa riparakun altupiña kasqanta.

Chaysi, huk qaqa ukuman, t´uquman winarapusqa warmichataqa. Chaysi, chaypi kay waynaqa kunturman tukupusqa.

Hinaspansi, huk killa, iskay killa hinañas uywachkan warmichataqa; aychawan, tukuy imaymananwan: aycha kankata, aycha t´imputa ima quspa. Chaysi wata hinaña kachkaqtinkus ña warminña kapusqa hinaspa, wawachata wachakusqa kay sipascha.

Chaysi, sipaschaqa tutapunchaw waqayuchkan taytanmanta:

"¿Imaynataq taytayri sapallan qipan? ¿Pitaq taytaytari qhawachkan? ¿Pitaq uvijachaykunata qhawachkan? Pusapuway maymantan apamuwaranki. Chayman pusapuway", nispansi valiyukun kunturtaqa.

Chaysi kunturqa mana kasunchu. Hinaspansi, huk punchaw huk q´intichaqa rikhurisqa. Chaysi, q´intichaqa nin: "¡Ay, q´intichalláy q´inticha! ¿Piñataq qam hinaqa? Raprayuq kanki. Mana nuqa kaymanta imaynatapas urayuyta atinichu. Wata masñan pusaramuwan, waynaman

59

here. He brought me here a year or more ago, a condor who turned into a man. And now I've become his woman. I've even given birth to his child."

The hummingbird said, "Don't you cry, young lady. I'm going to help you." Then the little hummingbird said, "Today I'll go and tell your father where you are. Your father will soon come looking for you then."

And the girl said, "Oh, so you do know my house, hummingbird? There are lots of pretty flowers in my garden. I promise that if you help me, every single one of those flowers around my house will be only for you."

When she said that, the hummingbird joyfully returned to her village. There, it said to her father, "Hey, I know right where your daughter is. She's the wife of a condor. Only, I don't think there's any way for us to get her down from where she is. I know, let's take an old donkey along," and he told the old man what his plan was. They laid the donkey out on the plain. And while the condor was busy eating it, busy eating the old donkey, the hummingbird and the man got the young woman down from the cliff. And in her and the child's place, they put two frogs: one small one, one big one. So they left behind those frogs inside the niche, inside the cliff niche. The old man was able to get his daughter down from there and take her home.

Next, the hummingbird went to where the condor was, and said to him, "Listen, condor. You can't guess what terrible thing has happened in your home." That's what he said.

"What happened?" the condor wanted to know.

"Your wife and child have turned into frogs." The condor flew straight back to see. Neither his wife nor his child was in the cliff niche any longer; just two frogs were. He sure was surprised, but there was nothing for him to do. Now the little hummingbird spends each and every day among the flowers in the young girl's house.

tukuspa huk kuntur. Chaymi kunan warmin kapuni. Hinaspa ña wawachaytapas wachakuniña", nispa.

Chaysi, q´inticha nin: "Ama waqaychu, yaw sipas. Nuqa yanapasayki". Chaynatas q´intichaqa nin: "Kunan willaramusaq taytaykiman maypi kasqaykitapas. Taytaykipas maskhasasunki", nispa.

Chaysi kay sipaschaqa nisqa: "¿Riqsinki riki yaw, q´inticha wasiytaqa? wasiypiqa askha t´ikakuna sumaq kachkan. Imaynapipas yanapawanki, chayqa chay wasiypi kaq t´ikakunapas qampaqmi kanqa q´ala", nispa.

Chayta niqtinsi, kusisqa q´intichaqa kutirin llaqtaman. Chaysi, nimun taytanta: "Ña yachaniña maypichá ususiyki kachkan.

Altupi t´uqu ukupi kachkan. Kunturpa warminmi. Icha manan atisunmanchu hinallata pusanpuyta", nispa. "Aparikusunchk huk machu asnuta", nispansi q´intichaqa yachachin machulaman. Chaysi rinku; hinaspa, aparikunku machu asnuta. Chaysi churayunku pampallapi. Chayqa kuntur mikhuchkanan kama, chay machu-asnu mikhuchkanan kama, q´intichawan machulachawanqa chicata, sipaschata urayachipunku qaqamanta. Hinaspansi, apasqaku iskayta hamp´atukunata: huk huch´uyta huk hatunta. Chayqa, chay hamp´atukunata saq´inku t´uqu ukupi, chay qaqa t´uqu ukupi. Hinaspansi, urayramuqtin pusakapun machulacha ususintin.

Chayqa, q´intichataq rin kunturpa kasqanman. Hinaspansi, willamun: "Yaw, kuntur, manan qam yachankichu ima desgraciachá wasiykipi kachakn." Chayta nispa.

"¿Imataq pasarunri?" nispansi kunturqa nin.

"Warmikin wawaykipuwan hap´atuman tukurunku", nispa.

Chayqa, phawaspas kunturqa qhawaq rin. Hinaspansi, t´uqu ukupiqa manañas sipaschu nitaq wawanchu kapun; iskay hap´atullaña kasqa. Chaysi, mancharikuspa; manaña imatapas ruwasqachu. Chayqa, q´intichataq sapa punchaw sipaschap wasinpi t´ika ukullapiña sapa punchaw kaq.

The Quena

Quenas have become an almost hackneyed sound-icon of the melancholy Andean, usually playing the dreaded musical cliché "El Condor Pasa" on plaza sidewalks or in tourist restaurants. In this, Gloria's other simple story, the quena is returned to its freshness; the youngest son gets literally turned into a live reed. When he is carved and played, he signifies his sadness. One hopes that the little boy's preternaturally knowing voice is striking one of the notes compiled or composed by the brilliant musicologist and instrumentalist Jaime Guardia. "Since we are all mortal/Let us put our lives in order." Here, as in other stories where the woodcutter appears, one can discern the influence of European folk tales such as "Hansel and Gretel" and "Little Red Riding-Hood." The fact is, apart from scattered groves of eucalyptus trees, which aren't much good for building and are inferior as firewood, there is precious little wood to be had around Cusco. The figure of the woodcutter exists far more in imagination than he does in actual practice. Certain aspects of these stories reflect social realities. Other aspects are rooted in the parallel and autonomous world of the imagination.

The Quena

Told by Gloria Tamayo

Once upon a time, in a village, there was a woman. She was left a widow. That woman had three children. The two older children really hated the youngest boy. The mother spoiled the youngest a lot. And he had become a mama's boy. Seeing this, the older brothers strongly hated this youngest kid. One day, the three of them went out to hunt for firewood. When they got to an isolated ravine, the two older ones killed their younger brother. They then returned to their mother's house. And when their mother asked for the youngest, they said, "We didn't see him. He went along another path."

His mother waited for him all night long, she waited until the next morning. He didn't come back. A week went by, a month, and he didn't come back. The woman went walking around, crying, asking this person and that, "Have any of you seen my baby, or not?" Nobody could tell her anything. Nobody knew anything about how that youngest boy had come to be lost.

One day, a woodcutter was passing through that ravine, and there, lots of reeds were growing. The man cut off one of the reeds, and made himself a quena. And he began to play the little quena. At that moment, the quena began to cry "It's me, my sweet mother, my mama. I've been here all along. My brothers killed me, my brothers murdered me. I'm buried right here." The quena's cry told of all his suffering.

The man was startled, and said to himself, "Whose child could this

Qinacha

Huk kutinsi, huk llaqtapi, huk warmi kasqa. Chaysi, viuda qipapusqa. Kay warminpas kasqa kimsa wawankuna.

Iskay kuraqkuna sinchita chiqnikuq sullk´a kaq chicuta.

Mamansi kay sullk´a kaqta sinchita luluq. Chayrayku, aswan lulusqata uywasqa. Chayta rikuspas, kuraq wawqinkuna sinchita chiqnikapun sullk´a kaq warmata. Chaysi, huk kuti llant´aman risqaku. Hinaspansi chaypi ch´in niq wayq´upi wañuchisqaku sullk´a wawqinkuta. Chaysi kutipusqaku mamankupa wasinman.

Chaysi, tapuqtin mamanta nisqaku, "Mana rikuykuchu. Payqa ñannintan ripun", nispa.

Chaysi, mamanqa suyayun tutantin, paqaristinpis suyayun.

Manas kutinpunchu. Chay simanaña, killaña, manas kutinpunchu. Chayqa, hina waqaspa warmiqa purisqa, hukta-hukta tapukuspa: "¿Rikurankichikchu wawayta, icha manachu?" nispa. Manas pipas willanchu. Manas pipas yachanchu chay sullk´aq chinkasqanta.

Chaysi, huk kutin huk llant´a ruwaq risqa chay wayq´uman chaypis wiñayuchkasqa sumaqtaraq suqus. Chaysi, Huk suqusta kuchuspa, qinata ruwasqa chay runaqa. Chaysi, qinachanta tucayta qallarin. Chaysi qinacha waqayta qallarin: "¡Nuqaqa, ay mamallay, mama! Nuqaqa kaypi kachkani. Wawqiykunan wañuchiwan, wawqiykunan sipiwan. Kaypin p´ampasqa kachkani", nispansi waqayta qallarin, ancha llakillataña qinaqa.

Chaysi runaqa mancharikun, ichaqa: "¿Piqpa wawantap kayri kan-

be?" And he asked the quena, "Who are you telling me about?" He played the little quena again.

And it said, "My mother is that widow, the poor woman. She's been walking about crying, asking for me. Tell her where I am."

When the woodcutter told the widow, she said "I hope it's true, sir. Show me where he is, and I'll give you whatever I can."

So the man began to play the quena. And the quena let loose its cry again. "Oh, my sweet mother, I'm right here, buried. My brothers killed me this way." There they found the boy. The mother watered the reeds with her tears, and revived him. And they lived happily ever after.

man?" nispansi qinachata tapun. "¿Pimantataq willakuchkanki?" nispa. Llapa tucayullantaq qinachataqa.

Chaysi nin: "Mamaysi chay viuda, wakcha warmi. waqaspa purichkan, nuqamanta tapukuspa. Willayanpuway maypi kasqaytapas", nispa.

"Ichapas papay. Ima kasqantapas, qupusqayki. Willaway maypin", nispa.

Chaysi qallarin runaqa qina tucayta. Chaysi qinachaqa yapa waqallantaq: "¡Ay, mamallay, nuqaqa chaypin kachkani, p´ampasqa! Wayqiy-kunan khaynata wañuchiwan" nispa. Chaypis taripusqaku chicuta. Chayqa, mamanpa wiqinwan qarpachkallaqtinsi rikch´arinpusqa. Hi-naspa, kusisqa kawsasqaku.

The Clever Priest

    *

Miguel Waman was 72 years old at the time he told me this and all the other stories of his that are contained in this collection. Whether Miguel is a Catholic, pagan, neo-Incan, agnostic, or atheist at the end of the day is difficult to determine. He always seemed to delight in describing priests in the most ribald and "sacrilegious" terms possible. He never disguised his contempt for the particular village priest who reigned in San Jeronimo at the time I compiled "The Clever Priest." He found him a bit of a stick. Yet not long ago, Miguel paid for a mass to be celebrated in memory of the third anniversary of his wife's death. The same day, he and his daughter-in-law asked me to be godparent to one of his grandsons when the boy gets baptized. The liturgical forms of the Catholic religion seem to give him a certain comfort, yet he doesn't appear to have an especially optimistic view of how Catholicism might intervene in his life or afterlife. Miguel told this piquant tale with an irrepressible gusto, almost crowing by the time he reached the end. Yet it must be observed that "The Clever Priest" contains a clear and important reversal. The priest doesn't get away with his defilement of the nun and of Saint Peter. Saint Paul is there to administer divine justice in the form of mortification of the flesh. I liked this carefully irreverent story so much that I elsewhere rewrote it in verse as a song lyric, as part of the libretto for "The Serpent's Lover," my musical play about the Tupac Amaru rebellion.

The Clever Priest

Told by Miguel Waman

There was a parish priest and his sacristan. And a young nun, good looking, a babe, like your wife, was in the convent. First she would enter
making the sign of the cross to Saint Peter. She couldn't enter or leave
without always saying "See you later" to the saint. She greeted him, came
close, prayed, always observed him.

The priest was aware of all this, took note. "What can I do, what can
I do, how can I make her fall?" he said to himself. "How can I make
her fall?" One day, he said "Young lady."

"Yes, father."

"Tonight, young lady, Good Saint Peter is going to visit you."

Oh, man, she was happy, content, just happy. "As much as I love him,
surely he'll love me the same. That's why he's visiting me."

The priest set himself to thinking. He wondered "What can I do?"
He dressed himself in the saint's clothes, adornments. The saint himself ended up naked, without a stitch.

That night, he went to see the young lady. She had set out a beautiful altar, pretty flowers, candles. The priest climbed to the top of the
altar, all the way up to the cross. Incense was flowing. The lady, the young
lady, was overjoyed. It was just the two of them. He came down slowly,
slowly. "Father Pedro was to sleep by your side," he said.

"Oh Peter, my little Father, is going to sleep by my side!" She was
contented. And Peter, at midnight, just ate her right up.

But the sacristan heard it all. He had come in right behind the priest,

Huk Cura Yuyayninpi

Huk cura kasqa, parroco, sacristannintin. Hinaspa, señoritaqa *monjita salió pues, mamita, como tú mujer buenamoza.*

Primero entraba persignado al santo San Pedro. Yaykun napayukuq llusinpunanpaqpas *"Hasta luego"* nispas. Saludaykun, achhuyukun, rezayukun ima.

Curaqa qhawachkallan, está mirando. *"¿Qué cosa hago, qué cosa hago, en qué forma puedo hacer caer?" Está diciendo pues cura.* "Imaynata urmayachisaq". *Un día,* "señoracha".

"Papá" cura nin, "señoracha kunanmi taytacha San Pedro visitamusunki", nispa.

Ay caray kusisqa, *contenta pues, alegre pues. "Como tanto yo quiero me querrá el también pues",* dijo. *"Por eso me visitará".*

Chayqa pinsasqa curaqa napaq riki, curaqa yuyayninpi kachkan. Yuyayninpi nichkan "¿Imatan ruwasaq?" nispa. Santop p'achanwan churarukun, imaynan p'achaykiwan churarukuyman, aknata p'achanwan, llipinwan. Q'alalla santuqa sayachkan, q'alachalla.

Chaynintin rin señoritaqtaqa. Chayqa sumaqchata altarchata watasqa: sumaq t'ikakuna, lluy velakuna. Chayqa pataman siqan, pata puntaman. . . cruzchata. Inciensuchata t'akachkan.

Señoraqa, señoritaqa kusisqa; iskaychallanku. San Pedro altarpis kachkan, paytaq pampapi. Allichallamanta uraykamun, uraykamun. "Taytacha laduykipi puñuyunqa", nisqa.

"¡Ay taytay, taytacha puñuyunqa laduypi!" *contenta pues.*

dressed in Saint Paul's clothing. Peter and Paul have equal power, you see, as far as their holy feasts are concerned. Today you have Saint Peter, tomorrow Saint Paul. So what did the sacristan do? He'd brought a big whip, and a big stick. He beat the stuffing out of the priest, and whipped him all the way back to the manse. He just about killed him.

The next morning the sacristan came into the manse. "Father."

"Son."

"How are you, father?"

"Oh, a thief came in last night."

"Oh, father. Your body is in bad shape."

"Yes, he beat me all over. He hit me here, and here." Under his breath, he said, "And I'm kicking myself pretty good too."

"Oh, father. Did you know that Good Saint Peter is completely naked?"

"Oh, don't let anyone find out. Here, I'll give you some money. Go get some clean clothing, and put it back on him."

The sacristan had freshly laundered clothing put on the saint. He'd come back the night before and put Saint Paul's clothing back on him. And he'd beat the poor priest so hard, he'd just about killed him. The two of them kept on living in the same place, eating together, just as we are here now, like that. They lived a good life in common; the sacristan and priest were like brothers.

The sacristan wanted to confess what he'd done, but couldn't bring himself to do it. He'd say to himself, "I beat up on the priest." As he couldn't say it directly, he'd just say, "Oh father, father, forgive me!"

"I forgive you, my son, I forgive you. You're solid gold to me. You're like a saint."

The sacristan was in torment about not being able to tell. He was really suffering. "How can I die without telling him I whipped him?" He was suffering, in torment. "Father. Father, you went as Saint Peter, and I went as Saint Paul. I beat you. Forgive me, father."

The poor priest didn't know whether to shout or fall to the ground. What could he do? He'd known nothing about the sacristan beating him. He'd really believed he'd been beaten by Saint Paul.

Taytachaqa *a la media noche* mikhuyapunyá.

Naqa uyarichkan; sacristanqa qipanpi kachkan, San Pablop p´achanwan vistirusqa. *Pedro y Pablo son iguales pues,* fiestankupas: Kunan San Pedro, paqarin San Pablo. ¿Imata ruwan naqa sacristanqa? (*Buen lazo había*) allin lazuta apasqa, allin k´aspita. Thalla-thallata curata p´anayapusqa; hasta casacuralkama chayachimusqa. Yaqa wañuchipusqapas.

Tutachallamanta yaykurun nataqa casacuraltaqa. "Papá".

"Hijo".

"Imanantaqri papá".

"¡Ay, suwan yaykumusqa!", ninsi.

"¡Ay, papá! lluymá papá cuerpoykiqa"

"Lluytan p´anaykuwan. Kaypin p´anaykuwan". Sunqunpiqa, "allinta nuqa p´anaykuni", nichkantaqyá.

"¡Ay papá! ¡papá San Pedroqa q´alallataq kachkasqa!" ninsi.

"¡Ay, ama pipas yachachunchu! qullqita qusqayki. T´asarachinpuway. Ama kunanqa misapas kachunchu. T´aqsarachinpuy, hinaspa churayapunki".

T´aqsarachimun churayapun ropanwan. Payqa hamuspa hinalla. San Pablomanqa churapusqa p´achanwanqa allinta.

P´anayuspa hinalla, tirasta pobretaqa yaqa sipimusqapas hina.

Chayqa ña iskaychallanku kuskalla mikhunkupas, ankhayna kachkanchik, hinalla. Munaychallata kawsachkanku, wawqintin hinalla curawanqa.

Confesakun chaysis willakun. Mana imaynata willayta atinchu, chay p´anasqanta. "Chiqaqtachá taytacha p´anawan", nichkanchá, riki.

Chayqa mana imaynata willata atispa: "¡Ay papáy, papá perdunawankichá!"

"Perdonayki hijo, perdonayki. Qullqiy rantin kanki. *Eres como santo*".

Llakikuchkanpuni huk kay mana willakusqanmantaqa. Sacristanqa llakikuchkan. *"¿Cómo voy a morir sin avisar lo que he sobado?"* Llakikuchkan, llakisqa kachkan. "Papáy. Riranki San Pedromanta, nuqataq San Pablomanta. P´anayusqaytan, perdonaway papáy.

¡Ay cura mana kunpakuyta ni qapariyta!, ¿Imanayta atinchu, i? Anchaypiña yachasqa sacritán p´anayusqanta. Payqa creesqa chiqaq San Pablo p´anasqanpaqyá.

The Baker and The Lovers

Here is one of two somewhat overlapping tales Miguel recounted of a husband's revenge on his adulterous wife. But the woman's punishment is not such a clear victory for the husband. The wife's reappearance as an undead soul, in her funeral shroud, underscores the fact that the bond between the living and the dead in southern Andean society remains complicated and strong. The husband is compromised as much as she by her transgression. Besides, it isn't such a simple matter to get shut of a kinsman or a spouse, no matter what that person's sins. Although—as will become apparent in the other stories about condemned souls in this collection—there are specific formulae for freeing these souls (and therefore, by extension, oneself), there exists no guarantee that they will not reappear later in some other, usually malevolent, guise. The baker in this tale, with his crafty attempt at a quick fix, learns this very lesson. Usually, the liberation into heaven is not complete until the sinner gets absolved, often accompanied by a physical blow, and turns into a white dove, imitating Christ's ascension.

The Baker and the Lovers

Told by Miguel Waman

There once was a baker. He ground grain and sold bread. So he regularly had to go fetch grain. One time he went to get some grain. When he came back, his friends let him know something about his wife. They said "Listen, brother, you need to go to bed instead. Your wife is sleeping with somebody else." He couldn't believe it. The next time he had to go out, he thought about doubling back. He wondered and wondered. So, the time after the baker said to his wife, "I'm going out for grain. I'll be back tomorrow."

Once she knew that, the woman said to the neighbor, her lover, "My husband won't be back until tomorrow. Come over; we can sleep here."

"Okay."

Not long after, at nightfall, the husband sneaked back. When he came in the house, his wife said "What did you come back for?"

"Nothing. I just left my machete behind. That's what I came back for."

Man, she got him out of the room as fast as she could. Then she said to her tryst partner, her lover, "Here, climb inside the oven and wait." She opened the oven door. When the husband came back in the room, the wife had hidden the lover's clothes underneath the bedstead. "Husband, why don't you stay here?"

"No, I have to go back. I only left my burro here. No, I really have to get back there," said the husband.

"No, don't leave. Spend the night here."

"I think I'll just go." He pretended to go off, and came back around

Panaderuwan Puñuq
Masikunawan

Huk panaderu kasqa. Hinaspa t´antachata masakuq; mayninpi vindikuq trigunpi. Hinaspas triguchanman ripun riki. Hinaspas warminmantaqa willanku riki, "¡Ay, wawqiyqa, puñuruyta rinayki! warmiykiqa huk-wanmá puñukuchkan". Mana creenchu. Chayqa hukta hampurun. Chayqa tapukun, tapukun, waqtantañataq, "Trigumanmi risaq. Paqar-inña hampusaq", nispa nin panaderuqa. Chay negociantiqa, "Paqar-inña hampusaq," nispa warmintaqa nin.

Niqtinqa, warminqa chay munakuq masintaqa nin: "Paqarinña qusayqa hampunqa. Hamunki; puñukusunchik kaypi".

"Bueno."

Chayqa ratullamanyá ch´isillanta qusanqa yaykurun. Chayqa yayku-ruqtinqa nin, "¿Imamantaq kutimuchkankiri?' nispa.

"Mana, navajayta saqirparisqani", nispa. "Chaymanmi kutimuchkani," nispa.

¡Ay, qusanta luculla dispidirqan! Chay nataqa, chay tumpaymasin, chay quiridantaqa, "Kayllapi kachkan, hornupi tiyarayamuchkay", nispa. Hornuman wisq´arun. Chayqa qusan, yaykuqtinqa, p´achankunatapas catrep pachanman khaynaman winarun. "Qusáy quidakunkichá."

"Manan, kutipullachkaqmi. Saqiyamullanin asnuyta. Manan, kutiri-pullachkanqmi", qusanqa.

"Mana, amaña kutiychu. Tutañatáq."

"Hinallata ripusaq." Pasapuq tukun. Yapaqa kutiramun, huk ladunta. Yaykuramuspa khayna puñuchkaqta tarirapun, huktawan.

the other side of the house. When he entered again, he found them sleeping together. "Now what shall I do?" He had a very sharp knife. And while the two lovers slept, shak! shak! he slit them both. Then he went off on his trip.

He went on his way, and came back the next day. "Oh, my goodness. My wife up and died. I wonder how she died?" He pretended not to know. And of course he'd done it himself. "Goodness, we'll have to bury her. I'm so sad!" He put on as though he was grieving. But he sure wasn't grieving. "Why should I be crying?" He buried her and felt peaceful. Once she was buried, he didn't give her another thought. They hadn't even had children yet.

He walked into the kitchen one day, and his wife sat there cooking like always. She'd come back, and wore her funeral shroud. She sat there peeling potatoes, wearing her burial cap. And her winding sheet. "God damn!" he said "Now what do I do? Why have you come back?"

"I've wronged you, my husband. That's why God made me return."

"No, wife. I want you to go away from here."

"Me? But where to?"

"I don't care where, only go away. Go on, with that, you know, that companion of yours." That other guy had also died, of course, the one she was seeing. The two of them wandered off, wearing their shrouds, wandered down toward the jungle netherlands.

Meanwhile, the dead man's wife was still alive. The wife of that other man lived on. He'd gone off with his lover, not giving her another thought. The baker went on working, and the dead couple didn't return.

"I wonder whether my husband is dead, or has just strayed off?" the other woman asked herself about her husband. But there was no use thinking about it. He wasn't there anymore. He'd gone forever. There was no point in saying a mass for him anymore. There was nothing to do.

The baker pretended to know nothing. He played dumb. Because the woman was going around clamoring about the loss of her husband. "They tell me my husband used to come around here a lot," she said to the baker.

"I don't know anything about it, missus. I've never seen him before."

"They say he was your wife's lover."

"Ha! I doubt they were lovers," he answered. And who can say where those lovers were wandering, in the meantime, draped in their shrouds? The two of them had no money. Because they say that condemned souls can't carry money with them. They have to drift with no possessions of

"¿Imanasaqtaq kunanri?" nisqa. "Aswanyá iskachallantaña salva-yarapusaq", nispas nin chayqa cuchilluchan karanchá, filucha. Iskayninkuta puñuchkaqta, masi-puñuqchata, ¡Qhaq!, ¡qhaq! iskayninta. Pasakapusqataq viajita.

Chayqa pasakapuspaqa. Paqariynin chayamun. "Akakallaw. Warmiyqa wañupusqataq. ¿Imaynapitaq wañupunri?" Waqtallantayá nichkan. Paytaq ruwachkan. Chayrí, "¡Ay enterrayapunachá kanqa, riki! Akakallaw", nispa. Paylla waqtanta chullku churakun. Chayqa manañayá waqanpaschu. "¿Imapaqtaq waqasaq?" Tranquilulla enterrayakapun. Entierro tukuytaqa, mana ni pinsanpaschu; nitaq wawankunapas kasqataqchu. ¿Chayqa kusiña yaykunanpaqqa tiyakuchkasqa kaqta warmin wayk´ukuspa i? Kutirakanpusqa chhayna nachallantin, murta-jachantin tiyachkasqa, papata bondachkasqa, ququruchuchantin ima. *con su hábito pues.* "¡Carajo! ¿Imanasaqtaq? ¿Imamantaq kutimunkiri?"

Ñan, "qamta qusay ruwarayki. Chaymanta kutichimuwan Taytacha", nispas nin.

(Nuqallachá riki) "Qamllachá warmiy puriripunki."

"¿Nuqaqa. Mayman?"

"Rinaykitayá. Ripuychik chaywan, chay compañeruykipuwan." Chayqa huk kaqpas wañurapullantaqsi, chay tunpaymasinpas. Iskaninku chinkapunku, habituntinkama yunka uraymanchá tirayapunku riki.

Chayqa warmipas, warmi naqa kakuchkallan, chay qharip warmin-pas kakuchkallan. Paytaq [chayllawan rinku]. Ni pinsanpaschu. Qha-riqa llank´akuchkallan. Manaña kutinpunkuchu.

"¿Maypin wañupuranku; desaparisipunkuchu?" Averiguansi war-miqa qusanmanta. Manaña kanchu. Manaña piensapunchu. Chayqa wiñaypaq ripun. Chayqa manayá misatapas misachipunchu; ni imapas kanchu. Ni yachaqpas tukunchu. Qhariqa chullku churallakuchkan. Chayqa nañataqsi manuchamun riki, chay qharip warmin. "Kayllatas hamunman karan qusayqa", nispa.

"Manan nuqaqa, señora, yachanichu; ni riqsinipaschu."

"Warmiykiwansi pantanman karan."

"¡Hah! Manañatáq pantanmanpaschá", nillansi paytaq hinallapuni. Maytayá chinkapullankutaq yapamanta, habituntinkamaña. Chay qul-lqinkupas kachkansi. Manas qullqintaqa condeqa apakachanmanchu. Q´alallapas purinmi. Nitaqsi sombrerunpas akna kanmanchu; aknallas.

Chayqa chaymanta hampunku. Hampuqtinkuqa, chay qusanqa pu-natañataq ripusqa. Punata riqtinqa, papata apamusqa, achkhata q´ip-inpi. Asnupi cargamusqa papata. Hinaspa cargamuqtinqa, phawaka-

any kind. And they can't wear their hats tilted back on their heads; they're always tilted down over their eyes, like this.

But one day, the two of them did return. When they reappeared, the husband was on his way up to the highland grazing pastures. As he went up toward the pastureland, he was carrying a big bundle of potatoes, loaded on his burro. Right about then, he spied a sheep. A ram, a big one, with big horns. He threw off his poncho and started running after it. He grabbed hold of the ram, and it started to bawl, "Baah, baah!" God damn! He bundled it up and threw it over his shoulder. "Oh baby, oh man! Now I've got a load of potatoes, and a big old sheep! Man, I am going to eat one hell of a big stew. All for me!" And he carried it off. He broke a sweat, weighed down as he was, and headed back toward the outskirts of the village.

As he carried the bundle along, all of a sudden the sheep touched his face, and said "Hey, do I weigh a lot?" Then the man noticed it was wearing a burial cap—a condemned soul. A flame was shooting out of its mouth. Worms were spilling from its nose.

Oh my God! He threw it down with all his might, and ran straight into his house. He threw open the latch and fell down on the floor. "Oh! Help! What's happening? How?" He couldn't wake up. When did that man fall? He stayed there sleeping for twenty-four hours.

chachkasqa riki naqa, uvijaqa. Allin anejo astapas, asta. Hinaspas riki, pumchunta ch´utirukuspa, qatikachaspa, hap´irun anejuta. "¡Bahh! ¡Bahh!", nichkaqta. ¡Carajo! contentu runaqa q´ipimun riki. "Añañaw taytáy. Papaypas carga kachkan, uvijaypas. Wira t´imputa mikhuyusaq, taytáy. Sapachallayqa", nispa, q´ipimuchkan riki. Hump´ipis api llasallataña, cantunta, chay llaqta circallantachá q´ipimuchkan riki.

Hinaspa naqa, aknata aknayusqa: "¿Yaw llasachu kasqani?" *Había sido con ququruchu, condenado pues. De su boca había estado saliendo candela. De su naríz derramando gusanos.*

¡Ay caramba! lo botó con toda su fuerza, y se entró a su casa, parece que ha entrado . . . ¡Qhah! Buummm se cayó al suelo. "¡Ay! auxilio. Imananmi, hayk´ananmi"; no se despertó.

¿A qué hora ha caído ese individuo? Había tomado, hasta 24 horas. Había dormido.

The Carpenter's Wife

In this version, the husband metes out a less extreme form of justice, and the wife's comeuppance, consequently, seems less ambiguous. The fact that she doesn't die at the husband's hands means she doesn't have to reappear to him as an undead soul. Miguel told me this story one day when we had been making adobe bricks out behind his house in Chimpawaylla, during our lunch break. His second wife, Ignacia (the first had died some years before) was some twenty-five years younger than him. She brought us a blanket of steaming corn and beans out to the field. Untying the knotted blanket, she squatted and ate with us, in utter tranquillity, nodding her stovepipe-hatted head as Miguel told his spousal revenge story and the three of us peeled our boiled corn.

The Carpenter's Wife

Told by Miguel Waman

A carpenter lived happily with his wife. But they didn't have any children; there was just the two of them. So, other men were always hitting on his wife. And the wife flirted with them too. Finally, she said to one of them, "My husband is travelling on such and such a day."

"All right."

"Come over then. We'll sleep together," she said. The carpenter, however, knew how she was. He pretended he was going on a two-day trip, and stayed on the outskirts of town. That night he came back, while his wife was sleeping with somebody else. He knocked on the door. Yes, he knocked on the door while she was sleeping with another. The lovers threw back their blankets.

"Hide inside the oven," she said. There was an oven right out there in the courtyard.

The carpenter had gone to get some wheat. He told her, "I left my scythe here, that's why I came back." Meantime, the lover was stuck naked inside the oven. Naked, didn't have a stitch on. All at once, the husband slammed shut the oven door. Just like that. He had a plan about what he was going to do. He was ready. The oven door was shut tight.

To his wife he then said "Let's make some bread right now."

The woman was scared to death. She was thinking, "There he is inside the oven, and we're about to make bread!" God damn! The carpenter started sticking thorny branches into the oven-pit, filled it up

Carpinterop Warmin

Carpintero sumaqta kawsakusqa, warmi-qhari. Mana wawachankupas kasqachu, iskaychallanku. Hinaspa, huk fastidiasqa warmita, warmita. Entonces warmipas bolata qusqataq. Chayqa, "Tal diata qusay viajita rinqa", nispa nisqa.

"Bueno."

"Chayta hamunki. Puñukusunchik", nispa nisqa. Ña yachasqaña chay. Waktanta iskay p´unchaw viajaspa, cantullapi kamusqa. Tuta chayamun, warmin hukwan puñuchkaqtinña. Takayamun punkuta. Punkuta takayamuqtinqa hukwan puñuchkasqa. ¡Khachakhachal! "Qamqa hurnu ukhuman winarukuy", nispa. Haqaynapichá patiupi hurnu karan riki, chayman.

Chayqa triguman risqa. Chayqa "Navajayta saqirusqani, chaymi kutimuchkani", nispa. Q´alachalla huk kaqqa hurnu ukupi kachkan, q´alatu numas. . . Imapas kachkan. (Hurnutaqa taparapun pacha) Punkuta wisq´arun pacha qusanqa. Yastá pues. Kaypiña, umapi kachkan llipin. Yachachkanña lliwta. Chayqa hurnuman wisqarun q´alata.

Chayqa warmintaqa nin: "Kunanmi t´antata masasun", nispa nin. Warminqa manchayukuchkan riki. "¿Imaynataq hurnu ukupi kachkan? Kunanri t´antata masasaqku." ¡Carajo! kiskata winayta qallarin hurnuman, espinata hunt´ata. Hurnup siminqa hatuntaq kachkan. Qaqata winayun riki; hinallapi kachkan. Chay ukullapi, q´alalla tiyachkan chiripichá riki. Q´uniy-q´uniytaq hurnu kachkan. Chayqa riki, aguantachkanchá riki.

with branches. The mouth of the oven was big, and he shoved the thorn branches in nice and tight. Inside, the lover was squatting there naked, in the cold. Then the oven started to get hot, and the lover tried to withstand it.

Then the carpenter said "No, let's not make bread; we'll roast suckling pig instead." He lit a branch, and tossed it in the oven. When the wood got burning good, the lover leaped out of the oven. The carpenter gave him a good beating. He gave both the woman and the lover a beating. The woman pretended to be innocent, and not to know that the man had been closed up in the oven. But the husband knew better. The woman pretended to be mad at him, as if she didn't know anything.

Later on, he caught hold of the lover who escaped, and slit his throat.

That time was potato harvest time. He went at night, and buried the man in a potato furrow, a ditch there. After he'd buried him, he said to his wife, "Tomorrow we're going to harvest potatoes."

"Okay," she answered.

"Make corn beer," the husband told her. The husband already had in his mind what he was going to do. So, where was that head of ours buried? He put his wife in that very furrow to dig up potatoes. The head was there, just the way he'd left it. They were doing this two or three days after he'd killed the man. The head was there covered up with dirt in the furrow. The woman found the man's head, her lover's head. The head jumped up all by itself, and stuck onto the woman's shoulder. While she was digging around to see what it was, the head jumped up onto her shoulder and looked her right in the face. "Go on and run off together," the husband said, pushing them away. Who knows where they disappeared to together? Nobody heard any more about them.

Chayqa, "Lechun-lechunakunqa; mana t´antataqa masakunqachu".
¡Hap´iyachin ruq´ita i! hurnu ukuman. Chaypitaq yawrachkaqtin, es-
capamun riki. Lliwta p´anaykun riki carpinteroqa. Chay qharitaqa
warmintawan p´amaykun. Mana yachaqpas tukunchu chay nawan
kasqanta, chay qharita hurnuman wisq´asqanta. Qhariqa yachachkanyá.
Warmiyá chullku churakun, mana yachaq, disimulada. Chayqa es-
capamusqanmanta hap´iramuspa, kunkanta qururusqa.
    Chay tiempu karan, papa allay tiempuchá kachkaran. Tutaraq rispa,
huk wachuman p´amparamusqa, papa wachuman, surcuman. P´am-
pamuqtinqa, "Paqarinmi papata allasun", nispas nin.
    "Bueno", nispas.
    "Aqhay", nispa qhariqa. Ña yachachkanña qhariqa imaynatas ru-
wanqa chayta. ¿Chayqa, maypichá p´ampasqa kachkan kay umanchik?
Anchay wachuman warminta churasqa allananpaq. Umansi kaqlla
kachkasqa. Iskay kimsa p´unchawllanman chayta wañuchisqanman ruwachkanku chayta. Hinaspa tapasqalla kachkan chay wachupi riki.
Tarirun chay warmi, chay qharinpa, pantaq masinpa umanta. Kikillan
k´askaramun kayman p´itayaramun uman. T´aqwiriqtin p´itaramusqa
kayman uman; aknaman uyayuq kaypi. "Phawayá ripuychik kuska", nispas qatirparinpun qusan. Maytachá chinkapunku wiñaypaq riki . . . chay
qharintin, mana kapunchu. Chaylla.

The Shepherdess

Ines Callali was another one of my Quechua teachers. Also known as La Gata (Cat Woman), Ines is a gifted instructor with a deep devotion to disseminating her verbal roots, and a disarming laugh that makes you feel she is about to betray a great secret to you. Repetition is used a good deal within any number of stories, but no one else with whom I spoke used it to quite as great a dramatic effect as La Gata does in this mixture of eros and death. Constant repetition increases the mood of foreboding and anxiety. One can easily imagine Ines and her companions swapping ghost stories, as she informed me they did as children, out in the cattle shed before bedtime, to scare the wits out of each other. The rhythm created by Ines's linguistic formulae, coupled with the playful winks of her cat-eyes at strategic intervals, also expressed a playful quality, as if she didn't expect her listener to take the macabre recitation all that seriously. On the other hand, the fact that Ines was a relatively young single mother, raising her child on her own, lent her telling of this seduction and abandonment a certain poignance.

The Shepherdess

Told by Ines Callali

A young woman, a young shepherdess always stayed alone in a hut; in an isolated highland sheep hut. Each day, the shepherdess took her sheep out to the fields to graze. That's how she spent each day, and while she was watching over them, herding, a young man came along. That young man started flirting with the girl, and said "Listen, girl. Are you all by yourself? Are you all by yourself?"

The young woman answered, "Don't pester me. Don't pester me." She wasn't interested in him. The next morning, the young woman went on out to the fields with her sheep to watch them, like always, to watch them.

Again, the young man came along pursuing her. "Hey, girl, do you like me, or not? Do you like me, or not?"

The girl answered. "Don't pester me. Don't pester me."

Each day, the girl kept on going out to watch the sheep. And that fellow was right after, after her. Handsome, elegant, with a hat of vicuna wool, a vicuna scarf, a well-dressed young man. As they walked along together, he said "Listen, girl, I care for you a lot. Are you listening to me?"

And the girl answered, "Okay." They came together, and loved one another. So each day they'd come together like that, there in the shepherdess's hut.

One day he said "Tonight I'll come to your house. I'll come to your bedroom." The young man started coming to her every night. He'd

Uvijiramanta K´ Achay-K´ Acha Waynawan

Huk sipaschas, uvijira sipascha napi, uvija wasipi sapallan tiyakusqa. Chaysi uvijirachaqa sapa punphaw uvija michiq riq kasqa, uvijantin. Michisqanpis, huk wayna rikhurisqa. Hinaspas nisqa; sipaschataqa turiyasqa chay wayna. "Yaw, sipas. ¿Sapallaykichu kanki?" nispas.

Chayqa sipaschaqa: "Ama turiyawaychu. Aman turiyawaychu", nispas. Mana munasqachu. Chayqa sipascha kaq paqarisnintinqa uvijantin rillanpuni camputa michiq, uvija michiq.

Chayqa chay waynaqa qatillasqataq. "¿Munawankichu, manachu, yaw sipas? ¿Munawankichu, manachu?"

Sipasqa nin: "Ama turiyawaychu. Ama turiyawaychu" (Chaysi nin).

Kaq, rillantaq sapa punchaw uvija michisqanman. Aypansi, chay runaqa: K´achay-k´achay, wik´uña sumbriruyuq, wik´uña chalinayuq, k´achay-k´achay waynaqa. Chay risqanpís kaq nin: "Anchatan munayki, yaw sipascha. ¿Uyawankichu, manachu?" nispas nin.

Chayqa sipaschaqa nin: "Ya". Ñas tupanakunkuña. Chayqa ña munanakunkuña. Chayqa sapa punchaw tupallankus, kay uvija michisqanpi.

Chaysi ninqa: "Kay tuta risaq wasiykiman", nispas nin. Chayqa, "Puñusqaykiman risaq". Chaysi chay waynaqa rin sapa tutalllas. Chaymantaqa yacharakapun sapa tutallas riq, uvijirachawan puñuq. Chayqa sapa tutalla risqanpisyá; ña unquqña sipaschaqa, unquqña. Chayqa ñas unquqña.

Chaysi nin: "Taytamamaywanchá parlanki", riki nin sipascha. "Tay-

go to where the shepherdess slept. Each night, he'd show up, until finally, the young woman became pregnant; pregnant. Now she was pregnant.

The girl said to the young man, "You have to tell my parents. You have to tell my parents. I'm pregnant now because of you. So I want you to come and tell my parents." But the young man didn't want to. He only appeared at night. He didn't want to.

One morning, she just grabbed hold of him as hard as she could. He'd gotten into the habit of going to sleep with her every night, and leaving in the early dawn. At three or four in the morning he'd go on his way. He wouldn't wait until daylight. So one day the young woman imposed herself, and said "No. Today you're going to stay. Why do you run off every day, so early, even before dawn breaks? Why, huh? What for? You must have another woman. That's what it is, right? That's why you don't want anyone to be seen with you." The young woman held tight to his poncho. "You're not leaving. You're not leaving. You're going to wait for daybreak. You'll wait here until daybreak comes."

When she seized hold of him, he cried "Let me go. Don't be that way. Let me go. Don't be that way. Let me go. Let me go!"

"No. No, I won't let you go. You'll wait for daybreak here. No, you'll wait. My parents want to meet you. We'll stay here together." She didn't want to release him, and grabbed hold of him with her entire body. She held fast to him; she held fast to him.

When he realized he couldn't get free, he shouted "I'm going to shatter! I'm going to shatter! Don't grab me. I'm going to shatter. I'm going to shatter."

"Shatter, then! I don't care. No matter what, you're staying right here." She held tight to him until daybreak. The sun was coming up. Some people were starting to pass by. And then, swoosh! The young man turned to a skeleton. He wasn't a young man after all. He was one of the undead ancestors, ancient, old. The woman was still pregnant, of course; still pregnant. At last, she gave birth to a skeleton, not a person.

tamamaywanchá parlanki. Ña unquqña rikhurini qampata. Chayqa
hamunkichá taytamamaywan parlaq", nispa. Chayqa waynaqa manas
munanchu. Tutañataqsi rikhurin, manas munanchu.

A la fuerzasyá huk tutamantaqa hap´irun. Sapa p´unchaw puñuq
rispaqa, tutachallamantas lluqsipuq. Las cuatruta, las trestaqa ña pas-
apuqña. Manas tempranukamaqa suyaqchu. Chayqa huk p´unchawsi
kay sipascha kallpata churarukuspa, "Mana. Kunan p´unchawqa qipankipuni. ¿Imaynapitaq qamri sapa p´unchaw ripunki, tempranuchallari,
manaraq pacha illariyta? ¿Imaynata, ha? ¿Imarayku? Kanpaschá
warmiyki. Chaychá, riki. Mana pimanpas rikuchikuyta munankichu",
nispas nin. Chayqa pumchunmantas hap´irun sipaschaqa. "Mana riwaqchu. Manan riwaqchu. Illarinantapuni suyanki. Kaypin illarinki!"
nispas nin.

Chayqa hap´ichkaqtin, "Kachariway. Ama chhayna kaychu. ¡Kachariway. Ama chhayna kaychu. Kachariway, kachariway!"

"Manan. Manan kachariykimanchu. Illarinkin kaypi. Mana, illarinki.
Taytamamaymá riqsiyta munasunki. Kaypin qipasun: Hinaspa, chaysi
mana kachariyta munachkaqtin, hap´iparukunsi warmi intirumanta.
Qaqata hap´irun; qaqata hap´irun.

Mana ripunanraykus nin: "Chhallmirusaqmi. Chhallmirusaqni.
Ama hap´iwaychu. Chhallmirusaqmi, chhallmirusaqmi."

"¡Chhallmiypis, imapas kay! Manan, qipankipuni kaypi", nispas nin.

Hinaqtinsi pacha illariykama hap´iyuchkan riki. Ñas p´uchaw hamuchkanña, chay. Ñas runakunapas ñas pasachkanña. Chaypis, ¡chhall!
Tulluman tukukapun chay wayna. Hinaspa manayá waynachu kasqa.
Chayqa unquq warmipis qipapun; unqusyapusqa. Chayqa wachakun tulluta; mana runatachu. Chaypi tukupun.

The Paṣtureland Girl

The fact that the incest taboo is nearly universal has long been a commonplace
of anthropology. Yet the consequences of violating the taboo vary widely from
one society to the next. What intrigues me about this account is the role of religious syncretism. The girl and her mother obey all the priest's instructions to the
letter, regarding the disposition of the dead father's corpse. But not only do the
women's strict observances of Catholic dogma fail to save the soul of the deceased
from the fires of Hell; the girl herself, though "innocent" of wrongdoing, must
suffer the same fate in the afterlife as her father. The presumably pre-Columbian
origins of the taboo remain so strong that Christian dogma cannot override them.
Both parties must pay for the illicit act. The harsher and more ancient interpre-
tation prevails over a newer one emphasizing atonement and redemption. Even
the priest himself is depicted as categorical in his rejection of "the Devil's child."
His only power, and quite limited role, is to facilitate the family's perdition—a
rather unpriestly activity, to say the least. Baptism of the fruit of incest appears
an impossible goal; in this reckoning, damnation is always already retroactive.
Time (as in "the nick of time") presents itself only as a perpetual vanishing point,
moving backward, away from the grandmother and her charge. The emphasis
of this tale lies elsewhere, in a place beyond salvation. To a sensibility formed
within a modern Judaeo-Christian/liberal republican cultural framework, in
which the rights of victims and the punishment of perpetrators get emphasized,
the ultimate outcome of this rape may seem troublesome, even incomprehensible.
But this folk tale is not a civics lesson. The ethos here, like Teodora's style of narration, is unflinching, almost existential. The endpoint of knowledge is neither
redemption nor self-enlightenment. The unsparing dialogue between the wake-
holding daughter and the offending father's corpse says it best:

"What does this world offer us?"
  "It doesn't offer us anything, father. We only know that it's a sin for a father to lie down with his daughter."

The Pastureland Girl

Told by Teodora Paliza

Now I'll tell you about a girl. There once were a farmer and his wife. They left their oldest girl, their daughter alone in the high pastureland, to take care of the sheep. So, she tended the sheep from one day to the next. She was growing into a young woman. And her father, by himself, would go up to the distant pastureland to visit her; but not her mother. One time, the father said to his daughter "I'm going to stay the night."

The daughter replied, "I don't think you should stay, father. Where would you sleep?"

"It's okay, I'll just stretch out right there. I'll sleep right by your side."

The daughter, frightened, laid out some bedclothes in another spot. "Father, sleep over here by yourself. I can't lie down to sleep with my father."

"No. We're going to sleep, that's all. Nothing is going to happen." That girl lay down to sleep, frightened to sleep. And then the father raped his daughter. "Don't tell anyone about this," he warned her.

After a time, the girl turned out to be pregnant. The father would go up to take her bread, sweets. "I'm going up to visit our daughter," he'd say to her mother, his wife.

"Run along, dear, visit her. I wonder how that daughter of ours is doing?" she'd say, and send him off.

He stayed up there two or three times. "Our daughter wasn't feeling well; that's why I stayed. I don't know what's wrong with her." But

Wachacha

Kunan willachkayki wachachamanta. Huk campesinus warmi-qhari kasqaku. Hinaqtinsi estanchkanman kuraq kaq chicankutaq, wawankutaqa saqimunku, uvija michinanpaq. Chayqa, chaypis p´unchaw-p´unchaw uvijata michin. Chay ña sipasña kapuchkan riki. Taytallan riq watukuq; mana mamitanqa. Hinaspas wachachaqa ña huk kutinqa, taytan nisqa: "Quidasaqmi", nispa.

Chaysi nin wachachaqa, "Manan taytáy quidawaqchu. ¿Maypitaq puñuwaqri? nispa nin.

"Manan, nuqaqa mast´allay chaypi. Ladullaykipi puñusaq".

Chaypi wachachaqa riki mancharikusqa puñunata mast´an. "Taytáy kay sapaqpiyá puñuy. Mana nuqa taytaywanqa puñuymanchu", nin.

"¡Mana! Puñullasunmi. Mana imapis kanqachu", nispas chay wachachaqa riki manchasqa riki puñuchkan, puñuchkan. Chayqa tayatan abusapusqa wachachataqa. "Aman rimariwankichu pimanpas", nispas nin.

Hinaqtinsi wachachaqa riki unquq rikhuripun. Taytanqa (hamun) riq, apaqsi t´antachata, misk´ichata. "Waturakamusaq wachachanchikta", nispas mamantaqa, warmintaqa.

"Phawayyá taytáy, waturakamuy. ¿Imaynachá kachkan chay wachachanchik?" nispa kachaq.

Iskay kimsa kutis quidakanpuq riki. "Malmi kachkasqa wachacha; chaymi quidarani. Imanakuchkanchá kanpas". Mamantaqsi mana creenchu imatapas. Bueno unquqyá, pusaqninpiña kachkan, ña isqun-

the mother didn't believe him. By then, the girl was well along in her pregnancy, into the ninth month. Her belly was really big. But no one knew about that. She stayed up there alone with the cows and the sheep. Until one time, when the father came to visit, she went into labor pains. "What's wrong?" he asked.

"My belly is hurting inside, father."

He said "Then let's go. I'm taking you to the village." He led her to the village. When they arrived, he said to his wife "What could be wrong with our daughter? I brought her down because she's having pains in her belly."

There was the girl. Her mother was taking care of her. "What can it be? Maybe she ate too many cold foods, and maybe from sleeping up there in the cold." She gave her some herbal tea. She prepared her some broth. "What can it be?"

"My belly hurts me, mother." She didn't tell her anything. The pains became more intense. And the old man was getting nervous. He didn't say anything either. She was suffering. At last she gave birth. And the baby was a little boy.

"What am I going to do with this little slut? Who is the father? Tell me." The mother questioned her and gave her hard slaps. But the girl didn't talk.

The baby was crying horribly. "Anh, anh, anh, anh, anh."

"What is he crying about? Oh, he needs to be baptized. Let's run and get him baptized," said the mother. The girl's mother bundled him up in diapers, a hat, put a shirt on him and carried him off. The baby was crying. They were crossing the threshold of the church.

Right then, the baby died. He died. "How can I take him in there dead?" So she started back toward home with the corpse. Then something amazing happened. She had almost gotten back to her house with the corpse, when once again, it started to cry, "Anh, anh, anh, anh, anh." The girl's mother said to her neighbor, next door neighbor, "What is happening with this child? I thought it was on account of his baptism. So I took him. As I crossed the doorway of the church, he died. And then, just as I was coming back to my own door, he came back to life. Now he's crying again." She took him three times, and the third time, she said "I'll just take him into the church dead. I'll tell the priest what happened." So she went in. When she arrived at the church, the child died again. She took him in to the priest. "Father, what's happening to this little angel? This is the third time in a

ninpiña. Hatuntaña apachkan. Ni pipas yachanchu chaytaqa. Wakap uvijap qipallanpis. Hinaspas huk kutin riqtinqa, dolorwan kachkasqa. "¿Imanantaqsi?" nispas nin.

"Wiksallaymi taytáy nanawachkan; wakrallaymi", nispas nin. Chayqa "Hakuyá. Llaqtata apayusayki", nispas nin. Llaqtaman pusayamun. Pusayamuqtinqa warmintaqa nin: "¿Imanakuchkanri chay wachachata? Wakra nanaywan kaqtimi pusayamuchkani", nispan.

Chay wachachaqa chaypi kachkan. Mamanqa atendichkan. "¿Imataq kanmanri? Chiri-chiri mikhusqanchá, chiripi puñusqanchá", nispas. Matikunata qun. Calduta haywan. "¿Imaykitaq nananri?"

"Wiksallaymi nanawan mamáy", nispa nin. Manas rimarinchu. Astawanña fuertiyuchkan dulurqa riki . . . Machutaqsi riki mancharisqa riki kachkan . . . rimarinchu. Ñak´ariyunsi. Por fin wachakapun riki. Hinaspas wawachaqa qharicha kasqa.

"¿Chay p´asñataqa, imanaymantaq? ¿Pin taytan? Willaway". Hinaspas allinta waqtayuspa, mamanqa tapun. Manas rimarinchu.Wawas fiuta waqan. Michikunaqa chay ratumanta pachas waqayuchkan. "Iñaw, iñaw, iñaw, iñaw, iñaw." Chaysi, "¿Imamantataq kayri waqan? Bautisninmanchá riki. Bautisachimusunyá, haku", nispas. Mamanqa apan riki pañalchawan, gurrucha, camisachata churayuspas apan. Wawaqa waqayuchkan. Iglisia ukumanña chayayuchkan.

Chaysi wawa wañurapun. Wañurapun. "¿Imayuqtaq wañusqatari apayusaqri?" Hinaspas Kasqanta kutichipullantaq ayachataqa. ¡Waw qiq! Wañusqa wasi isquinaman chayayusqa. Yapamantas, "Iñaw, iñaw, iñaw, iñaw, iñaw, iñaw", waqayuchkansi. Chaysi nin vicinukunata riki, wasimasinkunataqa nin riki, "¿Imanakunchá kay wawataqa? Kay hina bautisninmantachá", nispaymi. "apani", nispaymi. "iglisia punkupiñan chayaspa wañurapun. Kunan waq, isquinaman chayaqarmuqtiytaq, kawsarapun. Waqayuchkallantaq." Kimsakamas chayta apan. Kimsapiñas ichaqa, "Hina wañusqatayá apasaq. Señor curaman willamusaq", nispas nin. Chaysi riki nin. Chayayuchkaqtinqa, wañurapun wawaqa. Hinata apayun señor curamanqa. "Papáy, ¿imachá kay angilituwan pasanpas? Kaytawan kimsatañan chayachimuni. Hinaqtinmi kunan, huk hina, wañusqata hina apayamuchkani."

"¿Pitaq taytanri?"

"Manan rimarinchu por nada. Qusallaymi chayta riq. Estanchkapitaq, uvijachanchikkuna. Anchaywanmi watukuq. ¿Chaypis imapunin pasan? ¿Imaynataq?"

"Tapuyá qusaykita", nispas nin. Manas rimarinchu. Por fin, "Manan

row I've brought him here. Things being the way they are, I decided to just bring him in here dead."

"Who is the father?"

"There's no way my daughter is going to tell me. Only my husband goes up there to see her. She's up there in the pastureland tending the sheep. That's why he goes to visit. What happened up there? And how?"

"You should ask your husband," he told her. But the husband told her nothing. At last, the priest said "This child can't be a Christian. He's the Devil's child. I want you to go right back to your house. Bundle him up. Tie him to a heavy stone, and throw him into the river from the middle of the bridge."

"Yes, Father," she answered. But how can I throw him like that, if he's alive? I can't. He might still have a chance for salvation." And she went back home.

When she came into her street, the baby was still dead. Then he began to cry, "Anh, anh, anh, anh, anh." So she bundled him up. She took him, well bundled up, to the bridge. She tied him fast to a stone, and threw the baby right into the river. He was still in his cradle. The woman went back, weeping, to see the priest. "Father, when I threw the baby off the bridge, my husband also died."

"Then that man isn't a Christian either. That man is condemned, a condemned soul. How could he lie down with your daughter? Bring him to the church. We'll have to hold a wake for him in the chapel. Bring your daughter along too. She has to sit by his side, for three days and three nights. She has to sit by the corpse's side. That's the only possibility of his salvation." They put scapularies on the corpse, and prepared to sit with it all night.

At midnight, they heard the sound of the coffin opening. The corpse sat up on its own. "I'm tired, daughter," it said. "What does this world offer us?"

"It doesn't offer us anything, father. We only know that it's a sin for a father to lie down with his daughter."

"Ah!" That's all the corpse said: "Ah!" and boom! it lay down again. They remained there like that for three days and three nights. But there was no chance of salvation. Oh, the poor girl was so frightened she never slept. After three days and three nights, they took the corpse to the cemetery to bury it.

The priest said "Now your daughter has to stay in the cemetery, at the graveside, wearing scapularies and rosaries." They sat the daughter there at the graveside, and buried the corpse. Everyone else went

kayqa cristianuqa kanmanchu. Diablup wawanmi kayqa. Kunanmi
wasiykita kutipunki. Hinaspanmi waltharuspayki. Rumiwan con-
trapisaykuspayki, chawpi chakamanta mayuman wikch'uyunki."
Wañusqaña, wasi isquinaman chayaramun. Qallarillantaq waqayta.
"Iñaw, iñaw, iñaw, iñaw, iñaw, iñaw". Hinatas riki nawan waltharun.
Allintayá waltharuspas apan naman, chakaman. Wiksu, rumiwan aknata
watayuspansi, wikchuyun riki wawataqa mayu patachapi. Chay ratutaqsi
taytan wañurusqa. Pusan warmiqa. Puñunallapiraq kachkan riki . . .
Waqayuspas señor curaqta kutirin warmiqa. "Papáy wawa chanqayu-
ruqtiy, hinan kay wañurun."

"Manan chayqa, chayqa cristianuchu. Condenadun chay qhariqa,
condenadun. ¿Imaynataq wawanwanri tiyaranri? Chaysi apamuy iglisia-
man. Capillapiyá velakuchun. Ususiykitawan pusamuy. Ladunpi tiyanqa,
kimsa tuta, kimsa punchaw. Kay ayap ladunpi kanqa. Ichapasraq kanqa
salvaciunnin", nispas. Escapularionkunawan churaspansi, ayap ladunpi
tiyaykunku, tutayaykun riki.

Kuska tutas ¡K'irrrr! nispas nin. Kaqllapiqa riki bien hatarirun.
"Hananaw, wachacha. ¿Imallan kay mundupi ufricikuchkan?" nispas
nin.

Mana imapis taytáy ufricikunchu. Unico taytanwan ususinwan
puñukuyqa huchas kanman."

"¡Ah!" Chayllan rimay kachkan nispas, "¡Ah!" ¡Pún! kunpayakapul-
lantaq. Bueno hinas kimsa tuta, kimsa punchaw. Mana kanchu salvaciunnin riki. ¡Ay!, manas wachachaqa puñunchu riki, manchari-
kuyuchkan . . . Bueno kimsa p'unchaw, kimsa tutamanta pantiunman
riki p'anpaqta apapunku.

Chaypis nin: "Kunan pantiumpi, sipulturap ladunpi, kay ususiyki
quidanqa, nakunawan escapulariyukunawan, rosariyukunawan." Hinaspas riki ladunpi tiyachinku wachachataqa. Chayqa p'anpanku. Lluy
ch'iqirinpunku; hampunku; saqiyanpunku riki. ¿Kuska tutas, i? Nina
carruqa riki kukukuykusparaq achhuyun riki.

"¡Hola! Kaytachu munaranki", nispansi. Primiruta wikch'urparin
trenpi fierrumanta, pruq wikch'uyapun. Chaymanta taytanta nawan
chay trinchiwan hap'iruspas, ¡plan! Nina carrupi siqaychipusqa, con-
dinadu iskayninkus.

back to their houses. They went away and left her there. And what happened at midnight? A flaming chariot approached, pulsing with fire.

"Is this what you wanted, then?" the demons said to them. First they pitched the corpse out of the coffin. Then they grabbed hold of it with pitchforks, and carried it off in the chariot of fire. Both of them were damned.

The Hacienda
Owner's Daughter

Juan Velasco's Agrarian Reform Law of 1969 abolished haciendas in favor of "Peasant Communities," in an attempt to move an unjust concentration of land back toward the much older system of communal land tenure. The longstanding indigenous ayllus were superseded by land grabs that began in earnest when Peru's President Ramon Castilla abolished Indians' communal holdings in 1852, and the pillaging intensified in the early decades of the twentieth century. (There is an eye-opening chapter on this phenomenon in Jose Maria Arguedas's celebrated novel Yawar Fiesta.*) Chimpawaylla, where Miguel told me this story, was one of many sites where Velasco's reformist experiment took place. Yet when a cooperative peasant farmer such as Miguel Waman sat down to rest from planting, and allowed himself to dream in words, he dreamed not of abolishing the very concept of the haciendas by which he and his forerunners had been dispossessed, but rather of becoming the hacienda owner himself. Here, Miguel endows the boy in the story with the power of his ostensible nemesis, the dead hacienda owner. The storyteller's imaginative act becomes a form of grudging respect, ambivalent homage, for the "lordship" that the hacienda owner represents. (For a similar discussion of this cultural dialectic of satire and envy, see my discussion of the Los Majeños dance in the introductory essay to this collection.) Like many mythic traditions, this one rewards, not the kind of collective political action endorsed by Velasco, but individual heroism, exemplified in the courage displayed by the least of the least, the caretaker's son. At the same time, the Andean idea of gender complementarity and dependence on a co-equal surfaces; both he and the hacienda owner's daughter show mettle — she by putting the various suitors to a test in good-humored seriousness, and he by passing the test. He needs her in order to experience a sense of completion, and she needs him for the same reason. She tells him: "'Where I go to stay, you have to go too. We go together. Whatever I eat, we'll eat together.' That was their understanding." The daughter is presented not merely as a conduit to the suitor's empowerment, or the vessel of her father's will, but as the mistress of her own destiny. Ultimately, what she has is hers to give or withhold as she sees fit.*

The Hacienda Owner's Daughter

Told by Miguel Waman

There was a rich hacienda owner. He had an only daughter. One day, he told her all about his life; how he'd have to soon depart this world; how he'd have to die; how he'd have to leave his daughter alone; how she could make someone fall in love with her. He told all those things to his daughter. He told this daughter all she needed to know.

That gentleman hacienda owner died, and his daughter remained alone—a good-looking girl, tender and sweet, plump and shapely. And as she found herself all alone, a young man, young like you, sought her hand.

"I want us to marry, me and you."

"Charmed. I accept."

"Cross your heart?"

"And hope to die."

"We'll get married?"

"Let's get married."

But the young woman warned him: "Where I go to stay, you have to go too. We go together. Whatever I eat, we'll eat together." That was their understanding. They began to walk down the road together, like fiances. Out in the fields, the moon was shining as if it were day, the moon shining like that. It was as bright as day, and the young lady had gotten all dressed up and put on some makeup, got out her purse, like a damsel, a real lady.

Haciendayuqpa Ususin

Huk haciendayuq kasqa qapaq. Ususichan ch´ullachalla kasqa. Hinaspa lliwta willasqa vidanta: Imaynatas ripunqa; imaynatas wañupunqa; imaynatas wawanta saqinqa; imaynata enamuradunta ruwanqa chayta, lliwta, ususinman willasqa q´alata chayqa ususinpaqmá.

Wañupun chay wiraqucha haciendayuq, sapallanñas wawacha quidan buena moza sipas, *terneja pues*, phatuy-phatuy wirasapa. Hinaspas riki sapallanña quidaqtinqa huk enamurakun, qam hina wayna, joven. *"Yo te quiero para casarnos."*

"Encantado te recibo."

"¿Chocamos?"

"Ya, chocamos."

"¿Nos casamos?"

"Nos casamos." Bueno willan riki naqa, chay niñaqa: "Maytachá risaq qipayta hamunki. Kuska risun. Imatachá mikhukusaq, kuska mikhusun", nispa nin. *En esa condición* yastá quidasqaña, yastá casado hinaña sumaqta purichkanku. Chayqa khayna hawa llaqtapi killa p´unchaw hina kachkan, khayna riki killa. Hinaspa p´unchaw hina kaqtinqa riki señoritaqa cambiarukun, pintasqa bulsunniyuq, dama pues, *señora nomás pues.*

Enamuraduntaq aknata ladunta richkan. Hinaspa riki cantunman chayanku. Richkallan k´uchuntakama. Purichkanku cantunman. Chayayuqtinku pantiunman; punkuman chayayuqtinku, qaparispa joven

Her fiance was walking by her side. And they reached the edge of town. They reached the corner of the village, the outskirts. They arrived at the cemetery. As soon as they got to the gate, the young man let out a holler and ran away. He left the young girl all alone. He didn't have any desire to meet up with her ever again. The boy got scared out of his wits, and didn't say anything to anyone about what had happened.

So, another boy proposed to her. She accepted.

What was inside the cemetery? You don't know? In a niche in there, she had prepared roast lamb, spiced to perfection, juicy lamb. And whenever someone proposed to her, she had the meat prepared and put it inside the niche. She had a little key. And that key was the key to the niche.

Another fellow proposed to her, in the very same way. When she opened the cemetery gate, he hollered and ran away as fast as he could. Now it's four down, five down. None of them could face her afterward. The girl's still there, all by herself. So the caretaker's son got sweet on her. That boy would have been young, yes. "I'm in love with you, honey."

"Charmed. Wherever I go, we'll go together. Whatever I eat, you eat. Then we'll get married in the morning."

Oh yeah, the boy was overjoyed! He said to his mother, "Mama, that young lady said she and I will get married. Oh, mama! If I die, then I die, right? I don't know exactly where we're going, but we're going there tonight."

He rubbed his skin with alcohol. He was going in high spirits. They arrived at the cemetery, him right by her side. The cemtery was at the edge of town. It was a moonlit night. She opened the cemetery gate with her key. Creeeak! It opened. He was at her side, and didn't let go of her. That little tiny key was right in her purse, that little bitty key was the key to the niche, just small. And with that, she opened the little iron gate covering the funerary niche.

After she opened it, she pulled out a big platter of roast lamb. That's what she took out. Crack! She gave the young man a big old chunk of it, right into his hands. He took the whole thing right into his hands. The girl began to eat. The boy also ate his fill with gusto. Because, well, it was good meat, lamb. In the morning, they went back to the village. Right away, they married.

The other fellows who had proposed to her almost went crazy. "Why is she going with him, and not me?" They almost came to blows among themselves. There were a lot of suitors, but none of them suited her. No, she went with that man, that companion who had accompanied

ayqirikapun. Sapallanta niñata saqiyamun. Manaña munanñachu astawan tupayta chay niñawan. Chay joven manchakapun nitaq pimanpas willanchu, chayta chhayna pasasqanta.

Hukñataq enamurakun. Aceptan.

¿Imas kachkaran chay napi? ¿Mana yachankichu? Chay nichu ukupi preparasqa aycha kanka, sumaq cundimintuyuq, sumaq kanka. Chayqa sapa pichá enamurakun, chayqa kay llavitapas haqay nichup llavinta.

Huk enamurakun, kaqllataq. Pantiunta kichayuchkaqtin, qaparispa ayqimullantaq. Yastá tawaña, pichqaña. Mana pipas kutiyuq kanchu. Sapallan niña kachkan. Mayurdumup chicunñataq aficiunan. El hijo ya sería joven pues. "Munakuykin mamacita."

"Encantado. Maytachá risaq risun. Imatachá mikhusaq mikhunki. casarasun paqarisninta."

¡Ay kusisqa chicuqa riki! "mamá, ima señorita casarasun niwan. ¡Ay mamá . . .! Wañupusaq chayqa wañupusaqchá, riki. Maytachá risaqkupas, tutas risaqku. . . "

Alcoholkunawan qhaqurukun. Allin animasqa rin, riki. Pantiunman chayan, ladullanpi. Campupiraq pantiunqa kasqa. Killa p´unchaw kachkan Pantiunta kicharun llavinwan. ¡Khaq! kicharin. Ladullanpi mana kacharinchu. Llavichan kasqa bulsunninpi, huch´uy llavicha chay pantiun llavichachá riki, huch´uycha. Chay nichu llavichachá aknacha riki, aknacha llavicha. Chaychawan chay pantiun, chay bocanichuta rejachayuqta kichayrun riki.

Kichayaruqtin palanganapi aysaramun riki kankataqa. Chayqa aysaramun. ¡Qhaq! Llik´irparin aychataqa intiruta quykun makinninta naman, chay jovenman. Paypas intiruta hap´in. Niña mikhuyta qallarin. Jovenpas lucupaq mikhuyta qallarin. *Era pues rico,* kanka, *un asado de cordero.* Hampunku paqarisnintaqa. Casamiento kapun pacha.

Yaparaq lucu tukuyusqaku chay enamuradunkuna. "Imaynatan kaywanraq, mana nuqanwanchu", nispa. Yaqa maqanakusqakupas. Askha enamuraduqa kasqa, pero mana mayqinpas caesqachu. Chay hombrellanman, chay compañasqanman compañasqakuchu. Anchay kawsa pirdikapunku. Sichus conpañankuman karan, kuskalla kankuman karan, casarakunkuman chaywan karan. . .

Menos pensaduwan casarakapun, mayurdumunpa wawanwan.

Ha hecho pues modo posible. . . Kuska hampunku, yastá tranquilo. Uvijata ñak´ayukunku *por docenas* casamientupaq.

Jovenkuna maqanayukusqaku riki, "Nuqapas enamuradunmi karani."

"Nuqapas."

"Nuqapas."

her. That's why they lost her. If any one of them had just stayed along-side her, had stayed right with her, she would have married that one.

She married the least expected one, the caretaker's son. He did what he could. They came back from the cemetery, together and serene. And for the marriage feast, they slaughtered sheep by the dozens.

The other suitors finally got into a fistfight. "I was her fiance too!"

"Me too."

"Me too."

"How did she slip out of my grasp?"

God damnit! They just about died. Nobody had any idea that it was roast lamb in that funeral niche. No matter who courted her, she ac-cepted right off, and ordered the lamb to be roasted right off too. She had juicy meat roasted, and wrapped up in a bundle. With as many sheep as she had, as rich as she was, she was never at a loss for lamb.

That's how you find out about a man's weakness.

"Imaynapi hayk´aynapi khayna ayqikamurani."

"Nuqapas khaynamurani." ¡Carajo! yaqa wañuchinakapusqaku. *Nadie sabía lo que había en ese nicho carne asada.* Pichá fastidiaq enamuraduwan, aceptaq pacha, kankasqata apachiq pachataq. Q´ipiyachispalla sumaqta apachiq. Mana faltaqchu kanka, *tanto carnero, de un ricachón pues.*

Anchaynata qharip dibilidadnintaqa yachanku.

The Deserter

This rendition by 51–year-old grade school professor Agustin Farfan is evidence, to me, of how the oral tradition now must compete with television and movies as a medium of instruction and entertainment. It must be borne in mind that Quechua-speakers in the Sacred and Cusco Valleys are increasingly mestizo, urban, mostly bilingual, and subjected to a swirl of competing media. "The Deserter" sets forth a brand of machismo that is something of a departure from the norms of manhood endorsed by Quechua tradition. Bravery is desirable, to be sure, but when a demon or other emissary of the afterworld presents itself, bravado usually becomes tempered by a healthy respect for the power of the supernatural. That is why even the manliest of heroes (or heroines, for that matter) tends to have recourse to some form of supernatural sustenance to counter his foes. This soldier, however, simply brazens it out, in a cavalier fashion more suited to a television army sergeant confronting a human enemy than a monstrous archetype out of the oral tradition.

The Deserter

Told by Agustin Farfan

Once there lived a husband and wife, in the country, in a village. And above the village were grazing lands. A lot of cattle, sheep, horses, and other kinds of animals were kept there. The couple were rich, but they didn't have even one child. Eventually, the man died, and the woman had to lay out his corpse all by herself. On all four corners around him, she placed and lit dried manure, good for burning. Then she went into the village. "I'll go recruit people to help me with the burial," she said to herself.

It happened that a soldier had deserted from his barracks. He was going along his way. He walked and he walked. After a while, he started getting hungry and thirsty, but he didn't pass a single house. Night was coming on. In the dark, he saw a light blazing far off. He said "Maybe I'll find food there. Maybe someone lives there." After going on a bit longer, he arrived there. "Hello, ma'am!" he called out. No one answered. Only the corpse of the dead man was stretched out there. "I wonder whether some food has been left for the burial." The deserter had a look around. He searched, and found food: stew, corn beer, liquor, that sort of stuff. So he ate and drank. Now it was getting to be late. He stayed up, as a one-man wake. And while he was sitting the wake all by himself, the chariot of fire came. It made the whole house quake. "Thum thum thum thum!" went the chariot of fire as it neared. Someone approached the doorway, and the

Desertormanta

Huksi warmi-qhari tiyasqaku, karan campupi, llaqtapi. Hinas kay llaq-tap hawan pata, punapi. Hinaspan askha wakan kasqa, uvijan, caball-lun, imaymana animalninkuna. Qapaqpuni kasqaku. Chaysi mana ch´ullapis wawankuna kasqachu. Hinaspa qhari wañurapusqa. Hinas sapallan riki warmiqa riki almanta chutarirun. Hinaspantaqsi tawa-tawantin esquinaman micha q´awata hap´iyachispa, llaqtaman risqa. "Valikamusaqyá kunan, p´anpaysiwananpaq", nispa.

Chayñataq huk suldaduqa riki cuartilmanta desertanpusqa. Chaysi purimuchkasqa. Purimunsi, purimunsi. Hinas yarqaypi, ch´akiypi, manas tarinchu wasita. Hina tutayachkanña. Tutayaqtin k´anchaychata riku-musqa karumanta. Chaysi "Haqaypiqa kanpunichá naqa, mikhunaqa. Runa tiyanpunichá", nispa (hamusqaku) risqa. Chayqa chayasqa. Chaysi "Señora", waqhayukunsi. Manas pipas kanchu. Almallas chaypi chuta-layachkasqa. Chaysi, "kay almaqqa mikhunakuna kachkanchá", nispa t´aqwirikun. Chaysi t´aqwirikuqtin, mikhunakuna kasqa: t´impu, aqha, tragu, chaykuna. Chaysi tumayun, mikhuyun. Chaysi tuta, ñas tutañas riki. Chaysi tutata velachkaqtin. Sapallan velachkaqtin, nina carru hamun riki. Wasitapas chukchurichisparaq. "Ukukukukukkukummmmm", nispas riki, nina carruqa hamun.

Achhuyamun huk runa punkuman. Pakarukun riki, taqi sikiman. "¿Imataq chayri?" nispa.

Chaysi riki naqa, saqraqa achhuyamun riki. "¿Lluqsirqamunkichu?"

man hid himself behind the granary. "What could that be?" he asked himself.

It was a demon approaching. "Would you like to step out?" the demon said to the corpse.

"Would you like to come in? Come on in," the dead man's spirit answered, and sat up. The two of them did a high-stepping dance together.

"Shall we go?"

"Yes, let's go." And the demon and its shuddering chariot of fire went out first.

The soldier jumped up and gave the corpse a hard blow. "So you wanted to go out, eh? That's why you were so happy," he said, and whacked the spirit-corpse with the butt of his rifle. The soldier had gotten his courage up. He ate some more food and drank some more corn-beer.

The chariot of fire came back a second time and a third. It came twice, and the demon said "The third time I'm going to carry you off." The soldier was waiting in the doorway the third time, his rifle at the ready. When the chariot of fire came, the demon said, "You should thank him. I'm not going to carry you off. You have a savior."

Once the chariot of fire had gone away, the corpse sat up again, and said to the soldier, "Oh, our Lord must have sent you. Our Creator sent you here to save me. For that, I give you my cows, sheep, money. And you can marry my wife," he said. When he said this, he changed into a white dove, and the spirit flew away. He just disappeared.

When morning came, the wife showed up with many neighbors in tow, to bury her husband. But there was no corpse there. The soldier told them everything that had happened. "This is what your husband told me," he said. So the soldier and the woman got married. Instead of there being a burial, there was a wedding. And they invited me to it as well.

Yes, I was there participating in the service. And I said "I'm going to bring this along for my good friend." It was some good roast meat. But some mean dogs came up right behind me, and stole it away from me. That's the end of the story.

"¿Yaykurqamunkichu? Yaykurqamuyá", ninsi. Alma tiyarirun. Hinaspas tusuyunku waputa riki.

"¿Ripusunchu?"

"Ripusunmi", nispa. Chaysi riki pasapun riki saqraqa, kukukukuyuspa carrunpi, nina carrupi.

Chay suldaduqa hatariramuspa riki p´anayun riki. "¿Kaypaqqa ganasniyki kasqa ih? Kaypaqqa kusa kasqanki", nispa p´anayun almataqa riki, armanwan riki. Chaysi riki kasqanpi animayukullantaq. Traguta tumayun; aqhata tumayun.

Chaysi nina carruqa kimsa kutikama hamusqa. Iskay kutikama; hinas, "Kimsanpiqa apasaykin", nispa. Chaysi nina carru hamuspa nisqa, "Agradece. Mana apaykichu. Salvaqniyki kasqa", nispa.

Chaysi riki chay alma, nina carru pasapuqtin, almaqa tiyarirusqa. Hinas suldaduchata nisqa, "¡Ay, Diosninchik kachamusqasunki, nuqa salvawanaykipaq! Kaymi tantu wakay, qullqiy, uvijay. Warmiywanyá qam casarapunki", nispa. Chayta rimaruspas, yuraq palumachaman tukuruspa, pasapun chay almaqa riki. Ch´usaqman tukupun.

Chaysi paqarisnintinqa riki, lliw askha vicinukunata pusayukuspa, warminqa hamun, p´ampanankupaq. Chaysi mana alma kapusqachu. Chaysi Suldaduchaqa willakapusqa kasqanta. Chaysi, "Khaynatan niwan", nispansi. Suldaduchawan casarakapusqaku warmi. Chayqa entierru kanantaqa, entierrup kanantaqa, casamientu kapusqa. Chaymanpas invitallawankutaq nuqaman riki.

Chaypi nuqapis kasqan mink´asqallataq kani. Chayqa nini, "Kaychataqa aparkusaq Señora Ankipaq", nispa; sumaq kankakunata. Hinas chay qipapi millay allqukuna kasqa. Chay qichurapuwanku. Chayllan cuintucha.

Watch Dog and Bean Blossom

This dog's tale provides an instructive contrast with "The Deserter." No one thinks any less of the man who volunteers to slay the head-choppers on account of the fact that he takes his ferocious, larger-than-life dogs with him to accomplish the task. On the contrary, he is rewarded for his resourceful ways. He alone is able to gauge the scope and precise nature of the threat confronting him. He is a good planner, as his trip preparations demonstrate. His ability to vanquish the head-choppers stands as a feat of psychology — stalling for time with a "magic" formula — and not a mere feat of physical strength.

Watch Dog and Bean Blossom

Told by Isidoro Wamani

There was a hacienda owner. This hacienda owner had a lot of workers—
a lot of workers. And on that hacienda there were several fierce head-
chopping monsters. They went around terrorizing people. So everyone fled to a nearby village. They left the hacienda abandoned. One
day the hacienda owner came to them and said "Today, I want you all
to come back to my hacienda. It's been abandoned too long. I want
twenty-five men to go back there. With that many of you, you won't get
killed. Nothing is going to happen to you."

Just then, one of the men stepped up and said, "Excuse me, sir, but
I don't want to go there with twenty-five men. I only want three. I want
three of us to go."

"Which three, then?" asked the hacienda owner.

"I want to go along with Watch Dog and Bean Blossom. Them and
me. That's all. Just the three of us want to go."

"How soon can you start walking?"

"I'll get moving in the next few days." In less than a week, he toasted
corn, milled flour, and packed his provisions. And on the designated
day, the three of them started on the path back to the hacienda. Him
and his two dogs, Watch Dog and Bean Blossom. When they were
crossing the first mountain pass, they came across a horse carcass.
Since the horse was dead, the dogs stayed there long enough to eat
it. Meantime, the man walked ahead. When he got to the next pass,

Guarda Casacha, Habas T´ikacha

Huk hacendadu kasqa, Hinaspa hacendadup chay runakuna askha kasqa, askha runakuna. Hinaspa chay haciendanpi millay ñak´achukunaña askha kapusqaku. lliw abusutachá ruwapuranku. Chayqa huk circallamanña, huk llaqtamanña astakanpunku, Chayqa hacienda wikch´usqa kapun. Chayñataqsi hacendadu nin, "Kunanmi haciendayta rinkichik. Unayña wikch´usqa. Rinkichik iskaychunka pichqayuq runa. Chaytaqa manachá wañuchimusunkichikmanchu. Manachá imapas pasamusunkichikmanchu", nispa nipuspa.

Chayqa chaymantamá huknin runa nin, "Manan nuqaqa papáy, iskaychunka pichqayuq runawanqa riyta munanichu, sino kimsallawan. Kimsallan riyta munani", nispa.

"¿Chay mayqinkuna?" nispa ninpas.

"Nuqaqa riyta munani Guarda Casachawan, Habas T´ikachawan, nuqapuwan. Chayllan; kimsantillayku riyta munayku", nispa.

Chayqa, "¿Hayk´aqtaq puririnki?" nin.

"Purisaq nuqaqa huk punchaw", nispa. Chayqa simananman hank´ata hank´ayunku. Hak´uta kutayukun. Fiambrita ruwayukun. Chayqa huk p´unchaw designado, puririn, puririn chay haciendata chay kimsantillan. Iskaynin allqullantin, chay Guarda Casachawan, Habas T´ikachawan. Chayqa chay primer wayq´upi puririqtinñataqsi, huk caballu wañusqa kasqa. Hinaspa caballu wañusqa kaqtinñataq, chaypi chayta mikhuspa allqukuna quidarukusqa. Hinaspa payqa avan-

there stood a head-chopper, with three mules. Three mules were there by his side.

The head-chopper said "Hello, friend. Where are you headed? Stretch out your neck."

"Oh, good friend! I'll tell you my poor story. Don't kill me yet. I'll sing it to you," he said, to stall for time. The head-chopper took the knife away from his neck and waited. "I'll sing three times," the man said. And after the third time I sing, friend, you can kill me." He sang:

Watch Dog, Watch Dog, bow wow wow.
　Bean Blossom, Bean Blossom, bow wow wow.

That was once.

Watch Dog, Watch Dog, bow wow wow.
　Bean Blossom, Bean Blossom, bow wow wow.

That was twice. The head-chopper was watching, knowing there was only one more time left to sing. He said to himself, "He's just singing, right?" But he was really calling his dogs. When he looked away, the dogs were already rounding the bend in the path. The man only had one more before he'd be killed. He sang:

Watch Dog, Watch Dog, bow wow wow.

With only the last verse left to go, the two dogs knocked the head-chopper to the ground and killed him dead. When they'd killed him, the man and the dogs went off, taking the three mules with them.

That's how it went with the first head-chopper and his three mules. The man went on, leading the mules in tow. He got up on one of them, and led the other two. While the two dogs were finishing off the head-chopper, he went on ahead with the mules. He arrived at another mountain pass. And there, of course, another head-chopper was waiting. The dogs had remained behind for a minute. And in that short while they lagged behind, in the first pass, they got distracted.

So anyway, when the man got to the second pass, the head-chopper was waiting there. There was another head-chopper waiting for him. The man was mounted on the first head-chopper's mule, leading the other two. This time, he had his gun at the ready.

The head-chopper said "Hello, friend. Where are you headed with those? Stretch out your neck."

The man answered, "Put your hands up." He was going to defend himself with a pistol.

zachkanña. Chayqa huk wayq´upiñan chayaqtin, chaypi huk ñak´achu kachkasqa kimsa mulantin. Kimsa mulantin kachkasqa chaypi.

Hinaspa: "Hola, tayta. ¿Maytataq kayta hamuchkanki? Kunkata huqariy", nispa nipusqa.

Hinaspa: ¡Ay, papacito lindo! Wakcha vidaytaraq takirukusaq. Amaraq wañurachiwaychu. Takirukusaq", nispa niqtin, atajayukusqaraq. Chayqa kunkanmanta, kunkanmanta cuchilluta huquruspaqa, sayarachisqaraq. Hinaspa, "Kimsakaman takisaq. Chayqa kimsakama takiqtinña papáy, wañuchiwankipas", nispas nipusqa. Chayqa ninsi.

Guarda Casacha, kuk, kuk, kuk.

Habas T´ikacha, kuk, kuk, kuk.

Hukllatas;

Habas T´ikacha, kuk, kuk, kuk.

Guarda Casacha, kuk, kuk, kuk.

Iskayña. Chaysi riki, hukta qhawarikuqtinqa, hukllaña faltarun takinanpaq. Chaysi chayqa "Takichkanchá", ninchá riki ñak´achuqa. Chayqa allquntataq wakyachkasqa; hukta qharawirukuqtinqa, ña muyuramuchkasqaña allqukuna. Chayqa hukllaña faltasqan wañuchinaypaq. Chayqa:

Guarda Casacha, kuk, kuk, kuk.

Hukllaña faltayuqtin ñak´achu, ñak´achuqa iskaynin allqukuna kunparuspa, lluyta wañurachipusqaku. Chay wañuchipuqtinku, chayqa kimsantin caballutaqa chay runaqa aysarikapunña.

Chayqa hukllaña nak´achuqa, kimsa caballuntin. Chayqa aysarikapusqa, pasapunña. Yastá hukninta muntayun, iskayta aysarikun. Chayqa chay runawan embrullanakuchkanankama, allqukuna embrullanakuchkanankamaqa riki (nak´achu) chay runaqa puririn. Chayqa huk wayq´uman chayallantaq. Chayqa chaypisyá riki huk ñak´achu kallasqataq. Chayqa allqukuna quidarukullasqataq Chayqa huk chikanta. Chayqa huk chikanta quidaruqtinqa, allqukunaqa distrayikuspa quidarusqaku.

Chayqa chayaruqtinqa huk ladu wayq´uman chayaruqtinqa, chaypi ñak´achu kallasqataq. Chayqa ñak´achu kallaqtintaq chaypi. Chayqa primer ñak´achup caballunman muntayukuspa pasachkaran, iskayninta aysarikuspa. Chayqa ña pistolanpas kasqaña chaypaqqa.

Chayqa: Hola tayta. ¿Maytan hamuchkanki kayta? Kunkata huqariy."

Niqtin: "Alto manos", nispa pistolanwanña defindirakapusqa.

"¡Ah, cumpañiruymá kapusqanki!", nispa nipusqa. Chayqa chaykamalla distrayirukusqaku. Chayqa allqukuna chayaramusqaku chaytaqa wañurachipusqallataq. Chayqa iskay caballuyuq chayasqa. Chayqa un-

"Hey, you're my buddy," replied the head-chopper. That's how they were talking. And in that short space of time, the two dogs arrived and killed the second head-chopper. The man went on to the next mountain pass with the mules. The head-choppers had delayed him. When he got to the third pass, there wasn't any head-chopper. Only in the first two passes. At last, he arrived at the hacienda. The hacienda was all dusty, all the belongings going to rack and ruin. The man had brought along all the provisions and food he'd need for his time there. "What can happen to me? Nothing is going to happen to me, as long as I've got my dogs." He stayed there two or three weeks, a couple of weeks. Then he started back. It took him another week or so to return, a good long time.

His family hadn't seen him all that time, and his wife and children were already in mourning. "He probably died. In this amount of time, he would have arrived. He should have been here a while ago." Everyone was in mourning.

The man arrived, leading five mules loaded down on one side with gold, on the other with silver. He arrived with Watch Dog and Bean Blossom behind him. "What are you all in mourning about?" he asked. "Help me unload this gold and silver." He told them what had happened at the hacienda. He came back with all the riches he'd loaded onto the mules. That man lives very well today, with his two dogs. That's how he returned. That's it.

ayña hark´asqachayá. Huk ladu wayq´upiqa manaña ñak´achu kas-
qañachu. Chay iskaynin wayq´ullapi kasqa. Chayqa haciendaman
chayan. Lluy pulvullañas hacendadupiqa, lluy, imaymanan cusas-
ninkuna chhayna kasqa. Chaykunata cargayukuspa, chay caballuku-
napi cargayukuspa, huk semana wayk´uyukuspa. "¿Imallas pasawanqa?
Allqukunantintaq kachkani. Chayqa manachá imapas pasawanman-
chu riki." Chayqa ñas iskay kimsa semanaña, chunka pichqayuq p´un-
chawñas chaypi kachkan. Chaymantaqa puririnpunsi. Chayqa huk se-
manapis chayayapullantaq, huk semanatataq hark´asqaku, unayña.

Chayqa ña chicachakunapas, ñas warminpas lutukamaña kasqa.
"Wañunñachá. Chayamunmanñachá, khaytukuy. Unaypiqa chaya-
munmanña." Lluy lutukapusqa.

Lluy lutukapusqa.

Chayqa huk ladunpis quri, huk ladunpis qullqi. Lluy pichqa caballu
aysariyusqa. Chay runaqa chayanpusqa, chay Guarda Casachantin,
Habas T´ikachantin. Chayqa, "¿Imamantan lutukuchkankichik? kay qul-
lqikunata descargaychik", nispa chayanpusqa. Chayqa hacendadu-
mantapas nuticiata apamun. Lluy cosaskunatapas, lluyta cargayukuspa
ima hampusqa. Chayqa chay runaman ña allin runa kasqa, chay (kimsantin) iskaynin allqullawan. Chayqa chayanpusqayá. Chayqa chaypi
tukukapun.

Wayrurkumacha and Chinchirkumacha

*This variation on the preceding story is especially interesting because its pro-
tagonist takes the form of a fearless and cranky old woman who loves dogs a lot
more than she does people. It is true that male and female roles are in some respects rigidly defined and unequal in highland Peru. But a woman can nonetheless, under the right circumstances, become a heroine in much the same way as
a man can become a hero. Quechuas admire no one so much as the person (of
whatever sex) who knows how to live by his or her wits. I had to believe that Rosa
Callo, who told me this story, along with her mother Teodora and her daughter
Iliana—who together ran a household and a store without the help of any men—
could identify with this woman's uncompromising independent streak.*

Wayrurkumacha and Chinchirkumacha

Told by Juana Rosa Callo Paliza

An old woman lived in a village. And she was a rich old woman. She lived all alone, and owned sheep and llamas. She had all kinds of livestock; but she lived alone. Every morning she would get up, work her fields, and look after her livestock. As I mentioned, she lived there all alone.

Some thieves said to one another, "Hey, let's rob everything from that old hag. It's about time we killed her." But she had some dogs. And she would cook meals just for them. So the dogs were really big. They ate what she cooked up in her pot; she would cook them food. The thieves said, "She sure does treat those dogs good." The two dogs were really big. Solid. The thieves said "Man, that old woman babies those dogs so much, look how huge they've gotten! All the more reason we should rob her. She doesn't even have children. What does she need all that livestock for? It would be a good thing if we robbed her." So they kept their eye on the old woman, and waited.

She walked about with the dogs. And the dogs, in truth, were fierce. Anybody they saw, those dogs would kill. The thieves said "Why should we be scared of those dogs, just dogs? If it wasn't for those dogs, we'd already have killed her dead. We'd knock off the old lady, and round up her livestock." Oh, those crafty crooks were making plans! "But how?" they kept thinking. "Hey, I know, let's roast some guinea pig. It will have a strong aroma, and we'll put it up here on the hillside. While the dogs are gobbling it down, we'll tie up the old lady. And if she hollers, we'll just kill her. That's how we'll rob her." So they left it at that.

The aroma of the roast guinea pig really did draw the dogs. They fol-

Wayrurkumacha, Chinchirkumacha

Huk llaqtapis riki huk payacha tiyakusqa. Hinaspansi qapaq kasqa uvijanpas, llamanpis. Uywansi imaymana kasqa; sapallansi. Hinaspa payqa tutamantas hatarin. Hinaspa chakranta ruwan; uywanta qhawan. Hinaspansi sapallan tiyakun chaypi. Chaytas suwakunaqa qhawasqaku riki. Hinaspansi riki nisqa, "¡Ay, haqay mamakumantaqa suwaramusun lliwta! Sipiramullasunña", nispansi. Chaysi, hinataqsi allqukuna kasqa. Chaysi payqa mikhunatas wayk´ukuq riki, paypaq. Chaysi allqukunaqa wirallañas. Chaysi payqa chay mankacha mikhusqa wayk´usqan, mikhunacha wayk´ukusqan. Chaysi nin: "Chay mayllichallawansi uywaq allqukunata." Hatunkunasyá allqukuna kasqa, iskay. Chaysi wirallaña. Chaysi nisqa suwakunaqa: "¡Ay haqay payaqa sumaqtaraq allqutapas uywachkan, wiray-wirayta! Chaychus mana suwamusunman. Mana wawayuq mana imayuq. ¿Imapaqmi paypa ima uywanpas kanqa? Nuqanchik allin kanqa, suwamunanchik", nispansi. Chaysi awatiyasqaku riki payachataqa.

Hinas allqullantin purin riki. Allqus isu sí phiñallaña kasqa. Pitachá runata rikuq, chayqa wañuchillaqñas allqukunaqa. Chaysi, "¿Imaynatachá kay allqukunawan, allqullanmi manchachiwanchik? Mana allqun kanman chayqa ñan sipiramusunmanña, lliwta. Uywantapas qatiramusunman, thunkuruspallaraq payataqa," nispansi. ¡Ay, chaysi astutu suwakunaqa pinsanku riki. "¿Imaynan?" yuyayukunkus. "Aswan, nata, ay quwita kankarakamusun. Hinaspa q´apachkaqta kay q´asa pataman chararusunchik. Chayta allqu raqrachkanankukama, nuqanchik yaykuspa payataqa riki thunkurusun. Chaychus qaparkachanqa, chayqa sipirusunchik riki. chaykama suwasunchik", nispa. Chaysi riki, hinata riki.

lowed it. The thieves had cooked four or five guinea pigs. While the dogs gobbled them up, those bad thieves sneaked right in. The old woman said "Oh no, somehow or other they've gotten in! Now what?" The old lady picked up a stick to thrash them with. "How dare you rob me! It's me who is going to kill you all. If that's how you want it, okay, I'll kill you." Finally, they grabbed hold of the old woman. And she said, "Okay, you all want to kill me. I only ask you one little thing."

"What's that?"

"I only want to sing," she said. "I only want to sing. When I'm done singing, you can kill me. If you want to, cut off my head. If you want to, strangle me. "If I sing—that is, if you all agree to let me sing—then I'll give you silver and gold. Afterward, I'll even show you where it is."

The thieves thought about the silver and gold, and answered "In that case, let's let her sing. Then she'll tell us."

"As soon as I'm done singing, I'll tell you." So she began to sing in a loud voice.

Wayrurkumaaaaaacha! Chinchirkumaaaaaacha!

And what was that? Those were the names of the two dogs: Wayrurku-macha and Chinchirkumacha. She yelled it out again:

Wayrurkumaaaaaacha! Chinchirkumaaaaaacha!

The dogs heard her voice. This time, the dogs came running. Oh, they had almost reached her! "Now I'll sing for the third time." And for the third time she yelled out their names.

Wayrurkumaaaaaacha! Chinchirkumaaaaaacha!

Her dogs definitely heard that one. Then they got there, and started biting the thieves. That's how they saved the old woman.

The thieves didn't get a chance to kill her. She said to the dogs, "All right! You all saved me. So today, we're going to slaughter my best sheep, and eat it together." That's what the old woman said to her dogs. "Today you saved my life, by killing those robbers." The dogs had torn the thieves to pieces. They killed every last one of them. There had been three. The dogs bit them all over their bodies, and killed them. The old woman was in high spirits, and said "Today, if I didn't reward you as you deserve, I just couldn't feel happy. After you saved my life? Today, we slaughter a sheep so I can offer a meal to you." And she slaughtered the sheep. She gave it to the dogs; put a hunk of meat next to each dog's head. "And I'll eat this. And you eat that!" she said to the dogs. How about that? I even brought some of it back for you. But those dogs took it away from me.

Chayqa chiqaqpaqsi allqukunaqa riki asnachikunku riki quwi kankata. Chaysi pasanku. Chaysi ay, tawa pichqa quwi kasqa riki. Chay p´atachkanankukama riki, chiqaqpaq suwaqa yaykun, ¡ay! Hinaspansi nin, "¡Ay chiqaqpaqsi qaqaynaniraqta riki yaykunku! ¿Chaysi? "¿Imatan kunan?" Kutipakamunsi k´aspiwan mamakuchaqa. "Qamkuna munankichik wañuchiyta. Chayqa hukchallata mañaykuchkaykichik", ninsi. "¿Imata?", ninsi.

"Takirukullasaq", ninsi, "Takirukullasaq. Takirukuqtiyqa, wañuchiwanki. Aunque sea, quruwankipis. Aunque sea, siq´uwankipis", nispansi mamakuchaqa nin. Chaysi, (¡Ay taytay cuernos chaytaraq niwachkanki a ver takiyta an!) "Takiqtiyqa, takiyrachiwaqtiykiqa, quri-qullqiy kachkan. Chaytapas t´uqsiyrusaykin, maypin kachkan chayta."

Chayqa suwakunaqa riki quri-qullqiraykuqa, "Hinatapasyá takichun", nispa. "Willawasun."

"Chaysi takiqtiyña, willasaykiqa", ninsi. Chaysi takin, riki.

Wayrurkumacha, Chinchirkumacha.

nispansi qaparkachan riki. ¿chayqa, imas kasqa? Allqukunasyá sutin kasqa: Wayrurkumacha y Chinchirkumacha. Entonces qaparkachansi riki:

Wayrurkumacha, Chinchirkumacha.

nispa. Chayqa chaytasyá allqukunaqa uyarimun riki, Huktas, phawamunku riki allqukunaqa. ¡Ay, chaysi chayta chayaruspa! "Ña kimsakamallan kakisaq", nisqas. Chayqa kimsakamasyá chhaynata qaparkachasqa:

Wayrurkumacha, Chinchirkumacha

nispas. Huktas allqukunaqa uyarirun riki. Chaysi chayamun; huktas p´atayun riki suwakunataqa. Chaypi riki qispikapusqa.

Manas sipisqakuchu. Chayqa riki nisqa, "¡Ay, vaya! Kunanqa ay, qamkunamá kasqankichik. Kunan mayqinchá uvija kachkan. Chayta ñak´aspa mikhusunchik", nispa mamakuchaqa nin riki allqunkunata. "Qamkunarayku kunanqa salvakuni, sipiwanankumanta kay suwataqa." Ñut´utasyá t´isayusqaku allqukuna riki suwakunata. Llipinta sipiyusqaku; kimsachus hina kasqa. Chayta lliwta qhamsayun; wañusqayá. Chaymantasyá, animanparispa nisqa, "¡Ay, nuqaqa kunanqa!, manan imata pagapuqtiypas, cuntintuchu kayman, ¿khayna viday salvawasqaykimanta? Kunan uvijata ñak´aspa mikhurachipusqayki", nispansi uvijatas ñak´an. Allquman riki churayun; huknin allquman uman laduta kankankusyá. "¡Nuqataq kayta mikhusaq! ¡Qamtaq kayta mikhunki!", nispansi allquman ¿ih? Chaysi nuqapas chaymanta apakamuchkarani. Quyuwaranku. Chayllan chay.

The Man-Bear

One of the most widely disseminated folk tales of the southern Andes is "The Man-Bear." There are dozens of variants, with certain overlapping constants such as the kidnapping of the young woman. A priest also usually puts the boy-bear through a series of labors which he accomplishes in unexpected fashion, much to the priest's vexed chagrin. As in the cycle of comic vignettes about the fox and the mouse, the structure is episodic; individual tellers, while adhering to an essential core, decide which episodes they will include and which they will delete. I find this simple explanation more persuasive than "deep structure." I believe, as Clifford Geertz does, that the truth, like the Devil, lies in the details. As with the fireworks towers erected in the main square for patron saint celebrations, the individual flashes of the explosions have a more legitimate and logical claim on our attention than the armature which sustains them. The man-bear is also figured in the ukuku dance named after him, which can be seen at many a highland festival from Paucartambo to Pisaq, as part of the ever-changing panorama of masks, innovations in dance steps and flourishes of costuming and personal adornment. One aspect of the ukuku story is clearly Oedipal, detailing the son's need to protect the mother and slay the father. The version featured here was told to me by Buenaventura Rocca Molina, who took a break from his labors repairing a street to hold forth. His boss gave him an extra-long lunch break so that he could tell me his version, in the City Hall of San Sebastian. The boss and other laborers sat around on wooden chairs or on the floor and listened, clearly enjoying the recitation of a story that all of them appeared to be already familiar with.

The Man-Bear

Told by Buenaventura Rocca Molina

There was a shepherdess, a mestizo girl. She used to take her sheep up to graze. One day, a young man-bear came by, dressed in a black suit. "Hey, girl, what are you doing?"

"Well, boy, I'm grazing my sheep," she answered. "And you, where are you from?"

"I'm from a long ways away, and I've brought my own sheep to graze." Another time he came, bringing oranges and bananas. He picked some up along the way. He'd gathered them together so he could trick the girl. "We have these on my hacienda. Wouldn't you like to go to my hacienda? I've been looking for a servant girl for my hacienda," said the young man.

"I'll go ask my father," said the girl. "I wonder what he'll say? If he says yes, I'll also bring along my younger sister, and we can leave behind sheep-herding. She and I can come together."

The next day, the man-bear came back to the same place. He was a man-bear with a black suit. He came back bringing lots of fruit. And he distracted the younger sister with the fruit, so he could go off with the older sister. But when the girl didn't want to go off, he said "Well then, let's play piggyback with each other. First give me a ride on your back. Then I'll take a turn giving you a ride on mine." The man-bear let her give him a piggyback ride first. Then he gave the girl a ride on his. They each took three turns, and the third time, he carried her away. He bore her off to a cliff-cave. He opened a door in the cave, and they went inside.

Ukuku

Huk uvijiras, mistisachas kasqa. Chay uvijata michikuchkasqa. Hinas ukukus achhuyusqa nantin, yanakama tirnuntin. "¿Imata ruwakuchkanki, yaw chica?"

Niqtin, "Uvijatan, niño, michikuchkani", nispa nisqa. "¿Qamri, maymantataq kanki?"

"Nuqa chay karumantaraqmi uvijata qatikamuchkani, michikunaypaq", nispa. Hinaspañataq huk kutipiqa risqa, naranjantin, platanusnintin. Entonces chayta pallayuspa, riqtin, chicata ingañasqa. "Chhayna nuqaq haciendaypi. ¿Manachu haciendayta ripuwaq? Haciendaypi nuqa impliaduypaq munachkani." Chayna chicata nispa.

Entonces, "Papaytaraq tapuyamusaq. Ima ninqachá", nispa. "Chayqa huk sullk´achaytawan pusakamuspa, chay uvijata paqarin saqisaq", nispa. "Nuqawan risunchik", nispa.

Paqarisnintin, yapamanta kutisqallataq ukukuchaqa. Ukukuqa kasqan yana tirnuntin. Frutakunata apariyukuspa kutillasqataq. Entonces chay sullk´achanmanwan ingañaspa, frutata saqiyuspa, chicata pasachipun. Chica mana ripuyta munaqtin, "q´ipi-q´ipichapi entonces pukllasunchik", nispa. Primirta nuqataraq q´ipikachaway. Nuqañataq chaymanta q´ipiykachasayki", nispa. Q´ipiykachachikusqa primirta ukuku. Chaymantañataq chicata q´ipiykuchkasqa. Kimsakama pukllaqtinku, chicata q´ipiyukuspa siqayachipusqa ukukucha, huk qaqa wayq´uman. Chay qaqa wayq´uman pasayachipusqa. Punku kichalakapusqa qaqata; chayqa chayman pasayapusqa.

So the girl began to live together with the man-bear. After a time, the girl gave birth; she gave birth to a little boy-bear. He started to grow up. And whenever she would cry bitter tears, the man-bear said "Don't cry. I'll bring you back anything you want to eat: beef, anything at all. Don't cry."

The boy-bear, the little child, was getting ever bigger. One day he said to his mother, "What are you crying for? Where does your mother live?"

"My mother lives very far from here."

"Then why did you come to this place?"

"Because your father brought me here. He tricked me. That's why I feel so sad now."

"Well then, let me suckle at your breast a little longer. Suckle me well, and before long I'll be able to fell that door with a single blow." At last, he hit the door and knocked it down. The boy-bear helped his mother to escape.

The old man-bear had said to her that day "Today I'm going to bring you a cow, pure white. And once you have that pure white cow, you'll feel better about being here." While he was away, the boy-bear helped his mother to escape.

A hummingbird came whirring by. "Hummmmingbird, I'm a hum-mmmingbird. And your wife has left you for the arms of another. You might as well give up."

"Listen here, you damned jackass. What did you say to me?" He knocked the hummingbird down. He broke the hummingbird's leg. The hummingbird said "Please stick my leg back together with your snot. Then I'll tell you where your beloved ran off to." The old man-bear then climbed up to his cave to leave a cow he'd been carrying on his back.

His woman wasn't in the cave, that girl wasn't in the cave anymore. The boy-bear had helped her go off. He said to his mother, "Mama, don't be afraid—but my father is going to catch up with us. If red smoke rolls off of him, that means I'll win the fight. If white smoke rolls off me, that means he'll beat me. Then my father will eat up both of us." The father did indeed catch up with them, and started hollering "Now I'm going to eat up both of you." When he had almost caught up with them, the boy-bear pulled up a tree by its roots. He began to thrash his father with it. The two were thrashing each other. At last, the boy-bear killed his father.

The boy-bear arrived with his mother at his grandmother's house

Chayqa chay ukukuwan tiyapusqaku naqa, chay chicaqa. Chayqa uña ukukuchata wachakapusqa chay naqa, chicaqa wachakapusqa. Chayqa allinchaña kasqa. Chayqa nañataq, ukukuñataq riki, kuyata waqaqtin, ukukuñataq nisqa riki, "Ama waqaychu. Ima munasqaykita; wakatapas, imatapas apamusaykin, mikhunaykipaq. Ama waqaychu", nispa.

Chayqa chikan allinchaña kasqa, uña ukukucha. Chaysi mamitanta nisqa, "¿Imamantan waqanki? ¿Maypin mamitayki tiyan?" nispa.

"Mamitayqa tiyan karupiraqmi".

"¿Imamantaq hamurankiri?" nispa.

"Chaymi chhayna papayki pusamuwaran. Ingañaspa nuqataqa. Chaymi chaypi kunan llakipi rikukuni," nispa.

"Entonces imanayraq, astawanraq ñuñuway. Allinta ñuñu-ruwaqtiykiqa, nayusaqmi, kunanmi nuqa chay punkuta saqmaspa kicharusaq", nispa. Chayqa punkuta saqmaspa, kicharuqtin, mami-tantaqa iscapachinpusqa riki chay ukukuqa, uña ukukucha.

Chayqa machu ukukuqa riki nisqa, "Kunanmi aparamuchkayki yu-raq waka, puruta. Hinaspan kunan chay yuraq waka puruwan, kunan aswan allinta kanki chaypi", nispa. Chayqa chaypi kachkaqtin riki, chay ratuqa uña ukukucha pasachipusqaña mamitanta.

Chayñataq q´inticha achhuyyusqa riki. "Riww q´intichay, riww q´in-tichay. Ñan warma yanaykiqa hukpa brazunpiña siqayapuchkan. Amaña chhayna kaychu", nispa.

"¡Yaw asnu, carajo! ¿Imatan qam chayta niwanki?" Hinaspa ch´aqi-rapusqa. Chakichanta p´akirapusqa , q´inchichapta. Chayqa q´inticha nisqa, "Nachayta, chakillayta qhuñachaykiwan k´askayachipuway. Nuqa willayusayki . . . maytañas warma yanayki pasapuchkan", nispa. Chayqa wakata q´ipiyukuspa ukuku siqayamuchkan riki.

Chayqa manaña kapusqañachu wasinpi naqa, warminqa ka-pusqañachu, chay chicaqa. Ya apamuchkasqañan. Chaysi na riki, uña ukukuchaqa nin: "Ama mama manchakunkichu, sinokisqa (si nuqa-manta) papaywan tarparamasun. Chayqa papaymanta puka q´usñi sa-yarinqa, chaypi ganasaq. Si nuqamanta yuraq q´usñi sayarinqa, chaypi nuqata ganawanqa. Iskayninchiktan mikhullawasunchikña kunanqa pa-payqa", nisqa. Chayqa papanqa tarparamuchkasqaña riki, qapariyuspa, "Kunanqa iskayninchikta mikhuwallasunchikña", nispa. Chayqa tar-paramuchkaqtin, narapusqa, huk k´aspita t´iraruspa saphintinmanta. Chaywan papanta q´asusqa riki; q´asunayukusqaku riki. Chayqa papanta wañurachipusqa chay ukukuchaqa.

Chayqa ukukucha nachkayuqta mamitanpuwan abuilachanpaman chayanpusqaku riki, llaqtaman. Chayqa chay llaqtaman chayanpuqt-

in her hometown. When they got to town, they went to live with the grandmother. From the waist up, he was a bear, and from the waist down, he was a man, but hairy all over. The woman's father only gave the boy-bear certain things to eat. No meat, and not much of anything. He only gave him a small portion on a plate. One day, his grandfather said, "Run along and tend to our sheep and our pigs." And he sent the boy-bear off.

Well, the boy-bear ate the pigs. He threw the remains in the mud, with the feet sticking out. Later, he told his grandparents, "The pigs sank into the mud, and I lost them." The same thing happened with the sheep, just the feet sticking out. Nothing was left; his grandparents were losing everything.

Finally, they said to their daughter, "Oh, what are we supposed to do now? Whatever that is, it's no child. What on earth did you bring here?" Having said that, they got the boy-bear a job working for the village priest.

By then, the boy-bear had grown to full size. The priest said "Let's send a bunch of young men to push the boy-bear out of the tower. That way he'll die." So he sent the boy-bear up into the tower, after he was all grown up. Then he sent a bunch of men up after him, to push him out. "Take him by surprise," the priest said to them. But when they came up, the boy-bear grabbed them in both his arms, all those men, and he threw them out of the tower. A lot of men died.

The priest couldn't do anything to him. He said to himself "Oh! What is he? What is he? Is he an animal, or what?" Then he said to the boy-bear "Today I want you to drive those horses and burros down to the jungle-lands for me. And I want you to bring me back firewood from the jungle-lands." The priest made him up a travel bag of coca leaves and toasted corn. When that was ready, the boy-bear went off with the horses and mules, down toward the jungle, to search for wood. Along the way, along where they were walking, tigers, pumas, other wild animals ate up all the horses and burros.

The boy-bear said "Oh, no! Now what's my godfather going to say to me? Now where will I go?" So he rounded up all the wild animals, the ones who'd eaten his. He hit them one by one with a stick, and drove them back to the priest's house bearing the firewood.

When he arrived with them, the priest was scared. "Oh! What kinds of animals are those?" He commanded the boy-bear to take them back with the wood. "Run along, take those animals back. They could finish

inqa, abuilachanpaman yaykuyapusqaku riki. Chayqa kuskachamanta ukukucha, urachanmantaq runacha, piluchayuq. Entonces, chayqa (chay mamitanpanpiqa mana) chay papanpa apamusqanta, hinatachu mikhuchipusqa riki nata. Ni aychapas, imapas mididuchallata, platuchapi mikhuchipusqa. Chayñataqsi abuilachan nin riki, "Phawayllayá chay uvijanchikta, khuchinchikta michimuy", nispa uña ukukuchataqa kamachinku.

Chaysi uña ukukuchaqa khuchita mikhurapun. Chakinkunatataq wichayman, t´uru ukhupi:, nispa. Uvijatapas kasqantas, hinata ruwarapullantaq, chakillanñas. Manas imapas kanñachu, churayukapun.

Chayñataqsi nin riki, "¡Ay!, ¿Imatataq kunan chaytaqa ruwasunchik, chay natachaqa? Chayqa wawachus imachá kakunpas. Imatachá chaytaqa pusamuwanki", nispa. Chay niqtinñataq riki, huk señor curaqman impliakusqa riki uña ukukuchataqa.

Ña allinchaña kasqa. Chaysi ni riki, "Chay chhayñataq, chay runacha chaypachaqa, chay turripatamanta kunan chay, askha runakunawan taqayachimusunchik", nispa. "Chaypi wañupunqa", nispa. Chaysi turri pataman siqayachin riki cura chay runakunata askhata siqachillantaq riki, qipanta tanqayanpunankupaq. Chayqa: "Chay chicuchata wikch´uyanpunkichik qunqaylla", nispa. Chayñataq siqaruqtin, uña ukukucha riki iskay ladu makinwan, hap´iruspa runata, q´alata ukuman wikch´uyamun turripatamanta. Chayqa runa askha riki wañuyapusqa.

Manas imawanpas kayta atinñachu. Señor curapas nipunñas, "¡Ay!, ¿imataq chayqa? ¿Immachá chayqa? ¿animalchus imachá chayqa?" nispa. Chayñataqsi nin riki, :Kunanmi nakunata chay caballukunata, asnukunata nayuspa, yunkata qatiyun riki. Yunkamanta kunan llant´ata apamuwanki", nispa. Chaysi kukata, hank´ata, fiambrita ruwayapun curaqa. Chayta ruwayapuqtin riki, ukukuchaqa siqayapun caballukunantin, q´ala yunkata, llant´aman. Risqanpi chaypiñataq riki an, khayna purichkanankama nakuna, tigri, puma, chaykuna q´alata caballuntawan, asnuntawan q´alata mikhurapusqa riki.

Chaysi ukukuchaqa nin riki: "¡Ay!, ¿Ima niwanqataqqa khunan papayqa? ¿Maytataq kunanqa ripusaq?" nispa. Chay llipin animalta hap´iyuspa, chay animal mikhusqakunapi, sapankata p´anayuspa, llant´antin chayayachinpullantaq nataqa kasqan, curaqmanqa chayanpullantaq.

Chaysi chayayamuqtin, mancharikun riki. "¡Ay!, ¿Ima animalkunataq chaykunaqa?" nispa. Llant´antin yapamanta kasqan kutiriyapullantaq riki. "Phaway, kutiyachipuy chay animalkunata. Imatapas tukuwasun-

us off in no time." The boy-bear took them back. Just went right back with them.

Another time, the priest said "Oh! Now a condemned soul is walking about in town. Go see about it right away. It's there on the hacienda lands." When the boy-bear went, sure enough, a condemned soul was there. The hacienda owner had died. The boy-bear made a fake doll out of wood. He made the fake doll out of wood. He took his toasted corn along, and that doll, and went. He walked over to the hacienda to stay for a while, and set himself up. It was true that the hacienda owner had become a condemned soul. The boy-bear went straight into his room. But not a single man, nor anybody was living on that hacienda. It was deserted.

When night came, he slaughtered a cow, and began to eat. He was all by himself; with just that wooden doll by his side to keep him company. That night, while he was sleeping, he felt an arm fall down on him. It was the condemned soul. Then one leg, then a head. Then the condemned soul stood up.

He said to the boy-bear "Ahh, now I'm going to eat you!" The boy-bear grabbed a length of rope, and he and the condemned soul fought all night long. At one point, the wooden doll stood up and gave the condemned soul a hard kick. With its help, the boy-bear was able to defeat the condemned soul, and the hacienda owner left all of his possessions to the boy-bear. The boy-bear stayed on as the new hacienda owner. He lived with the hacienda owner's wife, and there he died.

manchá chaykunaqa", nispa. Chayñataqsi chaywan kutiyapusqa. Aswan kutinpusqa, hinalla riki.

Chayñataqsi, nillantaq, "¡Ay!, kunanmi chay llaqtapis Khunan, kunan kachkan cundinado. Chaymanyá aswan ripuy", nispa, "Chaypi haciendanchik", nispa. Chayqa chayta riqtinñataq riki, ciertupaqyá chaypi cundinado . . . Hacendadu wañupusqa. Chaysi k´ullu wawata ruwakun riki chay ukukuqa. K´ullumanta wawata ruwakun. Chaynintin siqayun riki, hank´antin ima. Chayqa chay haciendaman chayaruqtinqa tiyarusqa. Chhayna kayuchkasqa riki, cundinado kasqa chay haciendayup. Chayñataq ukukuqa yaykun riki, huk cuartuman riki. Pero mana runapas, imapas tiyasqañachu chay haciendapi. Ch´in kapusqa.

Chaysi tuta riki chayaspa hina, wakata ñak´akuspa, mikhuyta qallarin riki. Sapallan; chay k´ullu wawantataqsi ladunman kunpayakuntaq. Chaysi tuta puñuchkaqtin, huk ladu nallanraq, brazullanraq urmayun . . . patachaman, cundinado riki. Chaymanqa huk ladu chakin, uman. Chayqa riki sayaripun.

Chaysi ukukuqa nin: "¡Ay, kunanqa mikhuchkallaykiñan, kunanqa!", nispa. Chaysi chaypi riki ukukuqa waskhata, lazuta uqariyukuspa, p´ananayukunku cundinadowan riki tutantin. Huk ratunsi muñica, chay k´ullu wawan sayaruspan, hayt´an payñataqsi. Chay iskayninku por fin ukukuqa vincisqapuni riki. Chayqa ukukuman q´alata saqiyapusqa nankunata, cusasninkunata q´alata. Chayqa chay ukuku chaypi, napi, haciendayuq quidapusqa. Chay haciendayuq warminwan tiyapusqa, chaypi wañusqa. Chaypi tukukapun.

The Corn-Beer Seller

Maria Laura Ugarte, an impish and effervescent student in an English class I taught in Cusco for a couple of months, told me what is in effect a good joke. The occasion came about after I asked my students, as part of a conversation class, to tell me a story they knew from childhood in order to practice their pronunciation and perfect their ability to form complete sentences. The 26-year-old Laura, who worked at the time as a hotel clerk, while attending university, might not have seemed the most promising place to look for folk wisdom, given how eager she was to master English, get cityfied, and ply the trade of tourism. But I had learned by then that the style of cultural self-presentation of my prospective "informants" usually suggested little about their desire and ability to tell an engrossing story. Much more indicative, to me, was the fact that Laura was the class cut-up, who obviously liked to perform. She made a bargain with me: If I would teach her some Christmas carols in English, she would in turn tell me a couple of good'uns. My other students in the class, God help me, made me reciprocate their less successful attempts to narrate stories by teaching them the lyrics to a pop song by Supertramp. I love the spirited way "The Corn-Beer Seller" begins: "Little gringo, I'm going to tell you a story that will make you laugh." She was as good as her boast—it did.

The Corn-Beer Seller

Told by Maria Laura Ugarte

Little gringo, I'm going to tell you a story that will make you laugh. This happened in the little village of Ollantaytambo. A woman made a corn beer called chicha every day to sell. Anyway, one day, as she was making the chicha, working on making chicha, a mouse fell in the vessel. The mouse was swimming around inside it. And the woman said to herself, "Oh, this isn't a good thing. But how am I going to throw out so much chicha? Well, I'll just send the little girl off to sell it the way it is." So, in the morning she called to the serving-girl and said "Hey, girl, come here! Run and sell this, go off and sell this chicha. And don't tell anyone, don't breathe a word about how yesterday a mouse fell in it and swam around."

"No, ma'am, I won't say a word to anyone."

"Scuttle off and sell it at whatever price you can."

So off went the girl; she went off to sell the chicha. She was setting up her stand, when along came a man thirsty from working his fields. "Oh, yeah! There's a lot of chicha right there. I'll go over there to drink." Up he came to the stand. "Hey there, girl, how much is your chicha?"

"Well, sir, do you want it all?"

"I don't care; just give me all of it. I am really, really thirsty."

Some of the man's friends arrived right along behind him. He said, "Yes, I'll drink with my friends here. How much?"

"Take it all for two coins, sir," she said.

Aqha Qhatup

Gringucha, huk cuentuta willasayki asikunaykipaq hina. Ollantaytambo llaqtallapitaq kayqa sucidisqa. Huk warmi aqhakuq sapa p´unchaw, vendikunanpaq. Chaysis huk p´unchawqa aqhachkaqtinkus, aqhata aqhchkaqtin, upiman pasayusqa huk´ucha. Chaysis chullurapusqa huk´ucha. Chayqa, "Manañayá allintañachu", warmiqa ninsi. "¿Imaynatataq khaytukuy aqhatari wikch´usunman? Hinatachá vindichimusunchik warmachawan", nispas nin. Chaysis warmachata tutamantaqa nin, "¡Yaw, chicacha! Pasarullankiña, kay aparunki, kay aqhata. Ama pimanpas ninkichu, willakunkichu huk´uchap p´unchawpi chhaqaypi chullusqanta."

"Manan, mamáy pimanpas willasaqchu."

Imallapiñapas phaway haturanpuy."

Chaysis chicachaqa pasan riki; aqhachantin pasasqa qatuq riki. Chaysis tiyachichkaqtin. Chaysis huk runañataq chakramanta ch´akisqa hamun riki. "¡Ay! hapaypi aswan aqha kachkasqa. Hakayllataña upiyaramusaq", nispa. Chaysis achhuyun. "¿Yaw warmacha hayk´an chay aqhayki?"

"Papáy, ¿llapantachu munanki?"

Llapantapas aunquesea qumuway. nisyuta ch´akiywachkan." Chay huk amigunkunañataqsi hatipamuchkasqa runataqa. Chayqa, "Chay amiguykunapuwan tumarusaqku. ¿Hayk´an?" nispa.

"Iskarallapiña tumarukuy papáy", ninsi.

"Iskarallaña, allin allin kachkan", nispas piensayukun paypaq. Tu-

"Two coins? Great, that's great," the man thought. He started drinking with his friends. By the end, he was left drinking alone. He'd stayed on by himself. Drinking down the last, he said "Man! Listen here, girl, how is it that you were able to sell me all that chicha for just two coins? It's got to be worth more than that."

"Oh, sir, I just have to tell you the truth. Last night, my mistress was making chicha, and a mouse fell in. That's when she told me 'Sell it at whatever price you can.'"

"Damnit to hell! So you made me, me, drink chicha a mouse had been swimming in? What the hell kind of thing is that?" He gave the clay vessel a kick and shattered it.

"Oh no, sir! Why did you go off and shatter the clay pot? Now my mister and mistress are going to beat me. What will I do now?"

"Huh! You're as cracked as your clay pot. Why cry for it? Why would they beat you over such an old, worn out clay pot?"

"No, it's just that this is the pot my mister and mistress always go pee in, and now you've broken it," she answered.

mayrachipun amigunkunata. Chaysis paysis tumayullantaqsis ultimuta. Pay qipakusqa. Chaysis tumayuspaqa nin, "¡Yaw!, ¿Imanaqtintaq yaw warmacha, khaynatari kay iskarallapiri qatuchkanki aqhatari? Manamá chhaynallachu valin riki."

"¡Ay papáy!, willayrukusayki. Ch´isi mamáy, mamaypa aqhasqanman, huk´ucha pasayrusqa. Chaysi chayqa 'Hinallapiña vindiranpuy' nispa niwan", nispa.

"¡Ah, carajo! Entonces huk´ucha chullusqantachá nuqa, nuqaman tumarachiwanki. Supaychus kanmanpas cuentuqa." Chayqa hayt´arapusqa rakichantaqa. P´akirapun.

Chaysis: "¡ay, papáy¡ ¿Imapaqmi khaynata rakichayta, kay rakichayta p´akirapuwanki? Kunanqa taytamamay maqaywanqachá riki. ¿Imanayukusaqtaq?"

"¿Imatataq chay raqramasiyki rakimantari waqanki? ¿Imamanta chaymantari maqasunkimanñataq; ña lluy usasqaña kachkanqá?"

"Manan, es que chayqa taytamamaypa hisp´akunanmi karan chay rakichaqa", nispa. "Chaysis kunan chay p´akirapunki", nispa.

What the Gringo Ate

Miguel Waman, like Maria Laura Ugarte, had a flair for comedy, sometimes subtle, other times broad. I discuss the circumstances of this story's narration in the introductory essay. I will say that for all his devilish pranks and guarded knowingness, Miguel sometimes displayed a naive sweetness—the other side of his piquant personality. Then again, I couldn't necessarily guess, on any given occasion, whether Miguel was really being naive or simply having me on. Once, when I was going off on a plane trip back to the U.S., he met me unexpectedly at the airport with a fiambre—the pouch of beef jerky, toasted corn, salty cheese, and tamales that campesinos take with them on long walking trips through the mountains. He told me he was afraid I would go hungry on the plane, and that I couldn't journey all the way to such a distant land on an empty stomach. When I replied that I would be served a full breakfast on the plane, he seemed unimpressed by this information. He stubbornly insisted that I take the fiambre with me anyway. If anything, "What the Gringo Ate" indicates that Miguel doesn't have a lot of confidence in gringos' powers of reasoning when it came to matters of the stomach.

What the Gringo Ate

Told by Miguel Waman

This gringo was coming along on horseback. A woman was selling breaded frog legs, served up nice and hot. The gringo ate two or three platefuls, all he could eat. "Man, is this delicious!" He got a bellyful! After he'd eaten, he went off on his horse. While he was going along the path, he saw a whole mess of toads heaped up on each other along the riverbanks. The gringo gathered up enough of them to fill his knapsack. Then he arrived at his lodging.

He lit up his camp-stove, breaded the toads with flour. He fried them up and ate them. But after eating them, in the middle of the night, he fell seriously ill. The gringo was in bad shape. When he was at the point of death, he called out to the landlady of the lodging. "Help me ma'am, I'm a goner!"

The landlady said to herself, "Ah, let him leave if he wants to! As long as he covers his lodging bill. He's crazy if he thinks I'm getting out of this bed. I could care less whether he leaves or not."

The gringo called out again. "Help me ma'am, I'm a goner!"

"Who the devil cares? What am I supposed to do about it? I don't care whether he pays me or not."

He called out to her a final time. "Help me ma'am, I'm a goner!"

"Well, then get going, will you?" In the morning, the landlady got out of bed. When she looked outside, the gringo's horse was still there. It turns out that the gringo was dead. The landlady got to keep all his money. She even kept his horse, and there wasn't anybody to claim it for the gringo.

Gringuq Mikhusqan

Gringuqa hamukunsi caballupi. Hinaspas riki huk señoraqa qatukuchkasqa ranamanta apanaduchata, sumaq ruwasqachata. Gringuqa mikhurunsi iskay kimsa platuta gustuta. "¡*Qué rico! mamita.*" ¡*Qué rico* mikhurqun! Mikhuruspaqa, ripun caballunpi. Ripuchkaqtinqa, mayupi hamp´atu tawqa-tawqa muntun-muntun kachkasqa, sapusapukuna askha. Alfurjasninmankama hap´in. Chayqa chayasqan wasipi, alujamientunpi riki nañaqa, griguqa riki. Primuschanta hap´ichispa, riki k´uyuruspa, hak´upi qhuspachispa, tiqtiyachispa, mikhuykun asaduta. Chayqa mikhuykuqtinqa riki, tutaqa grave kan. Mana allin gringuqa. Wañuy pachaypi, dueñunta waqakun, wasiyuqta kikin alujamientuyuqta. "*Mamita ya me voy*", nispa.

"Ah ripullachunñayá. ¿Imatataq kay pagachkantaq chayri sayarimuyman? Hina kachun; ripuchun."

Yapapas waqakun, "*Mamita ya me voy*", nispa.

"¡Caramba ! hinachá kanqa riki. Amapas pagawachunchu."

Ultimutaqa riki waqakullantaq; chaywan kimsa. "*Mamita ya me voy.*"

"Ripullayñayá." Tutamantan sayarimun alujamientuyuq. Sayariqtinqa, caballunqa chayllapi kachkasqa. Gringutaq wañusqa rikhuripun. Llapan qullqiwan quidakapusqa alujamientuyuq. Caballuntapas hap´ikapusqaraqtaq; niraqtaq gringumanta pipas reclamaq kanchu.

The Stupid Gringo

This one is nothing but a little joke. Quechuas enjoy the idea of turning the ta-
bles on those who have historically held the upper hand. One of the more com-
plex examples of this dynamic is Arguedas's famous rendition of the folk tale
"The Pongo's Dream."

The Stupid Gringo

Told by Miguel Waman

Once a gringo and his wife were coming along together on horseback. Nobody knows from what distant place he was coming, the gringo, this stupid gringo. But as he came along on horseback, instead of saying "Mount my wife onto the horse," he just said, "Mount my wife." That's what the stupid gringo said.

His servant answered, "But sir, you don't mean I should mount the lady?"

"Mount, her, damn it!" He showed the servant his revolver. When the servant saw the revolver, he didn't want to die, so he mounted the gringa, right in front of her husband.

The gringo said, "Now I'm going to kill this guy. I'll go to jail. I'm going to kick him. It's going to get ugly. But that's the way it is." Because the servant had been with the gringa. But what else could he do?

Who was at fault? The gringo was at fault. Instead of saying "Mount my wife onto the horse," he just said, "Mount my wife." He really didn't understand.

Asnu Gringu

Huk gringuñataq hamukusqa warmi-qhari caballupi riki. May karumantachá hamukun riki gringuqa, "Siqachiy señorata caballuman" ninantaqa, "Siqay señorata", ninsi. Chayqa gringuqa asnu gringuqa ninsi. "¿Papáy imaynata señoratari siqasaqri, patronaytari?" ninsi. "¡Siqay carajo!" Revolvirta qhawayachin. Revolvirta qhawaykachaqtinqa; mana wañuruymanchu, runa siqapusqa gringata, *delante de su esposo.* Chayqa, "Kunan kay runata wañuchisaq. Preso kasaq. Hayt´asaq. Aswan peor kanqa." Hinachá riki kanqa nispas nin. Chayqa runa kapunyá gringuwan, ¿imananqataq?

¿Pitaq huchan? Gringup huchan. *En vez que* "Caballuman siqachiy señorata", ninantaqa, "Señorata siqay", nispa. Manayá intindinchu.

The Rascal Priest

As I mentioned before, Miguel Waman does not hold priests in especially high esteem. Even more telling, however, is his expression, in this lampoon, of a cultural strain that has been called cholismo — *that is, the half-failed, and sometimes unwittingly self-parodic attempt of native Quechua speakers to assimilate to the dress, speech, and customs of Peruvian Hispanic society. The no-account layabout in the story uses his false status to take advantage of the trusting religious devotion of his hometown kith and kin, including the very father who has sacrificed so that his son can get ahead. The vagabond rustlers, on the other hand, know a bad habit when they see one. The rascal priest betrays himself, not so much by his partying ways as by his mis-speaking at a critical moment: "He couldn't even speak Spanish well." It was fascinating to watch Miguel, given his own liberal, heterodox, freewheeling mixture of Quechua and Spanish, enact the 'erroneous speech' of the priest. And he did so without the slightest self-consciousness, because it is not 'poor grammar' per se that indicts the seminary student, but rather the ruse of assimilation without the substance. In my native Kentucky, we'd call this "getting above your raising."*

The Rascal Priest

Told by Miguel Waman

A peasant farmer wanted his son to be a priest. He did what he had to. "A priest, like God, is to be feared. That's how I want my son to be," he said. "Not like me. I want my son to be good." He gave him a good education. He put him in the seminary to be educated and become a priest. Well, as soon as they enter into the seminary, they wear habits, like priests. They put on those habits, garments, like uniforms, from then on. Anyway, after a short time, the son left school. The father kept sending him money, food, all kinds of stuff, clothing, everything. He just keeps on sending it, and meanwhile, the son has turned into a rascal. He'd learned how to sing, to play an instrument. Did nothing but party. He's not a priest anymore. He left, and turned into a rascal.

One day, he sent word to his father: "Papa, I'm coming back to visit our village."

"Yes, my son is coming here. He'll say Mass."

He thought his son knew how to say Mass. No way. He went out to knock a few back and play guitar, that's all. A rascal. Yes, indeed!

God damnit! His father got together all his godparents to give him a welcome. At that time the train stopped here. Everyone waited for him in the station, with flowers. And they strewed the petals all over, as if he were the Lord himself. The priest got off the train wearing his habit, of course.

"Oh, what a pretty little priest!" And they kissed the hands of this

Cura Bandido

Huk campesino trabajador munasqa wawanpa cura kananta. Modos pusiblista ruwasqa. "Curaqa kay Taytacha hinataq manchana. Chhayna waway kachun", nispa. "Mana nuqa hinachu", nispa. "Allin waway kachun." Educan allinta. Seminariuman churan educakunanpaq, cura kananpaq. Chayqa curachaqa reciente yaykuspaqa; kanyá nanku vistidunku. Cura hina sotananku, vestiduchanku, unifurmiyuq hinayá kapunku pasaqpaqña. Chayqa unayllanman lluqsirapusqa. ¡Papanqa apachimuchkallan qullqita, mikhunata, imaymanata! p´achata, lliwta. Chayqa apachimuqtinqa riki, naqa curachaqa ña kachkan naña kay bandido. Yachan tucayta, takiyta. *A la jarana nomás. Ya no es cura.* Lluqsipun; *un bandido se ha vuelto.*

Chayqa: "Papá hamusaqmi llaqtanchikta", nispa nisqa.

"¡Ay wawaymi chayaramunqa! ¡Misa kanqaña!" *creía que ya sabía cantar misa. Nunca pues. Salía a echar copa y tocar guitarra nomás, un bandido.* ¡Ah caráy!

¡Carajo! Consiguió pues padrinos, madrinas para recibir. Chaypachaqa karan maquinayá, tren. Trenpi suyanku, estacionpi, t´ikantin. T´ikawan hach´inku sumaqta taytachata hina. Sotanantin curayá urayamun. "¡Ay añañaw, taytacha!" Makinkunata m´uchanku chicupta, chay bandidoqa, borrachupta. Chayqa much´aqtinku wasiman pasanku. "Papáy misayukunqachá", nispa.

"Mana, mana, mana. Paqarinña. Tukusaqraq educakuyta misakunaypaq. Mana mana." Bueno hinalla kanku.

kid, this drunkard. And after kissing him, they took him home. "Father, say Mass," they pleaded.

"No, no, no. Not until tomorrow. I have to prepare myself a little more to say Mass. No, no." Well, that's how he left them.

There were some mule-drivers. The mule-drivers stole a sheep from his father. They rustled his very best sheep. When they were making off with it, the priest asked them, "Why is you a-robbin' that sheepie? Papa gonna be ticked." He couldn't even speak Spanish well. So the mule-drivers got after him with their whips. They whipped that little farmer-boy, that priest, good.

The boy's father asked them, "Sir, how can you whip a priest? This fellow is a priest."

And the mule-drivers answered, "No. You'll be a priest before he will. Man, this son of yours doesn't know anything. He's an ass."

"Is that true?"

"Yes, it's true." He didn't know anything. The father had gotten him educated for nothing. He'd gone away from his homeplace for nothing. The man spent a lot of money. What for? All that expense, and for what? He turned into a rascal. He was nothing. He hadn't even learned to pray.

He said to himself, "I went to become a priest for no good reason." He was just a rascal. Knew how to sing; knew how to play. That's it; chase women, that's all.

His father sold his sheep. Sent him money. And him, getting drunk with it, having a good time. His father sent him a lot of money. "My son's going to be a priest," he said. But he wasn't a priest. Used to be, to become a priest, ooh, man! You studied hard. You could say a good Mass. Now a priest is like anybody else. Who gives a priest a thought?

Chayqa huk arrierukuna kasqa. Arrierukuna riki uvijanta suwaru-kusqaku. Allinnin uvijata cargaman churarukunku.

Hinaspa churaruqtinkuqa, "¿Imapaq suwakundo ovija? Taytay phiñakundo." *No sabía ni castellano pues hablar bien.* Chayqa arrieru-kunaqa waqtayapusqaku curachataqa. *Le habían dado latigazos pues, al cholito, al cura.*

"¿Papáy imaynataq taytachatari waqtankiri? Papayqa curañan", nisqa.

"Mana, qamchá curaqa kawaq. Mana, papáy kay wawayki imatapas yachanchu, asnun", nispa nipusqaku.

"¿Chiqaqchu papáy?"

"Chiqaqmi." Chayqa *no sabía nada, pues. Para nada se ha educado, para nada ha ido a su tierra. El hombre ha gastado mucha plata. ¿Para qué?* Khay-naniraqta gastunta apakun. Bandidoman tukupun. Ni imapas ka-punchu; ni rezaytawanpas yachasqachu. (Entiendichkankichu).

"Yanqalla", nisqa, "Kunan kani", nisqa. Bandidollataq kasqa. Takiyta yachasqa; tucayta yachasqa. Chayllata, inamurakuyta, nada más.

Taytantaq uvijakunata vindiyuspa, qullqitataq apachimuchkan. Pay-taq chaywan machayuspa guzayukuchkantaq. *Su papá pues mandaba bastabte plata.* "Waway cura kanqa", nispa. Manayá curachu kasqa.

Ñawpaqqa cura kanankupaq, ¡Upp! ¡Caramba! waputa estudiaqku. Sumaqta misata cantanku. Kunanqa curaqa como cualquiera. Cu-rapiqa piensankupaschu.

The Idiot

Pretty much all social groups offer some variation on the fool who is the butt of these jokes, whether he hails from a neighboring state or country, a different ethnic group, or whether he is simply an instance of moronic behavior by a "defective" example of one's own in-group. When I went to school as an undergraduate in Indiana, I heard lots of "Kentucky jokes," such as the one about the Kentuckian riding in the back of a pickup truck. When the truck crashes into the river, he drowns because he can't get the tailgate down. When I studied at the Catholic University on Peru's Pacific coast, my fellow students delighted in telling about the boneheaded exploits of a mischievous and dense little schoolboy whose name, as my bad fortune would have it, was Johnny. The brief vignettes about the idiot are usually told not singly, but as interlocking strands of jokes—as if to say, He did it again! The idiot has a stupefying thick-headedness that protects him better than the most hardened exoskeleton could. "Crazy February" is a reference to the peak of the rainy, growing season. There is an abundance of crops about to be harvested, and everyone is in the fat time of the year. Carnival is celebrated throughout the highland areas of Peru and Bolivia known as the altiplano, *and to a lesser extent at lower elevations. The idiot, of course, does not possess the power of metaphorical speech, much less abstract reasoning, so he is able to understand Crazy February only in his own literal-minded way. I really like the sweetness of the reversal at the end of the second version, when the mother, in the face of her renewed good fortune, decides that she really does have a good son after all. Like him, she is an expedient creature, who has a hard time remembering, much less drawing lessons from, what has befallen her. They say the acorn never falls far from the tree.*

The Idiot

Told by Juana Rosa Callo Paliza

Once there was a woman, and she had a son. The son was becoming a man, growing up, growing up. He was an idiot. Her husband had died. So she had to act as both his mother and his father. She travelled, had to get food for the both of them. Well, one time she said to him, "Oh! We've got to get together food for January, February, because in January, February, there won't be anything to eat." I'll bring us food for then. Shall we go? Let's you and me set off together. We'll bring food for January, February, because in January, February, we won't have even fava beans or potatoes either. The rainy growing season won't be over yet." And she added, "Pull the door to behind you. Make sure you pull it to." So, the idiot tore the door off its hinges. He pulled it right off. His mother called back to him, "Hey, come on. Hurry up."

"I can't yet, mommy. I'm not done pulling the door."

"Be done with it," she said. "What's that little knucklehead doing? What is that idiot doing?" He'd pulled the door off. And he was walking with the door in front of him. And the path was all twisty and turny.

As he rounded one of the bends, he said "Mommy, I can't walk on this path. I'm going to fall."

"What is that knucklehead doing?" his mother said, and turned around to see. He was carrying the door on his back. "Listen, you stupid knucklehead. What are you doing? Look at you, you pulled the door off its hinges. All I told you was pull the door to. Hurry back to the

Sunsu

❧ LOCO FEBRERO

Huk warmis kasqa. Chaysi wawan kasqa qhari, wawachan. Hinaspansi wiñan, wiñan. Sunsu kasqa. Qusan wañupusqa. Chayqa payllas ma- manmanta, taytanmanata riki. Viajan. Mikhuytas cunsiguimun intiru- manta. Hinaspansi, hukpiqa nisqa, "¡Ay enero, febreropaqyá huñu- kamuna, porque enero, febreropiqa manan kanmanchu mikhuna. Chaypaqmi apamusaq. (¡Yaw! ¡wasita qhawachkanki! nispansi nin, ma- naraq chaytachu nin ninsi). ¿Hakuchu? Qampuwan puririsunchik. En- ero, febrerupaq apamusun mikhuyta, porque enero, febreropiqa manan ni habaspas ni papapas kanqaraqchu. Chayraq puqunqa faltanqaraq", nispansi nin. Chaysi riki bueno, "Punkuta aysaymuy", nispansi, "Aysay- kamuy", nispansi nin. Sunsuqa punkutas wakhapun, a ver. Aysapuchkan. Chaysi nin naqa, mamanqa nin, "¿Yaw ñachu? ¡Apuramuyari!"

"Manan mamáy atiniraqchu. ¡Khunachallanmi punkuta aysara- musaq!"

"Utqayta", nispansi. "¿Ya chay maqt´aqa, imatachá ruwan?" ninsi. ¿Chayqa sunsuqa, imatas ruwan? Punkuta wakharamusqa. Punku qi- pantinsi puriyuchkan. Chayqa ñansiyá q´iwi-q´iwi.

Chaysi huknin q´iwipi, "Mamáy, maman atikunchu ñanchata puri- muyta. Urmayusaqmi."

"¿Imata ruwan kay maqt´aqa?" nispansi mamanqa kutimun. Chayqa punku q´ipintin. "¡Yaw, asnu maqt´a! ¿Imata ruwamuranki? Qhawariy, punkutaraq wakharamusqanki. 'Aysayamuy' nirallaykitaq", ninsi.

house, run, put the door back on its hinges," she yelled at him. So the idiot trotted back to the house, crying.

There he was, saying to himself, "Oh, how am I going to put it back, after I went and pulled it off?" The woman followed him back. She started complaining. She turned to her neighbors and said, "Can you believe what my child did? When I tell him 'Pull the door to,' he yanks it off the hinges." So, they helped her out. "I'm not taking him along with me anymore. He'll just have to stay in the house. And you, watch your step. Make sure you don't cause me any more problems. Now I'm going to go for January, February."

The idiot stayed there on the doorstep. Along came some men, some peddlers walking along. He called out to them, "Hey, hey, hey, mister! Are you January, February?"

Well, they were thieves. And they realized what was up. "Yes, yes, that's me."

"My mommy has saved all this for January, February, she said. So take this along with you." He gave them everything he had: money, food, corn, potatoes. They bundled it all up." The idiot said, "Oh, my mommy is going to be so happy! I gave it all to January, February." Then along came the mother with a bundle, a heavy bundle. And oh yeah, the boy's name was Manuel.

"Manuelito!" she called.

"Mommy, mommy. I have to tell you. January, February came."

"Janauary, February? What have you done now?"

"I gave them every last thing. I even gave them our money. Everything."

"Oh, no, not again!" The woman began to cry. "Get away from me, you knucklehead. What have you done? Now you figure out what you're going to eat. Go away—just somewhere!" She threw him out. "No, no, it can't be. Look for my stuff. Find it. Who could you have given it to? I'm going to kill you. Get out, before I squash you like a bug."

Off went the idiot. The idiot went away. As he was on the path, night fell. He said, "What will I do now? Oh, no. Where will I sleep?" The idiot tried to think. Then he had a thought. "I'll climb to the top of that tree. And I'll sleep up there." So he climbed up the tree. He slept into the night.

Soon, a bunch of men came along. They were a band of thieves. One of them, their leader said "Listen up! Each of you tell me what you've done."

"I stole this. I brought this," each one said.

Another spoke up. "Yeah, well I stole a pair of oxen."

"Phaway wasita; riy; colocamuway, churamuy kaqta"; phiñarikusqa. Chaysi sunsuqa waqaspa hampun wasinta.

Chayqa sunsuqa chaypis kachkan, "¡Ay, imaynatan winasaq, wakhay-wakharunitáq!", nispansi. Kutinpun warmiqa. Chayqa warmiqa rini-gansiyá, "¡ih, chayqa valikunsi chaypi tiyaqkunata! "Khaynata waway, a ver. 'Aysamuy punkuta' niqtiy, wakharanpusqa." Chayqa yanapankusyá. "Kaytaqa manañachá pusasaqchu imapaqpis. Hinallañayá wasipi quidaspa kachun. Qhawachkanki, yaw. Paqtataq imatapas ruwawanki-man. Nuqallañayá risaq enero, febreropaq", nispansi.

Chaysi sunsuqa punkupis tiyachkan. Hinaspansi, chaypi runakunaqa, chay hina niguciu ruwaq runakunaqa purichkan. Chaysiyá, "¡Yaw, yaw, yaw! Papáy, ¿Enero, febrerochu kanki?" nispansi nin.

Chayqa suwakunasyá kasqa. Cuentatasyá quyurukusqaku. "Arí, arí, nuqan kani. Mamaymi waqaychachkaran, 'Enero, Febrero' nispa. Kayqa apakapuyá", nispansi quyapun lliwta: qullqichata, mikhuykunatasyá, sarata, papata. Lliwtas q´ipiyachin. Chaysi, "¡Ay mamayqa kusisqachá kanqa! En-ero, Febreroman quyapuni", nispansi. Chaysi mamanqa hamuyuchkan q´ipintin, ati q´ipintin. Chaysiyá ah, Manuilchas sutin kasqa. "¡Manuilcha!"

"¡Mamáy mamáy! Willasayki, Enero, Febrero hamusqa."

Chaysi nin: "¿Enero Febrero? ¿Imatan ruwaranki?"

"Lliwtan quyapuniña. Chay qullqichatapas qupuni, lliwta."

"¡Ay, yaw!" waqayunsi warmi. "Lluqsiy maqt´a. ¿Imatan munanki? Ku-nan imaykitan mikhunki. Maytapas ripuyá", nispansi qarqun. Chaysi, "Ay, amalla, tarimuwaychu, maskhamuway! ¿Pimanmi quranki chayta? Wañuchisayki", nisni. Lluqsiy, manaraq sipichkaqtiy."

Sunsuqa ripun riki. Ripuchkansi sunsuqa. Chaysi tutayachiku huk ñanpi. Chaysi, "¿Kunaqa ima nasataq? ¡Ay!, ¿Maypi puñusaqri?" nispansi sunsuqa pinsayukun. Yuyayukunsi, aswan, "Kay mallki patallamanña wicharusaq. Chayllapiña puñusaq." Chaypis tiyan riki, mallkipi. Chaysi tutata puñuchkan.

Hinaqtinsi hamusqaku, askha runakuna. Suwakunasyá kasqa. Chaysi nin, "¡Yaw! Kansiyá chaypi huknin kamachikuq. Chasysi "Yaw qam, ¿Imatan ruwamuranki?"

"Nuqaqa kayta suwamuni. Kayta apamuni", nispansi nin.

Chaymanta hukpas, "Arí, nuqapas wakata masantinta suwakamuni."

"Nuqaqa corralnintinmanta qatiramuni uvijata, lliwta", nispansi. Cuentata quyukuchkan riki.

Chaymansi, "Nuqataqmi hamuchkarani suwaq. Hinaspanmi chaypi huk sunsuwan tupani. Chaysi, '¿Enero Febrerochu kanki?' nispa niwan. Chay, 'Arí', niqtiyqa riki qullqita lliwta", nispansi nin.

"And I ran a bunch of sheep out of their corral." They were all rendering accounts.

Then another said, "Me, I was coming around to rob. And I met up with an idiot. He asked, 'Are you January, February?' When I answered yes, he gave me all his money."

Meanwhile, the idiot was up in the tree listening. His bowels were full. He said, "What am I going to do? I'm going to mess myself." And he let go, all over the thieves.

The thieves began to shout, "What's this?" They ran off in a panic.

The idiot shinnied down the tree, and looked all around him. There were all the things he'd given to January, February: money, food. He returned to his house. "Mommy, mommy. I found January, February. They were up there."

"Ah, you knucklehead. So you're lying to me again?"

"Come see, come see," he said, leading his mother along.

His mother was saying to herself, "What's he done this time?" But there were all the things of January, February, cattle, everything, you know. The mother said, "My son is a good boy. I'm so glad he gave everything to January, February. Because I ended up with more."

Chaysi sunsuqa uyarinsi. Chaysi wiksan punkisqa riki sunsuq. Chaysi, "¡Ay!, hukta. "¿Imanasqanmi?" ¡Wahh! Entonces hip´ayamun riki. "Akayukusaqmi" nispansi hisp´ayun.

Chayqa suwakunaqa riki ayqirinkusyá riki. "¿Imataq kay?" nispa riki. Chaykamaqa punchawramunsisyá. Rasphi-rasphitas, urayaramun. Qhawan. Chaypisyá kachkasqa Enero Febrero qusqankunaqa: qullqipis, mikhuypis. Chaysi wasiman kutimun. "Mamáy, mamáy. Enero Febreruta tariramuni. Haqaypin kachkan."

"¡Uh, maqt´a ¿Llullakunkiraqtaq qam i?"

"Hakulla, hakulla", nispansi pusamun riki mamanta.

Chaysi mamanqa riki, "¿Imatachá payqa ruwan riki?" Chayqa enero febreroqqa, chaypisyá kachkan kusa, askha, wakakuna, imaymana riki. Chayqa, "Allinchá karan wawachayqa. Allinchá Enero Febreroman quran. Kunan astawan tarikapuni", nispan. Chayllan.

The Idiot

Told by Miguel Waman

§ CRAZY FEBRUARY

A woman's son had turned into an idiot, a moron. Once she was keeping a pig, fattening it up. "I'm fattening this up for February, so I can eat it in March," she said. But the idiot didn't understand, he was ignorant, a moron. "Oh, my mommy is raising it up for February, this pig is for Crazy February, sir," he said, calling out to a mule-driver, calling the mule driver. "Hey Mister, are you Crazy February?"

"Yes, that's me."

"My mommy is fattening up a pig. Wouldn't you like to take it away?"

Well! The mule-driver threw the pig up on his horse, and carried it off.

Then the mother came home. "Hey, where is the pig?"

"Uh, you said it was for February. Anyway, that February guy came by here. Yeah, and carried it off on his horse."

"Oh, no! Listen, you idiot—you're such an idiot."

§ MONEY

"Okay, if you're going to beat me, I'll just run away," the idiot said, and ran off. He carried on his back a bundle of money. So, as he was going along, carrying the money on his back, he came across some farmers sowing a field with oxen and a yoke, in an isolated spot. And he had a lot of money in his bundle. He had some big coins, and those little old-fashioned ones they don't use any more.

Sunsu

§ LOCO FEBRERO

Huk señorap wasinsi sunsuyusqa, sunsucha. Hinaspas khuchita, hatun
khuchita uywakuchkan, hatunllataña. "Kaytaqa febrero killa marzupi
mikhunaypaq", nispa.

Chayqa sunsuchataq mana yachanchu, ignuranti, sunsucha, "Ay mamantaqa febreropaqmi, loco febreropaqmi uywakuchkan khuchitaqa
señor", nispa waqhan arrierutaqa, arrierutaqa waqhan. "¡Ay!" nispa,
"¿Señorniychu kanki febrero loco?"

"Arí, nuqa kani."

Khuchita uywachkan mamitay. Apakapullawaqñá." ¡Bueno! Khuchita
caballupi cargayuspa, apakapun chay arriero.

Hinaspa mamanqa chayamun. "Yaw, ¿maytaq khuchiri?" ninsi.

"Febrero killapaq nichkarankitaq. Chaymi chay febrero hamuchkasqa. Chaymi caballupi apakapun", nispa nin.

"¡Ay! yaw sunsu kay sunsu, haqay sunsu."

§ QULLQI

"Bueno, maqawanki chayqa chinkakapusaq", nispas chinkakapun
sunsunqa; imantin qullqita q´ipiyukuspa. Hinaspas riki qullqita
q´ipiyukuspaqa, ripuspanqa, wakawan tarpuchkasqaku, yuntawan
may karupichá riki. Paytaq askka qullqi q´ipintin richkan. Chay
hatuchachaq nueve dicimuskunata uchuychakunata. "Papáy. ¿Tarpu-
kusunchu? Wakirukusun", nispas nin. ¿Qullqiwan wakikun, husk´ay-

"Mister," he said to a farmer. "Can I help you sow your field? We'll work together and split it later." They started to work, placing a coin in each hole they dug. They carried the money along in a blanket, right behind the cow, and sowed it in the ground, down to the last coin.

The idiot went back home. "Mommy."

"Listen, you idiot, where's our money?"

"Mommy, oh mom, that money is going to grow a lot. I sowed it with a farmer, and we're going to split the harvest," he said. She beat him and threw him out on his ear. That idiot couldn't do a single thing right.

§ BABY

They were taking care of a baby. And the mother said "Grab hold of that baby." While they were watching it, the baby started to cry.

"Oh, the little baby, the little baby's crying. Oh, he's got pus in his head," said the idiot. The crown of a baby's head has a soft spot, a fontanelle. Well, the idiot pressed down very hard on the fontanelle, and burst it. "Oh, the little baby had pus inside his head. That's why he's crying. And mommy, after I cleaned out the pus, the baby fell asleep." And when his mother went to look, the baby's brain had burst.

tas qallarin i? Qullqita ukhuyukuspa hinatas; wakap qipanta husk´an qullqiwan, hasta llipin tukurkunankama.

Ripunsi llaqtanta. "Mamitay."

"¿Maymi qullqi, yaw sunsu?"

"Mamitay, wachanqa askhata mamá. Wakiramuni qullqitaqa, tarpuramuni", nispa. Qarqumun; maqayun.

Chayqa ni imanakuyta sunsuta atinchu.

§ WAWA

Wawachatañataq uywachinku. "Hap´iy kay wawachata", nispa. Chayqa wawachaqa waqnansi, uywaqtinkuqa.

"¡Ay wawachata, ay, wawacha waqachkan! ¡Ay! kaychapimá q´iya kasqa", nispa (*quiere decir pus*). Pukyunchanchikqa suavichallaraq wawachaqqa. Hinachalla lluyta sunsu fuertita q´apirqarin ñutqunñintaraq, phatarachipun. "¡Ah, wawachaqqa q´iyamá kasqa umanpi! Chaymá waqasqa. Chayta q´iyata p´uqaruqtiy, puñuchkan mamá wawaqa." Qhawaykuqtinkuqa wawaqa q´ala ñutqunñinta phatarachipusqa sunsu.

The Fox and the Mouse

Stories about the stupid fox who is tricked, time and again, by the more astute mouse, are widely (and broadly!) told in the southern Andes. They represent adaptations, with minor variations, of stories that have long circulated in Europe, Africa, and the United States. Anyone who has ever heard tell of Bre'r Fox and Bre'r Rabbit will instantly recognize the archetypes offered here. It was a singular sensation, both familiar and strange — almost cognitive dissonance — to sit and hear a story told in Quechua, and to suddenly realize that it was "The Tar Baby," something I had heard and read in my own language various times before. The fox-and-mouse cycle probably comes the closest of any stories in the Andean oral tradition to sheer entertainment. There is much more physics than metaphysics in them. I like to think of these episodes as Quechua cartoons, as their style of narration is so reminiscent of Road Runner and Wile E. Coyote, repeating the same essential joke ad hilariam. The fox never learns anything from his previous mistakes, and is always freshly eager to be duped again. I was amused that after the fox is "killed" in one episode, its daughter conveniently appears in the next, to exact revenge on the mouse. The teller simply needs a pretext for continuity, so that, as in cartoons featuring fantastical violence, the next episode can begin without interruption. Sometimes the fox is plain old reincarnated, without any explanation. No matter how spectacular the death of the fox, there is never a corpse to be found. This outcome stands in stark contrast to the fate of condemned souls, who carry, if anything, a surfeit of flesh.

The Fox

Told by Juana Rosa Callo Paliza

§ GRINDSTONE

A fox was walking along, and came upon a grindstone. He said, "Oh sure, all you do is lie around here all day, not doing a thing. Me, I have to walk. I'm eating juicy meat, a bunch of it, as I'm going along. But you don't even move from that spot," the fox said to that grindstone.

The stone was a grindstone, and said "Huh! What do you care if I'm just sitting here? Who's talking to you anyway? Go on, keep on walking," the grindstone said.

The fox answered, "And what are you going to do about it?"

"Watch it! Don't mess with me."

"Who are you to lay about here night and day? Heat, wind and cold weather are coming down on you. Hey, when it gets cold, I go find shelter. When it rains, I go find shelter. The sun blazes, I go find shelter. But you just stay in this spot."

"Watch it! Don't keep pestering me. Watch it! I might have to kill you."

An eagle happened to be flying around there. An eagle was flying. He said, "What's gotten into you two?"

The fox said "Ah, he's just lying there."

"Watch it! Watch it!"

"What are you gonna do about it?"

"Brother, brother," said the eagle. "Show him what kind of man you are. I mean, what can he do?"

Atuq

❧ MARAN

Atuqsi purichkaran. Hinaspansi, chaypi maranqa kasqa. Hinaspas nin,
"¡Ah!, qamqa tiyalayachkallanki chaypi, mana imata ruwaspa. Nuqaqa
purichkani. Intiruta, wira-wirata, aychatapas mikhukuni purisqaypi.
Chaypi maqʼalayachkanki", nispansi nin atuqqa chay rumita.

Rumiqa, maransiyá kasqa, chaysi nin: "¡Ah hah! ¿Nuqaqa iman
qamman qukusunki tiyalayakusaqpis? ¿pin qamta rimapayasunki?
Purikuy-purikunaykita", nispansi nin maranqa.

Chayqa atuqqa, "¿Imanawankimansi qam?"

"¡Paqtataq! Aman nuqawanqa churanakunkichu."

"¿Iman qam laqʼalachkanki chaypi, tuta-punchaw? Ruphayraq
wayraraq chiriraq atichkasunki. Nuqaqa chiriqtinpas, machʼayukuni.
Paraqtinpas, machʼayukuni. Phuyuqtinpas, machʼayukunimá. Qamqa
chayllapi kachkanki.

"¡Paqtataq! Aman turiyamuwankichu. ¡Paqtataq! Sipiruykiman."

Chaysi chaytataqsiyá muyuchkan ankaqa. Ankas muyuchkan. Chaysi,
:¿Iman qamkunawan kachkan?" nispansi nin.

Chaysi atuqqa nin: "Kay laqʼalayachkan."

"¡Paqtataq! ¡Paqtataq!" nimunsi.

"¿Imanawanmansi nuqata?"

"Wawqicháy, wawqicháy." An ya, chayyá. "Riqsiyachiyá qhari kasqay-
kita a ver. ¿Imanasunkis kay?"

Chaysi maranqa nin: "A ver. Aman nuqawan churanakamuwankichu.

Then the grindstone said "Listen, you better not get into it with me. Watch it! Watch it!"

The eagle said "Hey, don't you two come to blows. Okay, what kind of contest could you have?"

"A race. I want to run," said the fox.

The grindstone replied, "Oh yeah, you run. Think you got the legs for it? What are you? Watch it! Watch your step! You may end up crying uncle."

The eagle said, "Okay, I have a rope. I'll tie it to your waist, and then tie it to the grindstone." They were on the crest of a hill.

The fox said "Sure, I can win against this thing. I'll run and drag you along behind," he said to the stone.

The stone replied "Don't get into it with me. Watch it! You'll end up crying blood."

So the eagle tied the fox and the stone together. They were up on the peak of a big hill. "You two will run all the way down there. Down there is the lake, and you'll run there, because this is going to make you thirsty. Let's see who wins this battle. Run all the way down there to get a drink of water."

They were tied together. And the stone was round, like a wheel. The stone took off and picked up speed. The fox cried "Enough! Oh brother, stop! Stop, please! I give up, you win! My tongue is hanging out! Give it a rest, give it a rest!"

The stone answered, "Didn't I tell you?" It was round. That's why it went so fast. And it dragged the fox along until it just about killed it.

§ RAIN OF FIRE

The fox was walking along, walking. All at once, he met up with the mouse. The mouse was digging into the earth, making a hole. So the fox said "What are you doing?"

Well, the mouse was making a hole so that it could give birth. The mouse was pregnant. But the mouse realized that the fox was stupid. She said "Oh my brother, my brother. The rain of fire is coming."

"The rain of fire?"

"Yes. That's why I'm digging a hole, to hide myself. This afternoon the rain of fire will come."

So the fox said, "Oh, no. I'd better cover myself up too." And he started to dig. Soon he said, "I can't do it."

¡Paqtataq! ¡Paqtataq!" Chaysi nin ankaqa: "Ya amaña maqanakusaychis-chu. A ver, ¿Imatan, imapin churanakuwaqchis?"

"Phawallasaqku. Phawasaq", nispansi atuqqa nin.

Chaysi niqtinsi, maranqa, "¿Ya, imas qamri phawawaq? ¿Chakiyuqchu kanki? ¿Iman kanki? ¡Paqtataq! ¡Chaymá! ¡Paqtataq! 'Papacháy' nimuwankimanraq."

Chaysi ankaqa nin: "Bueno waskhachaymi kachkan. Waskhachaywan qamman, (cinturay, wiksay) cinturachaykimanta watarusayki. Maran-tapas watarullasuntaqyá." Kay urquq puntanpisyá chayqa kachkan.

Chaymantas riki bueno, "A ver nuqayá riki ganarusaq kaytaqa. Pha-wayuspa aysakachayusaqraq", nispansi nin atuqqa rumitaqa.

Chaysi rumiqa nipun: "Aman nuqawanqa churakamunkichu. ¡Paq-tataq! waqawaq yawartaraq, a ver."

Chaysi ankaqa riki watan atuqtawan, rumitawan. Chayqa, uma muqukuspiyá kachkan, urquq uma muqunpi. "Chaymantas phawayun-kichks, haqayman. Haqay lamarqucha kachkan, chayman chay ch´aki, ch´akiymantayá phawayunkichik. Chayqa, mayq´inniykichikchá cha-yallan, chayman phawayunkichik unu tumakuq", nispansi nin.

Bueno, watarunsi. Chayqa maransiyá kasqa rueda hina, muyu. Chayqa phawayamunsiyá phawaylla, maranqa riki. Nataqsi, atuqtaqsi, "Ñas ¡Ay, wawqicháy amaña! ¡Amaña kunanqa! ¡Yastañan, ganaruwachkankiña! ¡qalluypas lluqsiruwanqaña! ¡Sayallayña! ¡Sayallayña!"

Chaysi riki, "¡Ah, chay niraykitaq!" Muyutaq karan rumi. Chayqa phawayamuchkanyá riki. Chayqa atuqtaqa asayanpusqa, wañusqallataña riki. Chaypi tukukapusqa.

♪ NINA PARA

(Chaymantaqa nas kasqa *este que se llama*). Purichkansi atuqqa, puri-kuchkansi. Chaypis tupan nawan, huk´uchawan. (Chaysi huk´ucha nin) Huk´uchaqa hasp´ichkasqas, allpata t´uquchkasqa. Chaysi nin: "¿Imatan qam ruwachkanki?"

Uh, huk´uchaqa t´uquchkasqayá wachananpaq. Chichukusyá kasqa huk´ucha. Chaysi huk´uchaqa yuyarun riki atuq sunsu kasqantaqa. Yachankuñasyá. Chaysi nin, "¡Ay wawqicháy, wawqicháy! ¡Nina paras chayanqa!"

"¡¿Nina para?!"

"Arí. Chaymi nuqapas t´uquchkani, pakayukunaypaq. Tardimansi nina para chayamunqa."

"Look, just cover up your head. Then the rain of fire will only burn you on the tail." The mouse showed him how.

The fox said "I still can't."

"Well, hide yourself there whatever way you can. I've already dug my hole." The mouse scuttled off, and came back with a branch of thorns. He went around and stuck them into the fox's behind.

The fox cried "Ow! Ow! Ow! There really is a rain of fire. I feel it pricking me." Meanwhile, the mouse ran off.

Before long, an eagle came flying around. He said to the fox "Hey, what are you doing?"

"Ohh, it's the rain of fire!" The fox was stupid, and the mouse had said, "Just cover up your head. That way the rain of fire will only sting your tail." But she had really pricked him with a branch of thorns.

So the eagle said "Hey, what are you doing?"

"My brother, isn't it raining fire on you?"

"No. There's not any rain of fire."

"What? The mouse said to me, 'The rain of fire is coming. So make a hole. Then it will just scorch your tail, if you can't make a deep hole.'"

"Oh, man." The eagle said, "Let's pull these out," and helped remove the rain of fire.

§ LAKE

"This time I'm going to find that mouse. This time, oh this time, he'll get it." Soon, he met up with the mouse. "Hey, listen here, this time you're gonna get it. Now I'm going to kill you good. 'Look, it's the rain of fire,' you said. And you stuck thorns in my bottom, right?"

"My brother, my brother! This lake is going to overflow. It will kill us all. That's why I'm drinking water out of it. I'm slurping it. Look, right out there, a gull is drinking. And they always know. This will overflow," the mouse said. "It will overflow, and we're all gonna die."

"Oh! For real?"

"Yes, of course for real. So you need to drink as much as you can."

"Well, okay." And the fox was stupid, you know, and started drinking, gulping down water. "My brother! My brother! My stomach is swelling up."

"That happens. Mine is swelling up too." The fox just kept on drinking. Pow! His stomach exploded.

Chaysi bueno, "¡Ay, nuqapas tapayukusaq!", nispansi riki hasp´i-
yuchkan napas. "Mana atinichu."

"Umallaykitapas tapayukunkichá riki. Nina para sikillaykitaña hap´i-
sunki riki." Chaysi huk´uchaqa ruwan.

Bueno, "Manan atiniñachu."

"Imaynatapas chaypiyá pakayukun. Nuqapas ñan t´uquruniña."
Chaysi phawarin. Phawarispansi, kiskawan riki, hawanmanta huk´u-
chaqa winayamun.

Chaysi, "¡Ay! ¡ay! Chiqaymi kasqa nina para. T´urpuyuwachkan".
Chayqa riki huk´uchaqa chaykamaqa pasakapunsiyá.

Chaysi , chaypis ankaqa muyumuchkan riki. Chaysi, "¡Yaw! ¿Imatan
ruwachkanki?"

"¡Ay, nina paran! Atuq sunsuqa umanta, huk´uchasyá nisqa, "Umal-
laykita pakayukuy. Sikiykitaqa hap´ichunpis nina paraqa." Chayqa,
kiskayá kachkan riki; t´urpuyuchkan.

Chaysi, "¡Ay!, ¿imatan ruwachkanki?"

"¿Manachu wawqicháy, nina para hap´isunki?"

"Manan. Ima parapas kanchú."

"¿Ima? Huk´uchatáq niwan, 'Nina paran chayanqa. Chaymi
t´uqukuy. Sikillaykitaña hap´ichiy, mana t´uquyta atispaqa' riki."

Hina, chayqa, "Kiskawan, ch´ankiwantaq kachkankí."

"¡Ayyy!" Chayqa riki chaypisyá urqupun nina parata.

⚡ LAMAR QUCHA

"Kunanyá maskhamusaq huk´uchataqa. Kunan-kunanyá yachanqa", nispas. Chaysi, huk´uchawan riki tuparun. "¡Ay, yaw, kunanmi yachanki!
Kunanqa sipillasaykiñan. 'Qhawariy. Nina para', nispa ¿Ch´ankiwan
winawasqanki i?"

"¡Wawqicháy!, ¡Wawqicháy kay lamarquchas phawayamunqa! Sipi-
wasun llapanchikta. Chaymi nuqapas tumachkani unuchata. Ch´un-
qachkani. Qhawariyyá, chinpapipas hakay gaviuta tumayuchkan. Ya-
chanchus. Kaysi phatanqa", nispa. "Phawayunqa; lliwta wañuchiwasun."

"¡Ah!, ¿Chiqaqchu?"

"Arí, chiqaqmi kachkan. Chaysi, atinaykikama tumanki."

Chaysi nin: "¡Ay, bueno!" chayqa atuqqa sunsuqa riki, tumayuch-
kansiyá riki nata, unutas upyayuchkan. "¡Wawqicháy! ¡Wawqicháy! Wik-
saymi punkiyuchkanmi."

"Hinallan, nuqaqpas punkiyuchkanña." Chaykamas riki sunsuqa tumayuchkan. ¡Pum! phatapusqa. Chaypi tukukapun.

You want to hear another? Another fox was walking along there. He met up with the mouse. "Listen, you went and said the lake was going to swallow us up, huh? Now you're going to get it," he said. "You killed my mother." He'd killed its mother, the fox's mother. Her stomach exploded. "Now you're gonna get it. I'm her offspring; you're going to get it."

"My brother! My brother! Don't think that way. It really will happen. Right now, look up. There's an eagle flying around up there."

The eagle confirmed what the mouse was saying. The fox said "Okay, okay, then I want to go up into the sky, if it's really going to rain fire." The eagle, too, had conned him into believing it. "So, let's see, how will we do this? Tie me onto you," the fox said.

"You and the mouse tie yourselves to me with this rope. And then we can climb way up to the sun. They say you can live inside the sun." So they went toward the sun. They tied themselves with the rope. So then they're climbing higher, rising, climbing.

Then the fox said to the eagle, "Oh yeah, you might say 'I fly high, right?' Well now, I'm also going high."

The eagle replied to the fox, "Don't get into it with me."

"Yeah, and what are you going to do about it, bone beak? What are you going to do to me? Look, you think you're the only one who flies high. Well, I can fly high too."

"Watch it! Watch it!" said the eagle. But the fox kept pestering and pestering. They were still climbing; the mouse climbed, and the fox climbed. And then the fox said, "Now I'm going to look down from a place higher than you. The mouse and I are about to reach the sun."

The eagle said "Now you're gonna get it. Not even your bones will be left. They'll crumble to dust when you fall to earth."

"Oh yeah? And what are you going to do about it?" The eagle cut the rope. Then, "My brother! Now I'm done, I'm done! Spread out a blanket. Spread out a blanket," the fox cried. The fox sped from heaven to earth. He turned to nothing. He plummeted to his death. That's the end, that's all. Pow! He blew to pieces, and no more fox. That's all.

¿Chayqa chay huktañataqchu? Atuqqa purichkansi riki chaypi. Chaysi, huk´uchawan tuparun riki. "Yaw, qamraq niwaranki lamarquchan millp´uwasun ih? Kunanyá yachanki" nispansi. "Mamayta wañurachinki." Mamantasyá, chay atuqpa mamantasyá wañuchipusqa. Wiksan phatapusqa riki. "Kunanmi yachanki. Nuqaqa wawan kani; yachankin." "¡Wawqicháy! ¡Wawqicháy! Amaraq chaypi pinsayraqchu. Chiqaypunis kanqa. ¿Chaymi kunan qharariy i? Haqay ankapas purikuchkan chayninta", ninsi.

Chaysi niqtinqa, chayrí "¡Arí, arí! Nuqapis hanaqpachamanmi ripusaq. Kanqapunis nina paraqa", nispansi. Llullayrakamunsi ankapis riki. Chaysi niqtinsi, bueno. "¿Iman kanqa? Waskhawanyá."

"Watarukuy huk´uchatawan, qampuwan kay waskhachawanyá. Chaysi altutas riki naman, intillamanña ayqisunchik. Intipiqa kawsaysi kanqa", nispa. Chaysi intimansi riki. Waskhataqa riki nanku, watamunku riki. Chaytas wichayuchkanku aknata riki, laqhayuchkankus, wichayuchkankus.

Chaysi, "¡Ah! Qamqa niranki 'Nuqallan altunta purini', ¿ih? Kunanqa nuqapas purisaqmi" nispansi atuqqa nin ankata.

Chaysi, "Aman nuqawan churakamunkichu" ninsi atuqta ankaqa. "¿Imanawankimantaq qamri, yaw tullusimi? ¿Imatan ruwawankiman kunan nuqaqa? Qhawariy, qamllachus altuta puriwaq. Nuqapas purichkaniñan."

"Paqtataq, paqtataq", nispansi ankaqa nin. Chaysi sinchitaña rinigachkan riki, rinigachichkan atuqqa. Wichayuchkankusyá; huk´uchapis wichayuchkantaq; atuqpas ichayuchkaran. Chaysi, chayman nin atuqqa, "May kunanqa, kunanyá altuykimataraq qhawayamusayki. Ñan chayachkaykuña intiman."

Niqtinsi, "Kunanmi yachanki. Manan kanqachu tulluykipas. Ch´usaqmanraqmi tukunqa, pampaman urayamuqtiyki", nispansi nin.

"¡Ah! ¿Imatan qam ruwawanki?" nispas. Waskhatas k´uturamun, ¡i! ankaqa riki. Chay, "¡Ay, wawqicháy! Kunanqa, kunanqa. Chumpi qusitata mast´ay, chumpi qusitata mast´ay", nispansi. Atuqqa phawayamuchkan altumanta pampaman. Manas pipis kasunchu. Ch´iqiqpaq, wañuqpaq chayamusqa. Chaypi tukukapun, chayllan. ¡Pum! phatasparaq riki. Mana kapusqachu riki. Chaylla.

The Mouse

Told by Juana Rosa Callo Paliza

§ THE TAR BABY

In a town, there was an orchard. An old man and old woman lived there. And they weren't able to work. They had no children. "What are we going to do?" they said. We'll grow nice little flowers. Then we'll sell them, to make a living. Because who is going to give us money? We don't have any strength left." So, they put flowers and some other plants into a pretty orchard. And sold them. That's how they made their living. But one day, what happened?

"Oh, no! What happened here? Just look at this, look, something came here to eat. A mouse gnawed all these, all the pretty, pretty flowers." The old man said, "I'm sure the mouse will be back today. Hmm, I wonder how he got in here." So they looked all over. Then they found the hole. The man said "Okay, this time I'm going to punish that mouse good." They made a doll out of tar, and put it next to the hole.

That night, the mouse came. "Good evening, friend," chattered the mouse to the tar baby. "Move aside; you're sitting in my path." They had made the tar baby in the form of a person. But it didn't answer.

"Friend, good evening. I'm greeting you. Move aside; you're sitting in my path. What do you want?" said the mouse to the tar baby. But the tar baby didn't answer.

"What's wrong with this guy? If I have to say it again, I'm going to kick you. Then you, sir, will be saying goodbye. I'm greeting you. I've said it several times now. But this guy isn't listening. In a minute, I'm going to knock this gentleman flat on his back," said the mouse. So,

Huk´ Ucha

§ BREA WAWA

Huk llaqtapis kasqa huerta. Hinaspansi machu payachakuna tiyasqaku. Hinaspansi, manaña llank´ayta atisqachu. Manas wawankupas
kasqachu. Chayqa, "¿Ima nasaqtaqri? T´ikallatañachá riki cuidasun.
Chayllataña riki vindispa, kawsananchispaq. ¿Pitaq quwasun qullqita?
Kallpanchispas kanñachu." Chaysi sumaqta huertapiqa riki t´ikata churan, imaymanata. Chaytas vindikunku. Hinaspas chayllawan kawsanku.
Hinaspa hukpiqa, ¿Imas pasan?

"¡Ay!, ¿Imaynan kanqa kay? (*este, que se llama*) Qhawariy khaynata,
a ver mikhuramusqa, na. Huk´ucha raqraramusqa khaynata, sumaq-
sumaqllanta "t´ikata", nispansi nin: Chaysi, (Kunanmi kanqa) "Kunanmi kanqa huk´uchaqa", machu payacha nin. "¿Maynintachá yaykumun ih?" Chaysi, maskhanku riki lliwta. Chayqa tarinku, (*este que se
llama*) t´uquta. Chaysi nin: "Ay, kunanqa huk´uchataqa allintan casti-
garusaq", nispa. Chaysi muñicuta ruwanku breamanta. Chaywansi
t´uquman riki churanku.

Chaysi riki huk´uchaqa tutataqa riki hamun. (Buenos) "Buenas
noches papáy. Hatariy; purinaypi sayachkanki", nispas huk´uchachaqa
rimapayan breata. Breamantasyá muñicuta ruwanku, runata hina.
Chayqa manas contistakunchu.

"Papáy, buena noche. Napaykuchkayki. Hatariy, purikunaypi
kachkanki. ¿Imatan munanki?" nispansi huk´uchaqa nin breata. Chaysi
manasyá contistanchu breaqa riki.

"¿Imatataq kaytari? huktayá hayt´asaq. Hinaspa chaykamayá kanqa

he kicked him. And his paw got stuck in the tar. It got hung up in the tar.

"Listen here! Let go of me friend, at once. If you don't, I'll have to hit you again. I'll blow you apart. I'll pop you right in the eye. I'll knock your head askew." He punched the tar baby with his paw, and that got stuck too.

"I still have one hand left." He punched it with another paw, and that one got stuck too. "Turn me loose, friend, turn me loose. I've got one paw left." He kicked. And that paw got hung up, just like the other ones.

"I've still got my tail to whip you with. I'll rip your stomach open with my tail-whip. Watch it! Turn me loose, turn me loose." Then what happened? He gave it a good whip with his tail, smack! It swirled around a few times, and got stuck.

"All right, now you'll see! I've still got my head. I'll knock you down; my head will knock yours off." This time, he gave him a hard knock with his head. He gave a blow like this with his head, and it stuck in the tar.

And that's how he did himself in. In the morning, the old man and old woman came. "Hmm. Who's been here? This is who it was." They took hold of the hollering mouse and burned him in the fire.

kay wiraquchaqa", ninsi riki huk´ucha. Hayt´ansi. Chakan hap´iraka-
pun. riki breapiqa. Breapiqa k´achkan.

"¡Yaw! Kachariwayá papáy, apurayta. Manas, kachkanraqmi huknin
makiy. T´uqhachisaqyá; ñawinpi allinta churarusaq." Hukmanraq
umanta aparusaq. Saqmansi makinwan. K´askarapullantaqsi.

"Kachkanraqmi huknin makiy. Huknin makinwansi saqman. Mapas.
"Kachariwayá papáy, kachariway. Kachkanraqmi huk chakayqa. . .
Hayt´ansi. Chaypis k´askarapunmi riki, makinpis."

Chayqa, "Kachkanraqmi surriaguyqa. Surriaguyyá phatarachisunki-
raq wiksaykita", nin. "Paqtataq. Kachariway, kachariway", ninsi. ¿Chayqa
imas pasan? Huktan chupanwansisyá dalin riki, ¡hurrs! Chayqa asta-
wansi muyurirun riki. K´askarapun.

"¡Ay, kunanqa ahora!, kachkanraqmi umay. Tumbayusayki; chaypiqa phatarachisayki umaykita." Chaysi hukta riki, umanta saqman riki.
Aknata umanwan q´asun; breataq kachkan. Chayqa k´askarapun.

Chayqa chaypis wañupusqa. Chayqa tutamantaqa machu paya-
chakunaqa, "¡Ay!, ¿pin karan kayqa? kaymá kasqa", nispansi riki.
Hap´iruspanku qaparkachayachinku riki huk´uchataqa. Ninapis raw-
rayachinku. Chaypis tukukapun.

The Fox and the Mouse

Told by Isidoro Wamani

§ TAR BABY

A mouse was walking along. And the fox was feeling hungry. Because he felt hungry, he tried to corner the mouse. The mouse said, "Please don't eat me. We'll be good friends, you and I. You'll eat whatever you want. But don't kill me. I'll tell you where to wait for me. We'll be friends. Tonight, I want you to wait for me on top of that wall. I'll come in the night, and we'll sneak into the orchard." An orchard-keeper had a beautiful orchard there. So, they went in. They went inside there. The mouse started eating everything in sight. The fox too; flowers, whatever—they destroyed it all. And in the morning the two of them went back out to the countryside to wander.

That morning, the orchard-keeper came in. Everything was destroyed. They'd eaten flowers, everything. It was all chomped up. He cried in despair, "Who has done this? Ohhh! I can't believe it." The next day, he said "I'll lie in wait to see." So the next day he waited around. The animals didn't come. They must have guessed, because foxes have premonitions. So, they didn't come. Only the following day did they come. They went into the orchard. Once they were inside the orchard, they ate just about everything in it. They tore it up, turned it upside down. After he ate, the fox felt satisfied. When they had committed this terrible abuse, the man went around to his neighbors. "You can't believe how they tore up the flowers and everything else. There are dog tracks, tracks where a dog entered. It can't be any other animal. It really took advantage of me."

Atuqwan Huk´ Uchawan

❦ BREA WAWA

Huk huk´uchallaqa purikuchkasqas. Hinaspas atuqqa yarqaymanta-chá kachkaran. Hinaspa riki yarqaymanta kaqtin, huk´uchachata qatikachasqa. Chayqa: "Ama mikhuwaychu. Aswan amiguntin ka-sunchik, nuqawan. Askhata imaymanata mikhunki. Ama nuqata wañuchiwaychu", nispa. Chayqa, "¿Maypitaq suyawankiri? Amiguntin amiguntin kasunchik". Chayqa "kunanmi haqay punku qipallapi suyawanki, tutata. Chayqa tutata hamusaq, huertata yaykusunchik", nispa. Huk hortelanutaqsi sumaq huertayuq kasqa. Chayqa yaykunku. Hinaspas yaykunku chaypi. Huk´uchachaqa imakunatachá mikhu-pakamun. Atuqtaq lluyta riki, t´ikakunata ima, lluyta distrusapun. Chayqa tutamantantaqa lluqsinpunku camputachá iskayninku, may-tachus ripunku.

Hortelanutaqsi tutamanta riki yaykun. Hinaspa lluy distrusasqa. T´i-kakuna, imaymanakuna mikhurusqa. Lluy chaqusqa kachkan riki. Chayqa riki, "¿Imataq kayta ruwarunman? ¡Ayy!, ¿Imataq?" nispa riki, lluy disispirasqa kapun. Chayqa paqarisnintin: "A ver, suyapapusaqmi", nispa nin riki. Chayqa paqarisnintintataq suyapakun. Manas hamunkuchu. Adivinarunkus paykunaqa riki: atuqta watuqtaq. Chayqa riki mana hamunkuchu. Chayqa paqarisnintin hamullankutaq. Chayqa huertata yaykunku. Hinaspas yaykuspa. Hinaspa yaykuspa llapamta hortelanuqtaqa, lluyta imaymananta nayullankutaq, mikhullankutaq. Chaquyun, quspayun ima. Atuqqa contento riki mikhuymun. Chayqa chayñataqsi nisyuta abusuta ruwaqtin, nataqsi tapukachakun runaku-

As he told about this, one of his neighbors said "Are you a fool? Put a tar baby in the doorway. Right there. You'll catch your thief today. Man, you'll see what I mean."

So the man had a tar baby made, and placed it by the door. Then the fox and mouse came. The mouse said to the fox, "I'll go first and you follow." He went in through a little hole.

When the fox went to enter, there was a tar baby waiting. The fox said, "Sir, I need to pass by you." But the tar baby didn't speak a word. "Sir, I need to pass by you." He still didn't speak a word. "Sir, I need to pass by you! If I have to say it again, I'm going to punch you." The tar baby still didn't speak a word. So, the fox punched him. "Hey, what's going on here?" His hand had gotten stuck on the tar baby. "Hey, I've still got lots of wallop on on my left side. I'm going to knock you over." One of his paws had already gotten stuck. He hit him with the other one. That one got stuck too. "Okay! Now I'll kick you—kick you right over." Well, he kicked all right. That got stuck too. Only one paw was left. "The one on this leg ought to do it." He kicked. But now, all of them had gotten stuck. "Ha! Now I'll knock my head on yours and split you open!" And saying that, he got his head stuck. Now he was stuck fast. The tar baby wasn't letting go.

When morning came, there he was, yelling over and over "Turn me loose! Turn me loose! I won't eat any more flowers or anything else!" Early that morning, the orchard-keeper came. When he came, there was the fox, there stuck fast. And as he was stuck fast, the man killed the fox right there in the orchard.

Later, his friend said "Didn't I tell you right? Did you catch your thief well or not?" That's what the other gentleman said.

♪ MILK PUDDING

The mouse went to find himself another fox. He said to the fox, "Hey, you want to eat?"

"Yes, I want to eat," the fox answered.

"Then come on. There, in that house, there's milk pudding. I've tasted it," he said, and took the fox there. "There, an old woman and an old man make milk pudding." Well, this old couple ate part of the pudding, and covered it up. When it was covered, the mouse said "We'll eat this." When the old couple was fast asleep, they went in and ate. While they were eating, the fox stuck his head inside the pot. Once he'd put it inside the pot, he couldn't pull it out. So the mouse said, "Listen, come

nata. Hinaspa nin: "Khaynata lluyta t´ikakunata lluyta imachá nanpas. Hinaspa allqu yupillan, allqu yupillan chayta yaykusqa. Manan ima yupipas kanchu, Chhaynaniraqta maltratawan", nispa.

Niqtin, huk naqa, huk mistiqa nin: "¿Sunsuchu kanki? Huk brea wawata punkuman churaruy. Hinaspa riki chayman riki. Kunan chay suwaykita hap´inki riki. Runa rikullawankiyá", nin riki.

Hinaspa huk brea wawata ruwachimuspa, k´askachin. Chayman hamunkusyá. Chayqa, "Qipaytaña hamunki", nispa nin. Chayqa huk´u-chaqa pasayrun riki. Huk´uchachaqa pasayrun may k´uchuchantachá riki pasayrun.

Atuqqa yaykunanpaqqa, chaypi huk brea wawa sayachkasqa. Hinaspa nin: "Señor pasarukusayki", nispa niqtin atuq nin. Mana rimarinchu. "Señor pasarukusayki. "Mana rimarillantaqchu. Chayqa saqmansiyá. "¿Ya imanantaqri?" Makinsi k´askayparin chay brea wawaman riki. "Hay, kay lluq´i ladupimá kallpaqa kachkan", nispayá nin. Chayqa, "Saqmaspa apayrusayki", nisqa riki. Huk ladu makinqa K´askasqañas kachkan. Huk ninpuwan saqman. K´askarapullantaq. Chayqa riki "¡Ah!, hayt´aspa kunanqa hayt´aspa apayrusayki." Manan, hayt´allantaq riki. Chayqa k´askarapullantaq. Chayqa huk ladu chakillanña faltachkan. "Kay ladu chakiywanqa atirusaykipunis." Hayt´allantaq. Chayqa mana, q´ala k´askarapun. "¡Ay, kunanqa umaywan umaykita partirusayki!", nispa umanwantaq k´askallantaq. Chayqa k´askarapusqa; mana kacharipunchu brea wawa, riki.

Chayqa chaypi illaripun. Chayqa qapariyukuchkan: "¡Kachariway, kachariway! Manañan kunanqa t´ikaykitapas, imaykitapas mikhusaqñachu. ¡Kachariway!" nispayá niyuchkan. Chayqa tutamantaqa hamusqas riki. Tutamantan hamuqtinqa riki, chaypi riki, chaypi q´asuspa wañuchipusqa riki chay atuqtaqa riki chay naqa, chay este chay hortelanuqa.

Chayqa. "¿Anchaychu mana niraykitaq? Anchaychu mana chay suwaykita hap´inkitaq?" riki chay wiraquchaqa nin.

§ LICHI API

Chaysi huk´uchachaqa huk atuqtañataq tariramullantaq. Chayqa chay-tapas nin: "¡Yaw! ¿Mikhuyta munachkankichu?"

"Arí, mikhuyta munachkanku", nispa.

"Hamuy, yaw. Qhaqaypi lichi api kachkan, qhaqay wasipi. Nuqapas mikhuramuniñan", nispa riki pusayun riki. "Chaypi huk payachawan, huk machuchawan, chaypi riki lichi apita ruwakunku riki", nispas riki.

here, c'mere, c'mere. Here's a great big rock." He had the fox feel the old man's head with his hand. "Knock it against this," he said. The fox struck the pot against the old man's head, and the pot shattered.

As it shattered, the old man yelled "What's this? Has your lover come around, or what? Maybe that's why he's beating on me." Meanwhile, the animals ran off. As they ran off, the old couple was coming to blows. But there was nobody there. The animals stirred up a fight and ran away.

§ WALL

When they got in the clear, the mouse said "Hey, this wall is about to fall down. Let's go hold it up. I'll hold up my end." Then he left the fox alone holding up the wall, and ran off. Long after he fled, the fox kept holding it up with his paws. But the wall crumbled, and crushed the fox.

Chayqa wakinta mikhuspalla tapayunku. Tapayuqtinkuñataq riki, "Kayta mikhuruy", nispa riki. Ch´inchalla puñuchkanankamaqa huk-taña yaykuruspanku mikhunku, riki. Chayqa mikhuqtinku, umanta riki atuqqa riki mankamanqa churarapusqa. Chayqa k´askarapusqa mankantin, manka. Mana lluqsipuyta atinchu uman riki. Chayqa riki: "Yaw yaw hamuy hamuy hamuy. Kaypi hatun rumi kachkasqa", nispa riki, machup umanta riki llamiyachisqa riki. "Kayman q´asuy", nispa. Machuchaptaqa umanta q´asun riki. Hinaspa manka partirakapun riki.

Partirakapuqtinqa, chay machuchaqa nin: "¿Iman chay? ¿Inkay-kichu, iman chay? Hamun chaymi khaynata q´asuwan, haqayna khayna." Hinaspa paykunaqa pasakapunkusyá. Chhaynaqa pasakan-puqtinkuqa, ña machuchawanqa payachawan maqanayukunkusyá. Manasyá pipas kanchu. Chayqa maqanayachinku; hanpunkus.

§ PIRQAN

Chayman hamunankupaqqa ña huk huk´uchaqa "Yaw, kay pirqan ku-nan thuniyamunqa. Haku kayta tusapaysiway. Nuqapas hina tu-sapachkaniñan", nispa nin riki. Hinasllapi atuqtaqa saqiyun tusapach-kaqta riki. Payqa pasapun. Chayqa pasakapuqtin unayña riki makin chakin naruqtin ayqikapun. Chayqa thuniyamuspa atuqta ñit´ipullan-taq. Chaypi tukupun.

The Fox and the Mouse

Told by Aparicion Monje

§ ORCHARD-KEEPER

I'm going to tell you about an orchard-keeper who had three sons. An orchard-keeper had made an orchard. And he had three sons. He sent the first son to find out what animal was going into his orchard. But the son found nothing. That same night, he sent the middle son to see. But he didn't find anything either. Then he sent the youngest son. That one caught a mouse and hung it up on a string. The next morning the father came to find out what had happened. "Did you catch something?" asked the father.

"Yeah, I caught it. It was a mouse."

When he heard that, the father said "Great, now let's hurry over and punish it good. Yeah, now that it's hung up, let's get right over there and fix it."

As the mouse dangled there, the fox happened along. "My brother, why are you hanging there that way?"

"It's nothing, my brother. I'm supposed to get married to the orchard-keeper's daughter. But I don't want to get married to his daughter."

"You're going to marry his daughter? My brother, what if I was to marry her?"

"My brother, do you want to trade places? Should I hang you up?"

"Okay, hang me." When the orchard-keeper got there, the fox was hung. He started beating the fox. The fox cried "Okay, I'll marry your daughter! I'll marry your daughter!" And somehow, he escaped.

Atuqwan Huk´ Uchawan

Kimsa wawayuq hortelanomanta willasaykichik. (Chay) Huk horte-
lanos huertata ruwachikusqa. Chayqa kimsa chicunkuna kasqa. Huk
chicunta primirta kachasqa. Mana wawanqa tarillantaqchu. Kaq tu-
tañataq kaq, chawpi kaq wawantañataq kachallantaq. Chaypis ma-
nallataq tarillantaqchu. Kaq sullk´a kaq wawantaq tarillasqataqchu.
Chayqa hap´iranpusqa huk´uchachataqa. Chayqa huk´uchachata
warkuruspa. Tutamantaqa pasapusqa papanman willaq. Chayqa papanqa nin: "¿Hap´iramunkichu?"

"Arí, hap´iramunin. Nan kasqa huk´uchan kasqa."

Niqtinqa, "A ver, kunanqa supayta, allintapunin kunanqa castiga-
sunchik". "Arí, kunanqa warkusqañataq kachkan, apurayta as suq´amul-
layña", nin.

Chay atuqchaqa hamuchkasqa warkulayachkaqtinqa "¿Imamantan,
wawqicháy kaypi warkulayachkanki?"

"Manan wawqicháy. "Ususinwanmi casarasaq. Manan ususinwanmi,
mana casarasaq munasqaymanta."

"¿Ususinwan casaraytaqchu? ¿Icha wawqicháy nuqaqa casaray-
manmi?"

"¿Wawqicháy, warkurusaykichu?"

"A ver, warkuruway." Rinanpaqqa atuqqa warkulayachkanqa. Chaysi
suq´an riki atuqtaqa. "¡Casarallasaqmi ususiykiwan! ¡Casarallasaqmi
ususiykiwan!" Escapakunsi riki.

After he got away, he said to himself "Now I'm really going to eat that mouse. Where can he be?" He went along, walking, walking. In a field, the mouse was digging a hole. The fox said "What are you doing there, brother?"

The mouse answered, "Nothing, brother. The rain of fire is coming. I'm making a hole to protect myself from it. I'll be safe from it."

"For real?"

"Yes, for real." The fox helped the mouse dig the hole. When he hid his head, he kept trying to tunnel down. And as he was tunneling, the mouse pricked his hand with the "fire" of a thorn-branch.

"Ouch! The rain of fire really has come, that's what I'm feeling." He stayed under there a long time. He started to dig again. It just kept on coming. Finally, the fox took off running. It turned out he was covered with biting thorns. That's what had happened, and off he went.

§ BOULDER

"This time I'm definitely going to eat that mouse. He's made fun of me once too often." The mouse was leaning against the base of a cliff, just there at the base. "What are you doing here, brother?" the fox asked.

"Nothing, brother. That boulder is going to fall and kill both of us. How can we escape from it? I've been here holding it up as hard as I can."

The fox said "Here, brother, let me do it. But I wonder how I'll climb up there?" He climbed further up and started leaning against the boulder. And the mouse ran off. He stayed there a long time. "I wonder if that's true?" Then he ran a good distance away from it. Nothing happened. He went on walking.

§ GRAIN PUDDING

He ran into the mouse again along the path. "What are you doing here, brother?"

"Nothing, brother. Today I brought you some grain pudding."

"Where, let's see, where? Let me taste it. So where is it? I really want some."

"They're making it over there. Should we go see? Let's go. Do you want me to show you?"

❧ NINA PARA

Escapakuqtinqa riki, "Kunanqa chay huk´uchachataqa, kunanqa mikhuramullasaqña. Maypipas." Chayqa nispa nillantaq. Chay richkansi, purin, purin. Pampata t´uquyuchkasqa riki huk´uchachaqa. "¿Imantan ruwachkanki? kaypi wawqicha?"

Niqtinqa, "Manan, nina paran chayanqa wawqicha. Chaymi nachkani, pampata t´uquchkani wawqicháy. Nuqaqa may t´uquchantapas escapaymanchá. Escaparullasaqmi."

Chayqa nispa nin, "¿Chiqaychu?"

"Chiqayyá." Chayqa paypuwan yanapan t´uqutaqa. Chayqa pakarunsi atuqtaqa riki, pakaykarin. Chayqa pakaruqtinqa, hallpiparakamullantaq. Chayayuchkasqallataq. Chaymansi loco p´itamun riki. P´ata kiskawan tapayusqallas kasqa payqa. Chayqa hinas pasapun; siqayapun riki.

❧ QAQA

"Kunanyá kunan mikhuramullasaqña chay huk´uchachataqa. Nisyutan abusaywachkan", nispa nillantaq. Hinaspa qaqa sikipi tiyalayachkasqa. Qaqa sikipi tiyalayachkaqtinqa. "¿Imata ruwachkanki kaypin, wawqicha?"

"Mana, wawqicha. Kay qaqan pasayamunqa; ñit´iruwasunpaschá iskayninchikta. ¿Imatan escapasunman? Nuqallañan imaynatapas, (manachu) nuqallaña ñak´ayllaña aguantachkani. (Manachu) Siqayyá, siqayyá wawqicha." Niqtinqa nan, "¿Iman wichachkayman?" Siqayun payqa qaqa pataman. Aguantamuchkansi atuqchaqa riki. Pasapun riki huk´uchachaqa.

Unayñas, aguantayuchkan. Aguantayuqtinqa, "Chiqaychus imaynachá?" Pasallataq, p´itallantaq karuman atuqqa. Manas pasanchu. Chayqa tirayapunsi.

❧ MULLI API

Hina purisqanpi tupallankutaq. "¿Imata ruwachkanki wawqicha kaypiri?"

"Mana, wawqicha. Kunanqa kay mulli apichatan apamuchkayki", nispa nillantaq.

"¿May, a ver may? Prubachiway. ¿Maypitaq kachkanri? Astawan munachkani."

"Sure, show me."

"All right, let's go." And they went, and entered. Some people had made grain pudding. The fox and mouse ate as much as they wanted, chowed down. It belonged to an old man and old woman. They just ate and ate. While he was eating, the fox stuck his head in a pot. When his head got stuck in the pot, the mouse said "I can't find a rock, I can't find a rock."

"Can't we break it against something?" asked the fox.

"Here's something. Break it against this." So the fox smashed the pot against the old man's head.

The old man cried "What's going on? Who came? A robber, or who?" He started hitting. When he struck a match, he'd been smacking on his wife. And there was the fox with the collar of the pot around his neck. And off he ran.

ᕱ FIESTA

"He's gotten me three or four times now. This time, there's no way or nowhere for him to escape. This time I'm really, really going to eat him. He'll see this time." As he walked along, he came across the mouse. "Brother, today's the day I'm going to eat you."

"No, how can you say you're getting ready to eat me? Today we're going to a party. I've been hired for it. I'm going to play the drum. And you yourself get to play the whistle."

"For real?"

"Yes, for real." They climbed down the river bank. "Now each of us has to cross over here, brother. One by one, we'll each go over," said the mouse, and he crossed. He called back to the fox "Hurry up and cross, brother!" The fox went in, went along. When he got into the current, the river carried him off. That's the end.

"Haqaypiña ruwachkanku. ¿Hakuchu? Risunchik. ¿Pusasaykichu?"
"¿Pusaruway, a ver?"
"Entonces haku", nispas rinku riki. Risqankupi, hinaqa yaykunku.
Chay mulli api ruwachkanku, mikhuq q´alata; mikhuyparinku riki. Chay
machulachaqa payachayuq kasqa. Mikhurun, mikhurunyá q´alata.
Mikhuruspaqa uman cabirapusqa riki mankapiqa. Chayqa mankapi
tukurakapuqtinqa, chayqa, "Manachu rumillapas kan", nispas nillantaq. "Manachu rumi kan."
"Kaypi kachkasqa. Kaypi p´anaruy." Chayqa machulachap umana-
man p´anarun riki.
Chayqa machulachaqa, "¿Imana kay? ¿Pin hamuwan? ¿Suwachu,
iman?" Chayqa p´anallantaq. Mamakuntataqa maqan fusfuruta qitu-
ruqtinqa. Hinaspa chaypi atuqllataq collarnintin kapuchkasqa. Entonces escapakapun riki.

§ FIESTA
Chayqa, "Ña tawa kimsapiña. Manaña escapawanqañachu, ni may-
tapas. Kunanqa mikhuramullasaqpuniña. Kunanqa yachanqa", nispas
riki hamullantaq riki. Chaysi riki chaypi ay, kaqtin, purichkaqtinqa tu-
parullankutaq. "Wawqicha, may kunanmi mikhupullasaykin."
"Mana, chaywan hamuwachkanki, mikhupuwanaykipaq", nispa.
"Khunanqa risunchik natan, huk na, huk fiestamanmi risunchik.
Chaymi contratarakamunin, nuqataqmi tambormanta (nuqataqmi).
Personaykitaqmi rinki pitumanta", nispas nin riki.
Chayqa, "¿chiqaychu?"
"Arí, chiqaymi." Chayqa siqayunkus riki mayupatanta. "Kayta
pasasunchik kunanqa, wawqicha. Sapallanchik ch´ullallaña", nispa
huk´uchachaqa (pasaratan) pasaratanpun riki. "Wawqicha." Chayqa
nachanta richkansi, richkansi. Ña paypas yaykuyatamun. Chayqa mayu
apapun. Chayllapi tukupun riki.

The Boy Who Didn't Want to Eat

In this didactic lesson, the gothic Brothers Grimm come to mind, with their accounts of the horrible ends suffered by recalcitrant or misbehaving children. It was disconcerting to have this cautionary piece come out of the mouth of the sweet-natured Teodora Paliza. On the other hand, I was more than once impressed by the penetrating human insights in Quechua folk tales I heard, and by their tellers' willingness to casually entertain controversial subjects such as father-daughter incest, adultery, cold-blooded murder, or the suicide of a child. Social taboos against these behaviors do exist, but there seems to follow no impulse to censor what can be represented, sometimes quite graphically, in imagination. In Teodora's stories in particular, care is taken to build to a climax, to pepper the account with believable details, and to create a mood or state of mind. The mother's agitation, then her incredulity, followed by fear, shame, and remorse, are realistic, anchoring touches worthy of a gothic tale. As in "The Pastureland Girl" (also told by Teodora), parent and child share responsibility for the transgression, and must both pay a price, one that may strike us as extreme punishment, out of proportion to the pecadillo of spoiling one's offspring. Yet no apology is made for this severity. The one difference here is that the mother's observance of her prescribed penance does indeed—though barely and perhaps temporarily—ward off the child's ghoulish spirit. The pastureland girl is not so fortunate.

The Boy Who Didn't Want to Eat

Told by Teodora Paliza

Once there was a woman. She had only one male child, one son. She and her husband loved him with all their heart. They got in the habit of serving him first at the table, ever since he was a baby. That's how it went. If they didn't, he wouldn't eat his lunch. Only after she'd served the child would the woman serve her husband. Only afterward him or their girls. In this way, the boy grew to be a teenager.

One time, they gave some kind of party, I don't know what for ex-actly, but they said, "Let's invite our friends. We'll have a banquet for them." They invited the village priest, and other people. They made all kinds of dishes, cooked good food. Then they had their visitors come into the dining room and sit down. Of course they always served their child first; and they had already prepared a plate apart for him. But they hadn't sent it to the table yet. They had seated a couple of their visitors at the head of the table. And the son was seated down toward the middle. So the first plate didn't seem to come to him. In truth, he had been served first. But the child couldn't see that the first plate of the luncheon had in fact been his.

Then they were carrying plates to everyone. And they brought the child's plate to him. He was seated right there in the middle. They held it out to him. But he just sat there looking at it. He didn't want his lunch. The guests started criticizing him. The priest said "Go on and eat. Is there something wrong with it?"

"Eat, eat up, eat your lunch," they were saying. But he kept silent,

Huk Chicu, Mana Mikhusqamanta

Huk señoras kasqa. Hinaspas riki ch´ullalla qhari wawanku kasqa. Khuyay munasqa; khuyaytas munakuqku riki. Paymanraqsi primero platuta sirviyman acostumbrasqa, wawachanmanta pacha. Hinaspaykis hina kachkan. Mana, chayqa manas almusaqchu riki. Wawanman sirviruspañas, qusanmanpas sirviq. Chaymantañas payman, war-mankunamanchá riki. Hina, hinaña juvinchaña kapuchkan riki chicuqa, juvinchañas kachkan.

Huk kutinpiñataqsi fiestankuchus hina kasqa, no sé imatachá chaypi nisqa; (a nanki) u, "Invitasunchik. Banquetita ruwasunchik. Ami-gunchikkunata." Señor curatas invitasqaku, allin nakunata. Hinaspas mesataqa tanta mast´ayukun riki. Sumaqta wayk´uyachin. Chayqa ñas invitadukunaqa yaykumuchkankuña riki. Pasachichkankuña come-durman. Chaypiña nispa wawanpaqqa, siempre primerotapunis, platu-pas separadupi riki churachkanña riki. Pero mana apayachinraqchu. Cabecerapisyá riki huk visitakuna, allin nakuna tiyanku. Paypataqsi chawpiniqpiña riki. Manaraqsi paypaqqa. Ñasyá qarasqaqa. Ñasyá qa-rasqaqa, primeropi kachkan. Pero mana rikunchu riki chicu, primer plato qarasqanta.

Hinaspas riki lluymanña richkanku. Apayachin platuntaqa riki chicumanqa. Chawpipis tiyachkan, chaypi. Haywan. Hinaspas qhawachkallan, qhawachkallan. Mana munanchu almusayta. Hinaspas lluypas quijakunku riki. Sacerdotipas nin, "Mikhuykuyyari. ¿Imataq ma-nari allinchu?"

with his head hanging down, like this. Everyone else finished their lunch. They carried away the plates. And they carried his off too.

Then they brought the main course, well-served. But this time they made sure to bring his first. His mother went back into the kitchen and said "The child won't eat. Oh no, what are we going to do? He thought his banquet dish was brought last. But I made sure to serve his up first this time," speaking to the other children. They took it back out to him. But he kept silent, like this, sulking at the table, just sitting there. He didn't eat his main course, or even touch it.

The mother went back into the kitchen very upset. She was startled. "Why is he acting that way? I served his lunch up first. Only he didn't see that I did. I served him a big portion, just the way he likes it. How embarrassing for us. Our friends will say 'Their child has to be first. That's the kind of invitation we get.'" That's what the woman was saying within herself. That's what she was thinking.

The guests drank, ate, relaxed. As they were relaxing, one of the women guests went into the kitchen. "Listen, where is your son?"

"The child is inside."

""Well, we haven't seen him."

"I wonder where he is? He must be in his room. Run and see," she said to one of the girls. They went into his room. He wasn't there. The room was empty. "I wonder where he went off to?" The children all went around looking for him. They searched and called for him. But they didn't find him. It seems that somehow he'd entered into an old abandoned house. And what did they find in there? He had wrapped a belt his mother had given him as a present around his throat, and used a stone to counterweight it. He'd tied the belt to a stone and he himself had hung it from a tree. When he counterweighted it, he strangled himself, and his tongue was coming out of his mouth.

The children were frightened and ran away from there, shouting "Mama, mama. The boy hanged himself."

The mother answered, "Don't talk that way. Where would he have strangled himself?" She went to see. And in fact, he was dead. They went at once to the authorities, to give a deposition. They held a wake. In the middle of the wake, the boy turned to a condemned soul.

They buried him, and at night he began to cry out "Oh, mama! You are to blame. You taught me to be served first. Maaaama! Let's go away. We have to walk the earth together." The mother had placed all around scapularies and images of saints for the time the child was there. For that night, they had thorn-branches fastened all around the doorway.

"*Come*, mikhuyyari, almusayyari", nispas nichkanku riki. Hinaspas ch´inlla k´umulayachkan, aknallapi, mana. Almusayta tukunkuña lluysi. Platukunata uqaripunku. Paypatapas uqaripun.

Chayqa segundo platutas apayachillankutaq riki, lliwta. Pero paypaqqa primerusyá sirvikuchkantaq riki. Chaypipas yaykurun cocinataqa. "Niñucha mana mikhunchu. ¡Ay!, ¿Imanasuntaqri? Pinsanchá ultimu qarasqaypaq. Paypaqraqtaq primerutaqa qarachkaniqa", nispas mamitanqa riki warmankunawan parlan. Hinaqtinsi nan, apaykun. Chaymantas riki ch´inllalla, aknata, mesan k´umuyuruspallan, pasarapun, chicuqa. Mana mikhunchu ni imachatapas llamiyunpaschu, segundutapas.

Chaysi mamitanqa riki ukupin, "¡K´aq!" nichkan riki. Mancharikuchkan riki. "¿Imaraykutaq chaytari ruwachkanri? Paypaq primerutaqa qaraniqá. Mana rikunchu primirta . . . munaykun hunt´ataq. ¿Kunan p´inqaypichu quidasaqkuri? 'Wawamanraq primiruta. Chaytaq invitawanku', niwanqakuchá", riki nispayá, payqa sunqunpi pinsayuchkan riki. Hinas pinsayuchkan.

Hinaspayá ña tumapunku, mikhupunku, sayaripunku. Sayaripuspaqa cocinata yaykun riki señoraqa. "¿Yaw maymi niñuchayki?" nispas nin.

"Niñucha ukupichá riki kachkan", nispas.

"Manan rikuykuchu", nispas nin.

"¿Mayta pasarunri? Cuartupichá kachkan. Phaway qhawaramunki", nispas nin. Chaysi cuartuntaqa yaykurunku riki. Mana kanchu. Cuartunpipas ch´in. Hinaqtinsi, "¿Maytatatq pasanmanri?" nispas. Lluy warmakunantin puririnku maskhaq riki. Entonces maskhayamunku, waqyakachayuspa. Manas tarinkuchu riki. No sé, imaynapiñachá huk raqayta yaykurusqaku. Ya raqayta yaykuruqtinkus, ¿chaypi pimanqari? Rumiwan contrapesaykuspa, chay chumpi mamitanpa obsequiasqan, chay chumpiwan kunkamanta aknata watarukusqa. Watarukuspa rumiwan naman, chay mallkimanraq; pay kikinchá riki aparan. Chaywan contrapesayukuspa, ¡Phaq! Qalluraqchu hinankarayta saltamusqa.

¡Ay!, mancharikuspas riki warmaqa phawarin riki. "Mamitáy, mamitáy. Niñuchaqa siq´urkusqa." "¡Siq´urkusqan niñuchayqa! Ama rimapayawaychu. ¿Maypis niñuchari siq´urukuman?" Rin. Chiqaqta, ña wañusqaña. Chayqa kasqan ratus riki, autoridadkunamanchá riki phawarinku, parte ququ. Velapuchkanku riki chaypi. Velaqtinkus riki, condenaduña kapun chicuchaqa. Chaysi riki p´ampampunku.

P´ampampuqtinkus riki, tutata ih qaparqachaykun, "¡Ay mamáy!", riki. "Qammi huchayuq kanki. Primer, primer platumanqa yachachi-

The boy said, "You're lucky. The scapularies around your neck and the saints at your side are saving you. But I'll be back for you." Because they always try to come back.

The next day, the woman went to the priest for confession. She spoke clearly to the priest. "Yes, since he was a little baby, I got him in the habit of having the first plate, at lunch. That was my custom."

The priest gave her penance to do. "My child, we should never accustom our children to be the first ones served. They should always eat after. Nor should they swallow their bread down whole. In those ways a child ends up a condemned soul." For three days and three nights, that woman prayed before Mama Carmen and other saints. With scapularies and engraved seals.

The child's condemned soul shouted through the doorway. "Let's go walk together. You and I together will pay the debt." Through that process his soul was saved. Terrible, isn't it?

waspayki. ¡Waw! Hakuyá kunanqa. Kuskayá penamusunchik", nispas nin. Señoras riki ay nakunawan, escapulariwkunawan, santukunaman, niñucha kaspas. . . riki kachkan. ¡Ay!, chay tutaqa ay kiskakunawansi punkunta ch´ankiyamunku hinas. "Agradeciy, chay kunkaykipi, laduykipi kaqkunallan salvachkasunki. Pero pusasaykipunin", nispas nin. Kutiripun riki, lluy.

Paqarisnintinqa, confesakuqsi pasan riki, señor curaqta. Señor curaman willakunsi bien claruta. "Arí, desde huch´uyninmanta pacha, primer platuman yachachirani mikhuyta, almusachiyta. Yachachirani riki."

Chaysi penitenciata qun riki señor curaqa riki. "Mana hayk´aqpas, hija, wawanchiktaqa primer, primer mikhuymanqa yachachinachu. Siempre qipatapuni mikhuchina. Nitaqmi t´antapis enteruta quyman yachachinachu. An, chaykunamanta wawakuna condenakunku." Chayqa riki kimsa tuta, kimsa punchawchus hina, señoraqa riki hinallapi, Mama Carmenmanchus hina, chay santukunap qipanpi. Escapulariwkunawan . . . estampakunantintas . . .

Punkumanta qapariyuchkan riki. "Hakuyá puririsunchik. Qamwan kuskayá pagamusunchik", nispa. Haqayniraqta riki chay mudupis salvakusqa riki. ¿Takaw, i?

The Old Crone

This appears to be a version of "Hansel and Gretel," though the children are not lucky enough to have even the temporary temptation and solace of a gingerbread house. Instead, they get rocks and toads for supper. This story, like the one about the wayward shepherdess told to me by Ines Callali, gets regulated by the rhythm of her repetition. The synoptic retelling at the end by the surviving brother, far from being redundant, encapsulates the breathless rush of his horror. Storytelling, as this character proves, is not an extraneous cultural activity; whatever is perceived to be vital information must be narrated before it becomes truly real. Neither he nor his parents can believe, much less act on, the horrible reality of the sister's disappearance until it is put into words.

The Old Crone

Told by Ines Callali

Two children were sent by their parents to gather wood. So the children went off in search of wood: one boy, one girl. They went and they went. As they were going along to find the wood, they saw a hillside turned all white. The boy said "Look there! Wow! We'll gather a big bundle of wood up there. We'll have lots of wood to take back." They climbed up the hillside. When they arrived at the hilltop, though, there wasn't any wood. They were only horse bones. "This, oh, it's not wood! Oh! Where will we go now? We're going to have to go still further." They went, they went, and they went. They climbed up another hillside. There on the hilltop, they saw wood, all white. But it turned out not to be wood. They were cane reeds. They'd gathered no wood, and it was getting very late. For their journey back, it was late, it was dark and murky night. They said, "Now, where will we stay? Will we be able to get home?"

"We can't make it home. It's better if we just stay here, right here, I think."

"We shouldn't stay here," the little boy said. "We shouldn't stay here. Let's just go, anywhere." As they were travelling back, and travelling back, they spied a light inside a cave. A cave with a light inside. They called out, "Excuse us, ma'am, excuse us. Can we stay here? Can we stay here?"

Then an old woman, an old crone, came out. "Huh? What do you want, children? What do you want?"

"Excuse us, night caught us. Can we stay here?"

Saqra Paya

Huk hirq´ichakunatas taytamaman kachasqa llant´aman. Chaysi hirq´ikunaqa rinku llant´aman: huk qharicha, huk warmicha. Richkankus, richkankus. Chaysi richkaqtinku, richkanqtinku llant´aq (qharikuna), muqupi rikhurin, yuraqllaña. Hirq´icha, "¡Haqayqá! ¡Añañaw! Haqay llant´ata askhata q´ipisunchik. Askhata q´ipisunchik haqay llant´ata", nispas ninku. Chayqa chayamunkus chay muqukama. Muquman chayaruqtinkuqa, mana llant´achu kapusqa. Kasqa caballu tullulla riki. "¡Chay, ay mana llant´achu kasqa! ¡Ay!, ¿maytataq kunanri risun? Aswan risunchik tarukamanraq." Rinku, rinku, rinki. Chayqa muquta siqayunku. Chay muqu qipapi, huk llant´a yuraqllaña rikhurimullantaq. Mana llant´achu kasqa, tuqurulla kasqa. Chayqa mana llant´a kanchu, tardiña, tardiña tardiña. "Kunanrí, ¿ima llant´atan apasunchik?" Chayqa maskhankus llant´ata. Huk muquta rinku llant´a manas kanchu. Chayqa kutinpunankupaq, tardiña (manaña ni), limbu laqha tuta, laqha. Chayqa ninku, "Kunanrí, ¿mayman chayasun? ¿Chayayta atisunmanchu?"

"Mana chayasunmanñachu. Aswanchá qipakupullasunchikña kay, kaypi riki."

"Manan qipasunmanchu", qharichas nin. "Manan qipasunmanchu. Risunpunin, imaynapas." Chaysi kutinpuchkaqtinkus, kutinpuchkaqtinkus, huk mach´aychapi nina k´anchachkasqa, k´anchachkasqas huk mach´aypi. Chaysi nin: "Hampuyki, señora, hampuyki. Qhurpachaway", nispas nin. "Qhurpachaway, señora."

"Come on in. Sit down here," she said. She offered them potatoes to eat. Yes, potatoes to eat. But they weren't potatoes. She called them potatoes and gave them stones. Boiled stones. When they tried to bite into them, they were stones.

The children said to the old lady "These aren't potatoes. They're stones."

The old woman said "No, they're boiled potatoes. Eat them." Then she offered them meat, grilled meat. But it wasn't meat. It was toad flesh. Yes, it was toad.

The children said "Yuck! This is toad! This isn't meat. Old lady, this is really toad!"

"No it's not toad, it's meat," she replied. Then she said "Listen, children, listen." The little girl's brother was very skinny. But his sister was nice and chubby, yes, nice and chubby. They prepared to sleep. And the old crone, the old witch said "You'll sleep in this corner, by yourself. I'll sleep with your little sister." So the crone slept with the little sister. And the little boy slept by himself.

In the morning he woke up. Yes, in the morning he got up. The boy asked "Where did my sister go?"

"Oh, your sister went off to get water." The crone wasn't just a crone. She was a witch. She was a devil-witch. She was a troll-witch. And she'd eaten the little girl. The girl was nice and chubby. And since she was nice and chubby, the witch ate her. While they were in the bed, the witch ate her all up. That morning, she sent the boy off with a gourd, sent him off with a little gourd. "Bring me some water. Your sister also went for water," she said. So the boy went off with a gourd, but it was really made of his sister's head, of her skull. The boy was going along with his sister's skull, and came to the water's edge.

Then a toad began to croak, "Creak, creak, creak." The toad's name was Maria. "Creak, creak, creak, creak, creak, creak. You're carrying water in your sister's skull. You're carrying water in your sister's skull," she croaked. The boy heard that. He heard it just as he was dipping up the water. He was about to take it back to the devil-witch in a skull. Then the frog said "Creak, creak, creak, creak. Don't go back there." That's what Maria said. "The witch already ate your sister. And you're carrying along water in your sister's skull."

The boy looked at the skull. "Oh! Is this really my sister's skull? I won't go back." Oh! He hurled the skull full of water into the river, into the river. And he ran off as fast as he could. "Now she's going to try to eat me too."

Chaysi huk vieja, huk payacha lluqsimun. "¿Imachatan munanki, yaw hirq´ikuna? ¿Imachatan munankichik?"

"Hampuyki, tutayarachikamuykun. Qhurpachawayku."

"Pasaykamuy. Tiyaykuychik kaypi", nispas nin. Chayqa haywansi papachata mikhunanpaq, papachata mikhunankupaq. Manataqsi papachu kasqa. "Papa", nispas, rumita haywan. Rumi t´impus kasqa. Malliyuqtinkuqa, rumis kasqa.

Chaymantaqa ninsi, "Manan papachu kasqa. Rumitaq kasqa", nispas nin abuilachata.

Chayqa payachaqa nin: "Manan, papa wayk´un. ¡Mikhullay!" nispa. Chay payachataq kaq haywamun kay aychata, aycha kankacha. Manas aychachu kasqa. Hamp´atullataqsi kasqa. Hamp´atu kasqa.

Chayqa nin: "¡Ay, hamp´atu kasqa! Manan aychachu kasqa. ¡Hamp´atutaq kasqá, abuilay!" nispas nin.

"Mana hamp´atuchu, aychatáq", nispas nin. Chayqa bueno, "Yaw, yaw." (Wawqichan) Chay chicataq turachansi tulluchalla kasqa. Panachantaq wirasapacha kasqa, wirasapacha kasqa. Chaysi puñusqakuña. Chaysi mamakucha, payacha nin. "Qam haqay k´uchuchapi puñunki, sapallayki. Nuqa panachaykiwan puñusaq", nispa. Chayqa mamakucha puñun panachanwan. Chaymanta chicuchaqa sapallan puñun.

Chayqa tutallamanta rikch´arin. Tutallamanta hatarin. Chicucha, (mamakuchapis nispas nin) chicucha nin, "¿Maytaq panachayri?" nispas tapun.

"Panachaykiqa unumanmi rirun", nispas nin. Chayqa payachaqa mana payachu kasqa. Payachaqa diabla kasqa. Saqra paya kasqa. Duende paya kasqa. Hinaspas, chayqa mikhurakapusqa. Chay, panachanta wiracha kasqa. Wirasapacha kaqtin, mikhurakapusqa. Puñuna ukupi q´alata mikhurakapusqa. Hinaspa tutallamanta kachasqa huk putupi, putuchapi kachasqa. "Unuta aparamunki. Panachaykipas unumanmi rin, nispa. Chayqa putupisyá rin chicucha, pananpi umanpi, uma tullunpi. Pananpa uma tullunpi riqtinsi chicuchaqa, unu patamansi chayan.

Chaysi chaypi nin: "Tak, tak, tak, tak", nispas takimun hamp´atuqa. Chay hamp´atu Mariacha sitin riki. "Tak, tak, tak, tak, tak, tak. Panaykip tullu umanpi unuta apachkanki. Chicuchaqa uyarillansi. Unutaqa ñas, unutaqa ñas uqarirunña. Chay uma tullunpi apananña kachkaran saqra payaman. Hinaspas chayqa hamp´atu, "T´aq, t´aq, t´aq, t´aq. Amaña kutiyñachu", Mariacha nimun riki. "Amaña kutiyñachu. Panaykitapas chay saqra payaqa mikhunñan. Panaykip uma tullunpin unuta apchkanki", nispa.

The old crone started to chase him. She wanted to eat him too. Yes, the crone started to chase him. That devil-witch was chasing him. She cried after him "Come here, little boy. Where are you? Come here, little boy. Where are you? Where's my water?" The boy didn't answer a word. He ran for his life.

At last he reached his house. Yes, at last he reached his house. And his father asked "Where's your little sister? Where have you all been until now? Where did you sleep?"

"Night overtook us. We were looking for wood. We saw wood on a hillside. We went up the hillside. We saw wood there. But it wasn't wood. It was horse bones. It was cane reeds. Then it turned to night. And when it turned to night, we slept in an old crone's house. While we were sleeping in the old crone's house, that devil-witch, that dwarf-witch ate my little sister. Then she sent me off to gather water in my sister's skull. Then Maria said to me "You're carrying water in your sister's skull. Don't go back there. She also wants to eat you."

"Ah! Then let's go at once. I want you to show me that crone's house." They went to the house of that crone, that witch. There wasn't anything there. It had turned to nothing. It didn't exist anymore. That witch ate his sister.

Chaysi chicuchaqa qhawayun uma tulluta. "¡Ay!, ¿kaychu panaypa uma tullunqa? Manan Manan kutiymanñachu", nispa. ¡Ah! Uma tulluta, ununtinta ch´aqirparitamun mayu patapi, unupatapi. Hinaspa phawaylla ayqikun. "Nuqatapas kunanqa mikhuwanqachá riki", nispa.

Hinaspa, chayqa payachaqa aypamunsi. Paytawan mikhukapuyta munaran riki. Payachaqa aypamunsi. Chay saqra paya aypamun. Hinaspansi waqamunsi, "Yaw, chicucha. ¿Maypin kachkanki? Yaw, chicucha. ¿Maypin kachkanki? ¿Maymi unu? ¿Maymi unu?" nispas waqamun. Chicuchaqa ni imapaqpas ni contestamunñachu. Phawaylla ayqikapusqa.

Hinaspa chayan wasinta. Hinas chayansi wasinta. Hinaspas tapun taytan, "¿Maypin panachayki? ¿Maypin kunankama karankichik? ¿Maypin puñurankichik?"

"Hinas tutayawanku. Llant´an rikhuriwanku. Muqupin chay llant´a rikhuriwanku. Huk muquman riyku. Llantá rikhuriwanku. Mana llant´achu kasqa. Caballu tullu kasqa. Tuquru kasqa. Chayraykun tutayachikuyku. Tutayachikuspan, huk payachap wasinpi puñurayku. Chay payachap wasinpi puñusqaykupin, panachayta mikhurusqa chay saqra paya, chay duende riki. Hinaspa chay umachanpi nuqata kachawasqa unuman. Chay nay, Mariachañataq nimuwan, 'Panaykip umanpin ununuta aysachkanki. Amaña qampas kutiyñachu. Qamtapas mikhusuyta munasunki', nispan nimuwan", nispa.

"¡Ah! Chhaynaqa kunan risunchik. Chay payachap wasinta rikuchimuwanki." Rinkus payachap, chay saqraq wasinta. Manas imapas kasqachu. Ch´uralla kapusqa. Manaña imapas kapusqañachu. Chayqa saqra mikhukapun panachanta. Chayllapi tukupun.

The Farewell

The superstition related here is commonplace: condemned souls with unfinished business, however trifling, must formally take their leave and be forgiven by the one to whom the debt is owed. This recounting, in its brevity, almost falls into the category of an 'urban legend'—"Well, this is how it happened." Unlike the other stories of condemned souls in this collection, the emphasis is not so much on the consequences of the apparition's dilemma as on the fact that it 'really' occurred.

The Farewell

Told by Sara Vargas de Mayorga

A condemned soul said farewell to a friend, but when it still hadn't died, you see? Well, this is how it happened.

One day, a girl's parents told her "Okay, run along inside and take care of the children." They sent her in.

The girl ran inside. "Let's go together," she said. As she was going along the courtyard, she saw a furry dog with one eye. "Look, what's that? Is it a dog, or what?" she wondered. "What could it be?" But she wasn't afraid. In fact, she got closer to the dog. As she watched, it got bigger and bigger. And then, oh, that one-eyed thing became huge. Oh! Now the girl was scared, and started to back up. "What could that be?" Oh! All at once, she fell in a heap into the kitchen.

"Hey, what's wrong with you?" they asked her.

"Nothing, it was just a one-eyed dog."

All of them went outside to see. There wasn't anything. Not a soul, nothing, no dog. "What could it have been? Foolishness." They left the house. When they got to the corner, they heard that a friend had just died. The soul of the girl's schoolfriend had come just at the moment she died.

The girl said "Yes, it must have been her soul that came. That must have been what scared me. She turned into a dog, and came to say good-bye. She owed me money. Because of that money, she was coming to

Dispidikuy

Huk alma dispidikuq rin huk amigunpata, pero manaraq wañusqa, ¿no?
Ih, kayñataq pasan.

Huk kutin nin: "Bueno phaway chay cuartuta. Yaykuspayki qhawara-
muchkay wawakunata", nispa, chay kamachinku nispa.

Chicachaqa yaykun pkawaylla riki, "Rirusun", nispa, "kuskan."
Richkasqanpi hina, ñan patiupi rikurun huk allquchata, ñawillayuqtaq,
huk ch´akuchata hina. "Yaw, ¿Imataq haqayri? ¿Allquchu, imataq?"
nispa nin. Hina, "¿Imataq kanmanri?" nispa. Mana manchakuspa richkan riki. Astawasi achhuyuchkan allquman. Huktas, hatun, hatun-
mansi tukurapuchkan. Huktas ay, chayqa hatunman tukurapuqtinsi, hu-
k ch´ulla ñawi. ¡Ay!, manchaypi, qipanpamantas kutimun naqa riki,
chicachaqa, riki . . . "¿Imataq chayri?" nispa. ¡Ay!, huktas cocinaman
kunpayukun qipanmanta.

"¡Ay!, ¿ima, ima nasunkin?" nispa nin.

"Mana, huk allqun ch´ulla ñawillayuq", nispas nin.

Lluqsiramunkus llapanku qhawaq. Manas imapas kanchu. Chay; ni
ch´ulla, ni imapas, ni allqu. "¿Imataq kanmanri? Sunsiras", nispansi
nin. Hinaspa pasansi. Esquina anchaypis yacharunkus na, conpañi-
ranpa wañusqanta, riki. Compañiran chay almaq, almanpa hamusqanta
wañuqpata.

Hinaspa nin: "¡Ay!, seguruchá riki alman hamuran. Chaychá riki

say farewell." The girl started to cry. Crying, she said "Forgive me. And I also forgive you," After that, no more soul, nor anything else, appeared to the girl.

nuqataqa manchachiwaran. Allquman tukuspachá, riki hamuran dispidikuq. Nuqaman qullqin dibiwaran, nuqaman. Chaychá riki, qullqimanta dispidikuq nuqaman almaqa. Chay waqayun. Hinas waqayuspa, "En fin perdonaway. Perdonayki nuqapis", nispa riki nipun. Chayqa manaña astawan almapas, ni imapas rikhuripunñachu chicamanqa. Chayllapi tukukun.

The Coffin Contest

*The complicated co-existence between "those from above" and "those from below"
is a time-honored division. The negotiation of this division is depicted in* The
Huarochiri Manuscript *as a necessary marriage between those who need more
irrigation water and those who crave more land to till. Realpolitik upstages ide-
ology. Intermediaries such as the fertility cult goddess Chaupi Ñamca provide
a common reference point for religious syncretism, allowing competing popula-
tions, each with their own cache of goods and gods, to achieve both a practical
and a mythic synthesis, as an antidote to open dissent. Studies of the* hanan
and hurin *in the southern Andes emphasize the principle of "perfect" complementarity that rationalizes the inequities and hierarchies within Inca civiliza-
tion as a preferable alternative to constant caste conflict. Arguedas's novel* The
Fox Above, the Fox Below, *seizes on the folk figure of Reynard, himself a trans-
plant, as the emblem of Quechua highlanders who migrate to the coastal low-
lands to find their place among other races in the anchovy fisheries, sometimes
losing their identities, and even their lives, in the process. Those who cannily
learn to merge survive; those who do not perish. "The Coffin Contest" is yet another version of this ancient binarism. This battle of the tomb-titans temporarily upends the hierarchy, throwing its vote to the coffin of the disparaged, un-
derdog people, whose historical dispossession has made them tough and scrappy.
The type of bragadoccio depicted can be heard in just about any crossroads pi-
cantería tavern where Peruvian men from different towns gather to drink.*

The Coffin Contest

Told by Sara Vargas de Mayorga

There was a village in a cold, cold place. But as cold as it was, there was also a little valley there. And anywhere in it, people grew fruit, corn, and all the things that grow in hot lands. Lots of things grew in that valley. Those who lived higher up said "Okay, we'll bring ourselves subsistence from there." And those who always went to those fields grew large and tall, because they had all kinds of delicious hot-land food to eat. Those people develop better. They lived a good life there. And they said "Well, they'll just have to live a different way in the cold lands. We can easily be dominant over them. And this town will always be for us," said those who lived in the hot lands.

Meanwhile, the people who lived in the cold land said "Why are we like this, in our town, and our fields are just like this; Next thing you know, they'll even take these lands from us." That's how those people thought.

They kept thinking about that. And once, two coffins started to talk. "Because of the way it is in the cold town, I'm always having to bring corpses up here to the graveyard. You, on the other hand, don't have to carry anybody; not a soul, nobody, you. That's why you're better rested. And that's why now I'm stronger," said the coffin that lived in the cold land. See?

One night the two of them went out. The other coffin said "Okay, now what did you say about me before? Now I've stepped out here.

Ataudkuna Maqanakuy

Huk llaqtañataq kasqa sinchi chiri. Hinaspa, pero chiri kasqanpi, huk
vallichayuq kasqa. Paykuna maypichá chay frutatan, saran, imaymana
q´uñipi kasqan. Anchay naqkunaq, naq valliyuq kasqa. Chay vallimantataq paykuna nisqaku: "Bueno hinapi, kay, chaymanta kawsayta apakamusunchik. Chaymanta frutakunata apamusunchik", ninku. Hinamantaq chay estanciaman riqkuna hatunman tukupusqaku, *por cuanto
de que* sumaqtataq imaymana mikhunataq kan q´uñipiqa. Aswan mejorta runapis riki desarrollan. Anchaykunawan chaypi tiyapusqaku. Hinas, "Aswan chay chiri llaqtapiqa hina kachun. Aswan nuqanchik chayta duminakapusunchik. Hinaspa nuqanchikpaq kay llaqta kapunqa",
nispa chay q´uñipi tiyaqkuna kasqaku.

Hinas chay chiripi tiyaqkuna, "¿Imaynatataq khayna nuqanchik, llaqtanchikpi nuqanchikpapiri, esntancianchik hinalla kan; hinas paykuna
kunan qichupuwasunchikri?" nispa pensanku runakunaqa.

Hinas pensachkanku. Hinamansi ataudkunaqa riki. "Khaynaniraqta
kay llaqtapi, kay chiripi, sinchita nuqa q´ipini. Qamtaq mana imata
q´ipinkichu; ni almata ni imata qamqa. Aswan descansado qampaqqa
kan. Pues kunanqa nuqaqpas kallpay kachkanmi", nispas chay chiripi
chay chiripi tiyaqpa ataudqa nin, ¿ih?

Hinas huk tuta lluqsispanku. "A ver, ¿imatapunitaq qam ninki nuqamanta? Kunanyá nuqa lluqsimusaq. A ver, ¿mayqinninchikchá kallpanchik kachkan? Chaymi llaqtawan quidakapunqa: o bien chiriwan,

Okay, let's see which of us is stronger. Which town can lay claim: either the cold one, or the hot one. Which one will be bigger?" So they stepped out. "All right, such-and-such a night we'll meet," they agreed.

"Where will we meet?"

"Oh, let's meet just right on the Simp'i Bridge."

"No, let's meet right on the Ch'aqo Bridge. I'll look for you there."

"Ready when you are."

The coffins made a bet: the hot-town coffin and the cold-town coffin. Afterward, the cold-town coffin said "Man! Man, that's far for me to travel." But on the agreed night, he came out of the church. Ka-chunk! Ka-chunk! Ka-chunk! He sped downhill toward the hot land. At length, he got there, he arrived. "Hey, where's the coffin from down below? Will he show his face tonight? What's he doing?" He looked around, and looked around.

As he was looking, the other one from down below showed up. Ka-chunk! Ka-chunk! He was coming slowly.

A man was walking by there, in the vicinity of the bridge. He said to himself "I wonder what's making that Ka-chunk! Ka-chunk! sound? Oh my God, what in the devil are they carrying over there? Some demons are coming—it looks like coffins." The man was frightened. He climbed up to one side of the path. When he was off to one side, he said "Oh, what am I going to do now?" He was afraid. "I'll just let them pass by. Will the two of them meet up right here? And then what? Then what will I do?"

Meanwhile, the one coffin was looking for the other, looking and looking. "Is that you coming from down below?"

"Yes," said the other. All at once they grabbed each other and started fighting. The two coffins ended up as nothing but splinters.

And there was the man, above the path, looking on, scared. "What's going to become of me?" He was so afraid he was wetting himself. He didn't know what to do with himself. The coffin that had come from down below was all splintered. The man said "Oh, now what are these two going to do? They'll kill me. Will the Devil carry me off? Or what?" He couldn't imagine. He lay where he'd fallen, scared out of his wits.

The cold-land coffin said "Well, I beat you. I've smashed you to pieces. Now I'll go. And you go back down. Another day, we'll have an even better fight. That day, we'll teach each other a lesson, because this one wasn't even a good fight. Where's all that harm you were going to do to me? I overpowered you. Now the hot land belongs to me," said the cold-land coffin.

o bien q´uñiwan. ¿Mayqinchá kanqa hatunnin?" nispas nin. Hinaspas lluqsimun ¿ih? "Bueno tal tuta tupasunchik", nispa nin.

"¿Maypitaq tupasunchik?"

Simp´i chaka patallapi tupasunchik."

"Manas, Ch´aqu chaka patapi, chay patapi tupasunchik. Chaypi tiranakusunchik", nispa nin.

"Listo."

Apustayunkus iskayninku, ataudkunaqa: chay q´uñi llaqta ataudwan, chiri llaqta ataudqa. "¡Ay!" Hinaspas naqa, chay chiri llaqta ataudqa, ¡Ay! Karuraqtaq kachkan", nispas, "purinayqa" nispas, Huktas lluqsimun iglisiamanta ¿ih? "Thuqruq, thuqruq, thuqruq!", nispa. Phawaylla pasayun urayman riki (Aqumayu) q´uñi llaqtaman. Hinaspa pasayuspansi nin, chayarunsi. "¿Maytaq, chay uraymanta hamuqri? ¿Rikhurimunchu kunankama? ¿Imata ruwamun?", nispa. Qhawakun.

Qhawakuqtinsi, huktas naqa, uraymanta hamuqqa, ¿ih? "Thuqruq, thuqruq!", Susigullawansi hamun.

Hinas huk runas purichkan anchay, chay chakap pataman anchaniqpis kachkan runaqa, ¿ih? Hinaspas, "¿Imataq chayri, '¡Thuqruq, thuqruq!', nispari purin?" nispas nin ¿ih? ¡Ay, hinas!, "¡Atataw! Supaytaq qakaypiqa q´ipimuchkasqa. Saqrakunataq hamuchkasqa; ataudtaq", nispas mancharisqa. Na, pataman siqarun, ñanpataman. Ñanpataman siqaruspansis, "¡Ay!, ¿Imanasaqtaqri, kunanri?" nispas mancharikun. Ay, hinaspas, "Hinallayá pasarukuspasyá. ¿Kaypi iskayninku tuparunkuman, chayrí? ¿Ima nasaqtari?"

Qhawachkaqtinsi, ¡ay! Hinamanqa ataudqa, qhawachkansi, qhawachkansi huktas. "¿Qamchu uraymanta hamuckanki?"

"Arí", nispas. Huktas hap´inaykuyta qallarinku paykuna. Maqanayukunkus. Ñut´umansi tukurapun iskanin ataud.

¡Ay!, runataqsi chay patapi qhawayuchkan, manchasqa. "¿Imaynataq kunanri kasaq?" Mancharikuymantas na hip´ayukuchkanña kanpas. Mana riki atinchu imayna kayta. Ñut´us uraymanta hamuq, ataudqa, ¿ih? "¡Ay!, ¿Imaynataq kunan kaykunari ruwanakunqaku? ¿Imatataq ruwanakunqaku? Sipiwanqachu. ¿Nuqatawanchu? ¿Supaychu q´ipiwanqa? ¿Imananqa?" ¡Ay!, manas ni imaniyta. Hinallas kunparayan. Manchasqa tiyayuchkan runaqa, ¡ay!

Hinamansi, "Bueno, ñan qamta ganaykiña. Chhalluykiña. Ñut´uñan kanki. Kunanqa ripusaqmi. Qampas ripuyyá urayman. Huk punchawña astawan allinta tupanasunchik. Hinaspa chaypiña yachachinakusunchik, por que mana kunanqa allintachu maqanakunchik. ¿Maytaq nuqata ni imanawankichu? Nuqaqa nuqan duminayki qamta. Nuqa-

The other coffin replied "You're right, that's how it should be, brother. I'll come back another day. On that day, we'll really have a tough fight." Each went back. The one from below pulled its splinters back together and made itself into a whole coffin again. And with a Ka-bang! Ka-bang! it made its way downward.

The man, still startled, only got up little by little when both of the coffins had gone away. He went running all the way back to his house. He didn't arrive as a normal man, but rather vomiting foam from his mouth. His wife said "What's wrong with you? What happened to you?" The man couldn't even speak. He couldn't do anything but throw up foam. His wife boiled some aromatic herbs, ruda and some others. She boiled it with pig manure and some other stuff. At last, the man came back to himself, came into himself.

When he was himself again, he said "This is what happened. Two coffins had a fight on the Ch'aqo Bridge. The big coffin from the cold land came, that one that carries so many corpses. Because, you know, a lot of people die up there. That was the one who was stronger. The other one is just skinny. So, the big coffin won. That one was the winner."

His wife said "Can this be true? Did you really see that? No wonder you got so sick. I've heard you can get really sick if you see those coffins. I'm surprised they didn't just carry you off," she said to her husband.

The man said "Maybe that means they're going to win against us now. Those people are going to take over our town. Then what kind of life will we lead? We should go tell someone about this. We should tell the whole town. Maybe they can do something."

"How can you imagine people will believe you when you say that coffins walk? 'It's just a saying,' they'll tell you. 'Yeah, well let them fight each other. What do we care? Better if you don't walk around at night; let the coffins fight. People who are sick in the head from walking around, those are the ones who see coffins,' they'll say. Or maybe you're taking other men's women for lovers," his wife said, scolding her husband. "How come they never appear to me? You, on the other hand, see devils, all kinds of things. Those are for dirty, immoral people. You're worthless. Get out of here. Go live with the coffins. Take your stuff with you." The woman said this and a lot more to her husband.

The man walked away sadly. "Who can I tell this to? What kind of life is this? Who can free me from those coffins? They might appear to me again." He was scared, the man was scared even in the daytime. He always kept someone at his side. No matter who, but he wanted to walk around with someone. Finally, he told everything to a man he knew.

paqmi kay kay, chhaynaqa, kay q´uñi llaqta quidapunqa", nispas, chay chiri llaqtayuq nin, ¿ih?

¡Ay! "Hinamansi, bueno, hinayá kachun wawqiy. Huk p´unchawña hamusaq. Chaypiña riki maqanayukusunchik allinta", nispas nin ataudqa. Chaysi pasayapun kikillansi. Hina ñut´u kachkasqanta naman, askhaman huñurakapun kaq cajunman. Hinas, "Thaqlaq, thaqlaq!", nispas pasayapun urayman. Kaqtaqsi chay huk kaq ataudpas wichayman pasapun.

¡Ay!, chayraqsi runa mancharisqa, llapa, manaña ataudkuna kaqtinsi, chayraq sayarin, sayarin. ¡Ay!, puriq rin, ¡ay! Hinaspas wasinmanqa chayarapun. Manas runa hinañachu chayan, sinuqa, phusuquta aqtuspallañas chayan, ¡Ay!, hinas warmin nin: "Imanaramusunkitaq? ¿Imataq pasasunkiri?" nispa. Manas rimariyta atinchu. Phusuqullatas kutiyachichkan runaqa, ¿ih? ¡Ay!, hinaspas, por fin q´apachinsi imaymanawan warminqa. Nakunawan, rudakunawan, imakunawanchá, q´apayachichkan. Khuchi akatawan, imaymanawan q´apachin. Hinaspa, mana kutiyta atichkanchu. Por fin kutirimunsi.

Kutirimuspansi nin, "Kaymi pasan. Ataudkuna chay (Sint´i chaka), Ch´aqu chaka patapi maqanayukunku. Hinaspan chay punamanta hamuqqa ataud sinchi q´ipiq, sinchi q´ipiq. Por que sinchin punapiqa wañun runa, chaykuna. Chay aswan más fuerzayuq kasqa. As nallan kasqapas flacu, na, flacullan kasqapas. Hinaspa chay ganarapun. Hinaspan kunan chay ataudta hukkaqta ganarapun. Ganarapuqtinqa, riki."

Naqa, warminqa nisqa: "¿Chiqaytachu kanman? ¿Qam rikumurankichu? Chaymi ¡ay! entonces chayqa qhayqamusunki. Ataudkunaqa sinchi qhayqakuqmi ninkutaq. ¿Imayna mana q´ipirasunkipaschu?" nispas qharinta nin.

Hinas qharinqa nin: "¡Ay!, chaqaytan. Kunan chiqaytachá riki ganawasunchik. Llaqtanchiktachá riki hap´irakapunqaku chay punakuna. ¿Hinaspa imaynataq kasunri? Willaswanchá pikunamanpas. Llaqtamanchá willaswan. Chaychá paykuna riki nankuman", nispa.

"¿Imaynatataq ataudkunaq purisqanta qampaq creewasunmanchu pipas? 'Rimayllan,' chayqa ninkutaq. Chayqa hinaspayá, hinayá maqanakuchun. ¿Imataq nuqamchikmanri qukuwanchik? Qamqa amañayá tutaqa purinkiñachu, hinatan ataudkunaqa maqanakun. 'Hinatan purin chay mala cabeza runakunallapaqmi, ataudqa rikhurimun', nispataq ninku. Maypichá qamqa, pantachkanki pi warmikunawan", nispa riki astawan qharinta riki kutiriyun, ¿ih? "¿Imaynataq mana nuqamanri, rikhuriwanchu ni imapas? Qampaqtaq, saqrakunapas, imapas,

The man said "So, now they're going to come take our town away. What will we do? Let's go, the two of us, let's go find them. We'll go out at night and smash them to pieces. Yeah, we'll smash them to pieces, and no coffin will be able to come to your house then." Off they went to find the coffins. But they couldn't find the coffin from the highland. That coffin realized what they were doing.

Then one day, as the man was walking alone, the coffin appeared to him. It said "So now, you were looking for me, right? You were the one, huh? Now I'm going to carry you off. At daybreak, I'll carry you off," the coffin said, but it was still nighttime. The man was scared out of his wits. And the man simply died of fright.

rikhurimuchkasunki. Millay khuchi puriqkunallapaqmi chaykunaqa. Mana qamqa valinkichu. Pasayá. Ataudllawanña tiyamuy; q´ipichikamuypas", nispas warminqa riki niyun, imaymanata runataqa.

Hinas runaqa tristes purichkan, ¿ih? "¿Pimantaq willakusaq? ¿Imanasaqtaq kay vidaytari? ¿Pitaq chay ataudmanta khaynata librawanqari? Waqmantachá kunan rikhuriwanqa." Manchan, manchansi runaqa p´unchawpas, ¿ih? Manañas, huk ladullayuqña. Pillawanñapas kuskallas puriyta munanña. Por fin huk runamansi willayukun.

Hinaspansi, "¡Ay!, kunanqa chhaynaqa llaqtanchiktaqa qichupuwasunpaschá. ¿Imanasuntaqri? Hakuyá nuqanchik, lluqsispanchik iskayninchik. Tuta lluqsisunchik; ñut´uta ruwaramusunchik. Hinaspa nuqanchik ñut´uta ruwamuqtinchik, ataudqa manaña ripuyta atinqañachu wasinman", nispas nin. Chaysi tiranku maskhaq, na. Chaysi chay puna ataudtaqa manas tarimunkuchu. Ataudtaq chayqa riki cuentatas ruwakamuchkan.

Mana, qunqaylla purichkaqtin, huktas ataud sapallanman rikhurin, nispa, "Kunan, nuqamanta qam rikuwasqanki, ¿ih? Qam kasqanki, ¿ih? Kunan qamta q´ipisayki. Hina p´unchaw pachan q´ipisayki", nispa ataud niyun, tuta. Pero tutas kachkanpas. Mancharikamuchkan runa. Total chaypis wañurapusqa runa mancharikuywan. Chaypi tukupun.

The Wand

*Marital conflict doesn't get much worse than this. The wife shows the telltale
signs of the condemned soul: poor appetite and furtive behavior. As usual, the
husband quickly comes to suspect an adulterous affair. He should be so lucky:
her designs are necrotic, not erotic. The twist in this story is interesting; usually,
the spouse or other intended victim of the condemned soul is given supernatural
aid. In this case, however, the wife herself, though undead, is given the wand
by her equally departed grandmother, as a hedge for the inevitable moment when
the husband discovers that his mate is bringing more to the marriage than what
she promised in the wedding vows.*

The Wand

Told by Miguel Waman Lazaro

This one is about a condemned soul.

A young man got married; he took a wife, got married. And this newlywed man was given a boy for his servant. Also, the newlywed woman was given a girl to accompany her, just as if someone were to give you a servant, or your brother kept you company, and your wife was also given someone to accompany her. That sort of thing, they were supposed to help out. So, the girl cooked up hearty dishes, and the husband and wife ate them. They were young, so they were hungry. Then the grandmother died. When the grandmother died, they hadn't been married long. When she died, then what happened? That night, the grandmother came back in the form of a condemned soul. She took away the young woman while her husband was asleep. And gave her one of those magic wands. She touched her with it. The husband was fast asleep. The grandmother took the young wife to the cemetery at the edge of town. They dug up the grandmother's corpse. And they ate the flesh. They gnawed it down to the snow-white bones.

After that, she couldn't eat anymore with her husband. She had no appetite, she picked at her food, a spoonful or two. Then the husband's houseboy, the boy said "Sir, the mistress goes out at night. Maybe she has a lover or something. Another woman came to get her. Sir, don't drink your herb tea tonight; that makes you fall asleep." The husband made sure not to drink his herbal tea, that newlywed husband. He pretended to be asleep.

The wife and grandmother, sure enough, went out. He followed them

Chunta

Huk condenadumanta.

Huk niñus casarakun; warmiyuq kapun, casado. Hinaspas qhari novioman qumun huk chicuta muchachunpaq. Warmi noviamantaq khayna chicata qumullanta compañeranpaq, imaynan qamman qumusunkiman huk chicuta, wawqichayki compañasunkiman, warmiykipaqtaq ñañachan conpañanman. Anchhaynayá, acompañañanpaq qusqa. Hinaspas chicaqa wayk´uyunkus plato hunt´ankatas mikhuyunku, warmi qhari. *Como están joven, da ganas comer pues.* Hinaspas abuilachan wañupun. Abuilachan wañupun, riki, manaraq unay casado kachkaqtinku. Wañupuqtinqa, ¿imatan ruwan? tuta hamun abuilachan, condechaña. Pusan señoritataqa. Qusantaq puñuchkantaq. Aknata huk chuntachata, k´aspichata qusqa. Chayllawan aknata p´anaykun. Secuta puñuyapun qhari. Noviantataq pusan cantuman, pantiunman. Hinaspas chay entierruta t´aqwispanku. Chay ayata mikhuyunku. Rit´i-rit´iy tulluyuqtaraq p´atayunku.

Chay mana munasqachu mikhuytaqa qusanwan kuskaqa. Mana mikhuqchu, malli-mallichallata antujuchallapaq, cucharachallapi. Chayqa chay qharip chicunqa nisqa, muchachuchanqa, "Papá, Mamitayqa tutan lluqsin. Qusanpaschá kakun, imachá. Huk señoran hamuspa pusan. Ama papá matita tumankichu kunan tutaqa; chaymi puñurunki", nispa nin. Procuran, mana (Tumayta) matita tumanchu na, chay novio, qusan. Hinalla puñuruq tukun.

Yastá, pasanku. Qipanta qatin karullanta. Chayqa abuilachantin richkan chay noviaqa. Punkutas kichanku, ¡ran! Paytaq muyuramun

from a distance. They opened the door, creeeak! He went along after them to the edge of the village, climbed on the wall, and watched. His whole body shook. They dug up the body, took it out, and began to eat.

On the way back, he followed his wife closely. There was nothing else he could do. "How can I let her kiss me with that mouth? How can I let her, with that mouth that has been eating flesh—eating flesh!" the husband said, startled.

So what did that young man do? The grandmother, the old woman, had given the wife a wand. "If your husband hits you, you touch him with this," she said.

The next day, at home, the husband shouted "Bring the meal!" And the same way that we, as newlyweds, eat a full plate, he had her bring him a full, heaping plate. But the young woman herself couldn't eat. The husband ate hearty—you see? The husband emptied his plate. Then and there, he said "At night, you've been filling yourself up eating cadaver flesh." She realized then that he knew. And when he hit her, she turned the young husband into a dog.

He'd been turned into a big dog. Knew how to write, knew how to talk. But his body was that of a dog. And if you'd say, how are you? he'd come up to be petted. The dog walked around crying tears that looked like hailstones. From this house to that, at the public oven, like a servant. He helped out so that he could eat well. Finally, the dog ran off. His wife went on the same as always. The young man wandered wherever, whenever, for four or five years, or four or five months, anyway a long time.

One day, he came across some shamans. They gave him a hearty greeting, and asked him to sit down on the sofa. They offered him hot chocolate and petted him. Out of a cabinet, they took a wand and touched the young man with it. And in the same way he had become a dog, he turned back into a young man, a handsome young man. "Now what will you do?" they said to him. "You've had to suffer all this. Now make her suffer. We give you this wand."

He went back home. His wife hugged and kissed him. "Where have you been, my husband?" She pretended to weep, after what she did to him. Then, rapping her with the wand, he turned the wife into a large horse. She was a mean, unbroken mare. He put a saddle and bridle on her, and saddlebags. Then he rode her round and round the court-yard. The servant girl was hollering and crying.

So, he sold that mare to a mule-driver. That's how it ends. What an adventure, but the young man was saved. As for her, who knows where that horse is suffering, even today. She never came back.

chhayna cantuntachá. Siqaruspa qhawachkan riki. Hinaspa lluy cuer-
punkuna khatatachkan. Chakinkunapas hinayuchkan riki. Ayatas
urquramunku, t´aqwikapunku, mikhuyuchkanku riki. Hampunkuña,
hampuspa hijita ladunman achhuyun. Mana imatapas ruwayta atinchu.
"¿Ima kay simiwanchu much´ayuruwanqachu? ¿Imatataq aycha mikhuq,
aycha mikhusqan simiwanri?" nispa mancharakapun na qusan.

¿Chayqa imatan ruwan chay joventa? Chuntachata qusqa na abuilan,
chay paya. "Qusayki maqasuqtiykiqa, kayllawan p´anayurunki", nispa.
Chayqa, "¡Mikhunata qaramuy!" Phiña qusan. Imaynan recién casado
mikhurayku plato hunt´ata, aknaka hunt´anka qaramun. Mana
mikhuyta atinchu niñaqa. Qhariqa mikhurun gustunman (*Te das cuenta*)
mikhurun q´alata qhariqa. Anchaypiña nisqa: "Imaynataq tutaqa aya-
aychataqa gustuykimantaq mikhuyunki", nispa. Cuentata qurukun.
P´anaruqtin, hinan karay allquman tukurapun chay joven, qusan.
Se ha vuelto a perro grande. Sabe escribir, sabe hablar. Trasallachá allqu
riki. *Cómo está* niqtiykipas, abrazasunki lluyta. Chikchi-chikchimanta allqu waqaspa purichkan. Chay wasipi, kay wasipi, hurnupi, empleado
hina. Allin atiendisqa, allin mikhusqa. Chayqa chinkakapusqayá allqu.
Warminqa kaqlla kachkan. Chayqa imaynapichá, maypichá, tawa pichqa
watachus, tawa pichqa killachus, unayña purikun naqa, chay jovenqa.

Chaypi huk chhayna layqallamantaq chayasqa. Wapus napayukus-
pankus, sofá pata niñuta tiyarachinku. Chuculatita haywanku, abra-
zanku, lliwta. Vitrinachamanta urquyuruspas, k´aspichallawan aknata
p´anayurun joventa. Imayna trasantinmi allquman tukuran kaqta piji,
joven tukurapun, allin kaq jovenman. "¿Imatan qam ruwanki?" nispas
nin. "Kaytukuytañan sufrinki. Qam sufrichimuy. Kay chuntachayta
qusayki", nispas nin. "Kunanmi chayaqtiyki, warmiyki sumaqta adora-
sunki kay, diosta hinaraq. Warmakunapas qaparkachayunqa. Lliw kan-
qaku. Bueno, ¿imata ruwanki? Kayta ruway", nispas chuntachata qun.

Yaykupunsi. Abrazansi, much´ansi. "¿Qusay maypin karan?" Waqaq
tukun, pay chayta ruwachkaspa. Hinachata p´anayuruqtinsi hatun caballuman tukurapun warmin. *Había vuelto a yegua, mañosa.* Chucarataq.
Qaparqachayuchkaqta. Munturawan munturaykun. Bolsawan churay-
kun. Patiun-patiuntinta muyukachayachin. Warmakunapas qapariyku-
chkansi, niñaqa.

Chayqa arrieruman venderapusqa, chay yeguata. Chaypi tukukapun.
Imayna kasqanpas; pero salvakun joven; pero payqa, maypiraq caballu
kamuchkan sufrimun riki, wiñaypaq. Manaña kutinpunchu.

The Promise

This is the most "classic" version of a condemned soul story that I compiled, full of heartbreak, troth and betrayal, filial disobedience, impossible love. Rosa tended to favor more comic stories than her mother Teodora. She had a mobile face, jokey manner, and slapstick sensibility suited to lighter material. So I was surprised when she came out with this pensive offering. All the same, she seasoned it with ironic flashes, such as the moment when the fleeing newlywed wife appeals to the "heroic" mule-drivers for aid. The reasoned response of these questionably chivalrous sorts to her plea, just before they rush to help, is to observe: "We'll save this woman so that she can at least cook our food. She'll be good for something. That's why we're saving her." Food is, in fact, the most durable social glue, and it figures prominently in every important transaction in this story. The boy is killed by a falling sack of flour. His ghost brings his waiting bride a meal from his own wake (as in Hamlet, the funeral meats furnish forth the wedding feast). The first sign of the condemned soul's presence is the dog's inability to eat in peace. The condemned soul of the husband lacks appetite on arrival at the lodging. He tries to force down tea, but can't, thus awakening the landlady's suspicions. She, in turn, tells the bride the awful truth that awaits her: "He's going to eat you." The curse on her could not be more graphically or more frighteningly set forth. An upset stomach is a malaise that bespeaks ruptured social relations, disharmony within a living community, heralding a more general loss of vitality. A broken promise is, quite literally, hard to swallow, harder still to digest. Those who have sat at an Andean feast, whether domestic or public, will understand the exaggerated importance placed on eating well. A guest, hungry or not, declines proffered food at his own peril.

The Promise

Told by Juana Rosa Callo Paliza

There were a young man and woman, and they loved each other very much. The man said "If I die first, I'll take you with me." Each of them made the same promise to the other. They both agreed.

Their parents didn't want them to get married. They said, "Why would you want to get married to him? To her? You don't know anything about this life." Their parents were opposed to it.

The lovers said "Well, neither your mother and father or mine wants us to marry. So let's run off. We'll go to a faraway town. And there, we'll marry."

"Yes," both of them agreed. "Let's go. Tomorrow night you sneak out, and I'll also sneak out. We'll go away." They parted, and each went off to his or her house. The next night, they met on a hilltop outside their village. One said, "I brought some money."

"I also brought this. This is all we've got to eat. What should we do? It won't be enough."

"I'll return to my house," said the man.

The woman said "Yes, go. Run. I'll wait for you right here."

As he made his way down, the night was gloomy. First, he said to her, "I know where my mother and father keep their money hidden. I'm going to look where I'm pretty sure it's hidden. And I'll bring it with me. We can live on that a long time."

"Run along. Maybe I should go to my house too. But no. Since you're the man, you go; bring it back. I'll wait for you in this pass," said the

Juramento

Kasqas huk waynawan, huk sipaswan; munanakusqaku. Hinaspansi sin-chitapuni. Chaysis qhari nisqa, "Nuqa wañusaq primeruta, pusaka-pusayki", nispansi nisqa. Chaysi jurasqaku. Juraqtinkus, chaysi hina kanku.

Taytamamanku mana munasqachu casaranankuta, nispa, "¿Imawan-mi qamkuna kawsawaqchik? Mana yachankichikchu imaynan vida kayta; chaychu qamkuna." Manas munasqapunichu taytamamanku.

Chayqa chaysi, "Bueno, yakiña mana mamanchik ni taytanchik qam-papis, ni nuqaqpis munanchu. Chayqa haku; chinkakapusun. Ripusun karu llaqtata. Chaypi casarakusunchik."

"Bueno", nispansi iskayninkuqa ninku riki. Chaysi, "¡Ay, hakuyá! Tal paqarin ch´isi lluqsimunki. Nuqapis ch´isinta lluqsimusaq", nispa. "Ri-pusunchik." Chaysi ripusqaku. Wasinkumanta sapankanku puririnkus. Chaysi chhayna kay llaqtakama riki, urqu pata, anchhaynataña. Chaypis ninku: "Kay qullqillatan apamuni."

"Nuqapis kayllatan apamuni. Kayllata mikhunanchik, ¿chayri? Man-achá riki imapaqpis kanqachu."

"Aswayyari kutirusaq nuqa wasiyta", nispas qhari nisqa.

Chayqa warmis nin: "Riyari. Phaway; suyachkasayki kayllapi."

Chaysi tutataña rasphi-rasphitaña riki urayamun. "Yachachkanin ma-maypa, taytaypa qullqinta waqaychasqanta. Maypichá waqaychasqanta, rikuni. Chayta aparamusaq. Chaywan ripunanchispaq aswan karuta."

Chayqa, "Phawayari. Nuqapas riyman wasiyta. Pero mana. Qamqa

woman. They parted. He arrived at the house, and entered in the dark. His parents were asleep there. Those parents were rich. In one room, they kept a lot of wool. It was full of wool, and inside the wool they'd hidden the money. The son knew this. He felt around with his hand until he came across the money. As he was taking it out, a heavy bale of wool fell on him and pinned him. He cried out. Both parents woke up and went in with the dog to see what was happening. "Help me, help me," the young man called out.

The parents listened. "Who could it be? A thief, a thief, a thief." The father grabbed an ax in the dark, and hit the thief in the throat with it. "Now I got that thief," he said. In the morning they went to see who it had been. And it was their son. The parents began to weep, and they had to have him buried.

Meanwhile, the young woman was waiting, with her dog. From the mountain pass, she could look down on the young man's house. She said "Oh, he hasn't come back! I wondered who died? There's a funeral going on. Look, they're carrying a coffin to the cemetery." She could see everything. "What's wrong? He hasn't come back. What could have happened? And I wonder who died? Maybe he's helping them with the funeral," the woman thought. "Oh! What could it be?" She sat there with her little dog. He didn't appear. She looked all around for him. And the parents carried him to the cemetery, buried him, held a wake, everything. Now two, then three nights had passed.

When three nights had passed, her lover came to her. But he was already dead, you see. He went to her. When he showed up, she said "Hey, what have you been doing down there until now? You told me you were coming back. Who died at your house?"

He said, "Don't ask me about that. I brought you food. Eat this." As part of the burial in the cemetery, his parents had cooked food, made corn beer. And the man had wrapped some of it up and brought it to his lover. He said "Hurry up and eat this. We have to get walking soon. We've got a long way to go."

The woman said, "Sure, okay, let's go." She ate, and they set off walking at once. They were going along. The dog was skulking alongside holding a piece of food in his mouth. And the dog started to bark. "Woof! Woof! Woof!"

"What's wrong with the dog? Why won't he come near you?" said the woman. The dog kept its distance.

They kept walking. "We have a long way to go today. I brought these things: money, food. I brought everything. Today we have to go; we have

qhari hinayá phaway; aparamuy." nispansi. "Kay qʹasa patallapi suyawachkanki", nispansi nin warmi. Chaysi chayman pasanku. Chayqa chayamunsi; hinas tuta yaykun. Hinas taytanqa mamanqa puñuchkankus chaypi. Chaysi kasqa qapaq taytamaman. Hinaspas huk wasipis huntʹa millma kasqa. Chaysis millmap pachan, ukupis kasqa qullqi waqaychasqan. Wawanqa yacharanyá riki. Chayqa chaymansi suskhun nata, yaykunsi qullqiman. Chaysi winayukuchkan. Chaymansi urmayamusqa; chay millma tawqasqa, chayqa ñitʹisqa. Chaysi qaparkachan. ¡Ah, ya! Chay ripusqaku riki; iskayninkus allquchapuwansi risqaku. Chaysi riki, "¡Ay, kunanqa, ay!" Qaparkachayuchkansi runaqa.

Chaytas uyarin taytamamanqa. "¿Pitaq kanmanri? Suwa, suwa, suwa", nispansi hachata hapʹin. Hinaspansi tutataq. Chayqa kunkapi riki dalisqa. Chayqa, "Kunanqa suwata hapʹini", nispansi riki nin. Chayqa tutamantañas riki qhawarinku pikasqanta. Chayqa wawan kasqa. Chaysi taytamamanqa waqaspas nas, lliwta, enterrachin, lliwta.

Chaysi warmiqa suyachkansi allquchantin. Chay qʹasapatamantas wasin rikukusqa, chay waynaqqa. Chaysi nin: "¡Ay!, manataq hampunchú. ¿Pitaq wañunri? Entierrutaq kan. Qhawariy, entierruman apachkanku." Lliwtas qhawan riki. "¿Imataq? Manataq kutimunchu. ¿Imanantaqri? ¿Pichá riki wañun? Chaytaraq riki yanapamuchkan", nispansi warmiqa piensachkan. Chayqa, "¡Ay!, ¿imaynan kanqa?" Allquchallawansi tiyachkan. Mana rikhurimunchu; chaykamas lliwta rikumuchkan. Chaymanta riki lliwta apapusqanta, enterrasqankuta, velasqankuta, lliwta. Chaysi Chaymansi riki ñas iskay tutaña, kimsa tutaña.

Kimsa tutapiñas ripusqa, chay munaqnin risqa. Pero chayqa wañusqaña riki kachkaran. Risqas. Chaysi chayarunsi, nispa: "Yaw, ¿Imataq kunankamari ruwamuranki?; Kutiramusaqʹ, nispallataq rinki. ¿Pitaq wañuran wasiykipiri?" nispansi nisqa.

Chaysis, "Ama tapuwaychu kayta. Mikhunata apamuchkayki. Mikhuy kayta." Chaysi lliw pʹampanankupaq, hawallaqtapi riki waykʹunku mikhunata, aqhata ima. Chay qʹipiyusqas chayasqa chay runa, chay munaqnin. Chaysi, "Kayta mikhuy apurayta. Puririnanchikmi kunanqa. Karutan purisunchik."

Chaysi, "An, bueno hakuyá." Warmiqa mikhurunsi riki. Kaqllas purinkus, purinkus. Chaysi purichkankus hinata. Allquchas riki chaypacha riki mikhunantin suchuyuchkan. Chaysi nin allqucha, "¡Chʹiw, chʹiw, chʹiw, chʹiw!" nin nispa. "¿Imanantaq allqutari; ima nasqataq, ayqisunkiri?" Niqtinsi, pakakunsi allquchaqa.

Chayqa puririnkus. "Puri̇nanchikmi kunanqa karu. Kayqa apamunin: qullqita, kayqa, mikhuna, lliwta apamuni. Ripunanchikmi kunanqa

to walk a long way." They walked day and night, until the woman could hardly stand. Her feet were bleeding and full of blisters. The man kept driving her. "We have to walk a long way." So they kept walking and walking. They walked a long, long way.

Finally she said, "I can't go anymore. I don't have any strength left to walk. You told me that you loved me."

"It's true. That's why we're walking everywhere together." And they kept on walking.

At last, they arrived in a distant town, and found lodging. She said "I'll go in. We can sleep here. What do you think?"

He said, "No, you just sleep. I don't feel sleepy. Run on inside. If you're hungry, fix some of that food." So the woman went into the lodging.

Inside was a widow with seven children. She asked the young woman "Where are you travelling, missus?"

"I've been travelling all over the place. I left my parents' house. They didn't want me to marry my husband. So we're travelling to a far-off place. That's why I'm here," she said.

"And where's your fellow?"

"He's out there. He didn't want to come in. Could I make myself a cup of tea? I'm so thirsty from the walking. I don't have strength to walk another step."

"Sure, make yourself some." They made themselves some tea. And she took a cup out to her lover. He drank a cup, to keep up the ruse. The young woman went back inside, and the widow asked, "Aren't you all going to sleep here inside?"

"He doesn't want to. I guess we'll just sleep out there." She went back out, and there they slept.

That night, the owner of the lodging went out to see how they were doing. "Why on earth would that woman sleep out here on the bare ground? I wonder how they are. I'll go see, take a peek." She went out there with her dog. The dog started to bark. "Woof! Woof!" "What's wrong with him?" she said as she made her way. There were the two of them, sleeping face up. And while they were sleeping face up, a flame spewed from the man's mouth. Because he was dead. And the flame was going whooosh, from his mouth, when he snored, whooosh!

"Oh, how awful! What can this be? Oh, he's not a Christian. He's from the other life." She knelt down to pray. Yes, she prayed. "Oh, my goodness. How did this happen?"

The next morning, the young woman went into the lodging to "Missus, missus," she said. "Loan me your teapot, to make some herbal tea."

karutan puriysunchik", nispansi. Puriyuchkanku tuta-punchawsi. ¡Ay!, manas warmiqa yachanñachu. Chakinpis phata-phatallañas purisqanpi. Yawarpas ch´illchichkanñas. Qhariqa pusayullansi, "Karutan purisunchik", nispa. Chaysi puriyuchkan, puriyuchkanku. Hinaspansi ña karu, karutaña puriyuchkanku.

Chaysi nin: "Manaña atiniñachu. Manan kallpapas kanñachu purinaypaq". "Niwarankitaq 'Munakuykin'" nispa.

"Chayyá; kunan nuqapuwan kuskapuni purisun maykamapas", nispansi. Chaysi puriyuchkanku.

Chaysi huk llaqtaman chayasqaku. Chaypis, chaypi tarisqa huk. "Yaykuchkasqa. Haqaypi puñusaq. ¿imaynatataq khaynari?" niqtin, "Qamlla puñumuy. Manan nuqaqa puñumuymanchu. Phawayá yarqasunki, chayqa mikhunata ruwamuy", nispansi nin. Chaysi yaykun wasita.

Chaysi huk kasqa warmi, qanchis wawayuq, viuda. Chaysi, "¿May señoracha, maytan purimunki?" nispansi nin. Khaynatan purimuchkani. Mamaymantan, taytaymantan lluqsimuni. Mana munasqan qhariwan. Kunan karutaña purimuni", nispa. "Chaymi kaypi kachkani", nispan. "¿Maytaq nay, munaqniykiri?"

"Haqaypin kachkan. Manan munanchu yaykumuyta. Matichallatayá ruwayrukusaq. Ch´akiymantan purimuni. Manan kanñachu kallpaypas purinaypaq."

Chayqa, "Ruwakuyyá", nispansi nin. Chaypis ruwayuchkanku riki. Chaysi apan matita munaqninman. Chaysi tuman riki. Rikunallaqpaqchá tuman riki. Chayqa chayayunsi. Chaysis nin khaynata: "¡Ay!, ¿manachu kay ukupi puñunki?"

"Manan munanchu. Hakayllapin puñumusaqku", nispa nin. Chaysi pasanku; puñunkus.

Chaysi warmiqa tutata, chay alojakusqankupi warmi, rin qhawaq. "¿Imaynataq chay warmiri puñunmanri khayna, q´ala pampapiri? ¿Imaynataq kankuri? A ver, risaq, qhawaramusaq", nispa. Lluqsimun allquchantin. Chaysi allquqa, "¡Ch´iw, ch´iw!" nin. "¿Imanantaq kaytari?" nispansi puriyun. Chaysi iskayninku aknata puñuchkasqaku. Chaysi aknapis, aknapi puñuqtinkus, samayninpi nina lluqsisaq runamantaqa. Ñataq wañusqaña karan. Chayqa chaysi nina aknata ¡phuu! samayninpi ¡qhuu! "¡Ay, takaw! ¿Imataq kay kanmanri? ¡Ay!, kayqa manan cristianuchu. Huk vidan kayqa", nispansi nin. Chaysi kutin wasita chay warmiqa. Hinaspansi santo Cristun kan. Chaypis rezan haqayniraqta. "¡Ay!, rezayukuchkansi payqa. "¡Takaw! ¿Imataq kanman?"

Chaysi pacha paqariytaqa p´asñaqa yaykun riki. Chaysi nin: "Mantáy, mantáy", nispansi. "Mañayuway wich´ilaykita, mati ruwanaypaq."

"Go ahead. Where did you two end up sleeping?"

"Oh, down there."

"Listen, your fiancé is not of this life. He's of the other life—a condemned soul."

"What? Why do you say he's a condemned soul?"

"I saw last night. Flames were spewing from his mouth. I'm now going to tell you what to do to save yourself. I'll give you counsel. Today, you're leaving after you drink your tea, right?"

"Yes."

"And do you know why he's taking you off? So that you can ask God for forgiveness. And then he's going to eat you."

"That's terrible. Now what do I do? What advice can you give me?"

"I'm giving you this rope. I'm giving you a needle. I'm giving you a comb, and scissors. I'm giving you all this. Later today, you'll arrive at the river bank. Then and there, he won't want to cross over the river. He'll say to you 'Carry me on your back.' You should answer "I'll tie you with this rope so your feet won't slip." Then, throw the comb like this," she said, showing her how to do it.

Later on, the couple arrived in a distant town. They had really been walking. But before they'd left, the widow had said to her, "Even if he somehow gets himself untied, don't turn back around. Keep on going down the road. Don't go back. If you go back, he'll eat you. Now run along, get moving."

The young woman went. She said to her lover, "Let's go. I've made the tea. Let's drink it and go." Once again they walked and walked. As the widow had said, they arrived at a riverbank. She said "Oh, it looks like the path ends right here. We'll have to cross over."

"No, I don't want to go in the water," said the man.

The girl said "I'll carry you over. But first, I have to tie you up with this rope. I'll bind your hands and feet, so you don't fall in."

The man said "Yeah, do me like that." So she tied him up and carried him on her back.

The widow had told her that when they got in the middle of the river, she should toss him off and throw him in the water. They were crossing, and she had him on her back. When they got to the middle, she said "Oh, you're slipping, you're going to fall. Let me adjust the rope." Then she shrugged him off, boom! And threw him into the river. Then the young woman hurried on.

The condemned soul started to shout "Come back here. Now I'm going to eat you, eat you. Untie me. Now I'm going to eat you." He

Chayqa, "Ruwayyá. ¿Maypitaq puñumurankichikri?"

"Chay uraypi."

"Yaw, manan chay munaqniykiqa kay vidachu. Huk vida condenadun", ninsi.

Chaysi, "¡Ay!, ¿Imaraykun condenadun?"

"Rikuni ch´isi. Nina siminmanta phawamuchkaran. Kunanqa ninkichá salvakunaykipaqmi, kayta aconsejachkayki", nispansi. "Kunanmi pasapunkichik riki, kayta tumaspaykichik."

"Arí."

"¿Chaymanta, porque pusachkasunkiqa? Diosmanta perdon mañakunaykipaqyá. Mana Chayatiykichikqa, mikhusunkin", nispa.

Chaysi nin: "¡Ay! ¿Kunanqa imataq kanmanri? ¿Imatataq niwankiman ruwanaypaq?" nispa.

"Waskhachata qusayki. Ñaqchata qusayki. Agujatawan qusayki, tijerastawan", nispas. "Chaytan qusayki. Hinaspanmi kunan chayankichik mayup patanta. Hinas chayman, mana payqa munanqachu mayuman pasayta. 'Q´ipiway' nisunki. Hinaspa ninki: 'Manan chakiyki fastidianasunkipaqqa, watarusayki', ninki. Chaymantaqa kay ñaqchatapas khaynata ruwanki", nispansiyá yachachin.

Chaysi chhaynatas chayanku karu llaqtata riki. Chaysi puriyuchkankus chiqaqta. Chaysi nisqa, "Chaymantan kunan imaynapipas paskarukunman, imapas, chayqa amapunin kutimunkichu. Ñantaqa rillanki. Pero ama kutimunkichu. Kutimuqtiykiqa, mikhusunkin", ninsi. Chaysi chaypis, "Phawayyá, ripuy", nispansi nin.

Rinsi. Chaysi chhaynata, "Hakuyá. Kunanqa matita ruwaniña. Tumaykusun; ripusunchik", nispansi nin munaqninta. Chaysi yapamantas puririnku; purichkankus. Hinaspa chaysi chiqaqtas chayasqa huk nanman, mayup patanman. Chaysi nin: "¡Ay!, kay ñanqa kaypima tukun. Pasasunsi haqayta."

"¡Ay, manan nuqaqa yaykuymanchu!" nispansi qhariqa nin. Chaysi "Q´ipisaykichá", riki nin. Chaysi, "Bueno, waskhachawanyá watarusayki. Makiykitawan, chakiykitawan thunkurusayki, mana urmayunaykipaq." Hinaspansi niqtin: "Hinapasyá ruwaway", ninsi runaqa. Chaysi watan. Chayqa chaysi q´ipiyukun.

Chay señoraqa nisqa, chawpi mayuta pasachkaqtinku, "Wikch´uyrunkipuni, chhapchikuspayki", nispa.

Chaysi pasachkankus chhaynata riki. Aknata q´ipichkan. Chaysi chawpi mayupiqa, "¡Ay, suskhuchkankimá; urmayuchkanki! Allcharukusayki", nispansi. Aknata ¡pun! Mayuman kachayun. Chaysi pasarun warmiqa riki.

Condenaduqa qaparqachan, "Yaw, hamuy. Kunaqa mikhusayki.

shouted out her name. Her name was Emilia. "Listen Emilia, Emilia. Don't do this to me. Untie me, untie me," he shouted. The river current carried the condemned soul along, while she kept running. The footpath went along the river, and the woman kept running along it, as fast as she could. The condemned soul thrashed around so much, trying to get loose, that he ended up on an islet near the river bank on her side. Then he was able to untie his hands and feet. He started catching up to her. He said "Yes, now I'll grab you!" He was catching up, almost able to reach her.

That was when she threw down the comb. When she threw down the comb, a wall raised up. He shouted "Listen, Emilia. Why did you promise me that if I died first, I could carry you off with me, and if you died, you'd carry me off? After what we said, why are you leaving me behind?" He ran behind her, shouting.

The woman was still running along quickly. But again, he was about to catch her. So she threw down the scissors. When she threw down the scissors, a boulder, a huge one, appeared on the path. Again the woman was able to escape. He said "Come back. Now, this time, I'm going to eat you. We made a promise together. We promised one another. Now, no matter where it is, we have to go there together. Because God sent me back here." He kept after her.

She went on, and the condemned soul followed after. Then she threw down the needle. When she threw down the needle, it turned into water. He shouted "I'll catch you, I'll eat you this time." She ran and she ran, without knowing where she ran. The condemned soul couldn't cross over the river. In the place they were, there were no open fields. It was just river-cane and cold and wind they walked through.

Just then, she saw a group of men with a herd of mules who had come along with their helpers. They had four or five hundred mules, and were resting there. The woman ran up to them. "A condemned soul is pursuing me."

When she told them what had happened, the men threw their blankets over the woman to hide her. One of them said, "Which of us here is a man? Because he has to stand up to the condemned soul." The soul was coming along quickly. The men had brought liquor in some vessels. They stacked those around the woman so he wouldn't eat her. The soul started to claw at them. They acted like men, and went after him. And he gave as good as he got. The men started to lash him with their whips, and rip his flesh. "We'll save this woman. At the least, she can

Kachariway yaw. Kunanqa mikhusaykin", nispansi qaparkachan sutin-
mantas. Emilia sutin kasqa. "Yaw Emilia, Emilia. Ama ruwawaychu kayta.
Paskaway, paskaway", nispansi qaparkachayuchkan. Chaysi mayuqa
apayuchkan condenaduta. Paytaqsi pasachkan. Chaysi mayup patantas
kasqa ñanqa riki. Chaynintas purichkan warmiqa chakin. Phawaylla,
chaymansi chayan, ay ña naspa. Condenaduqa, chhayna wat´akachas-
qanpi hina. Chay laduman isla kasqa, mayup patanpi. Chayman chayan.
Chaysi paskarukun makinta, lliwta. Hinas chaysi tarpayuchkan, "¡Ay, kunanqa hap´isaykin!" Ñas tarpayuchkanña; hap´irunan kachkan.
   Chaysi wikchusqa nata ñaqch´ata. Ñaqch´ata wikch´usqtinsi, ch´anki
hatarin, ch´ankis. Chaysi qaparqachaylla, "Yaw Emiliacha. ¿Imapaqmi
niraykitaq (wañuqtiykiqa kutimusaqmi an) nuqa wañuqtiy, apasayki,
qam wañuqtiyki, apawanki? Chayraykutaq, imaraykun saqiwachkanña?"
nispansi. Ay, chaytas pasayuchkan, qaparkachayuspa riki.
   Chaykamasyá warminqa phawaylla puriyuchkan. Tarparuchkallan-
taqsi. Chaymansis nata, wikch´un tijirasta. ¡Tijirata wikch´uqtinqa,
qaqamansi tukuyun rumi, rumi! Chaytas yapamantas warmiqa puri-
yuchkallantaq riki. Hinaqtinsi, "¡Ay yaw! Kunallanyá, kunanqa mikhusaykin. Kuskan juraranchik. Juramentuta ruwaranchik. Chayqa khunanqa kuskallan maypipas kananchik", nispansi. Chaymantan Dios
kutichimuwan", ninsi. Purinsiyá.
   Chayqa chaytapis pasarunsi condenaduqa. Chaytaqa nata, agujatas
wikch´uyun. Agujata wikch´uqtinqa, unumansi turkurun. Chaypis qa-
parkachayuchkallantaq, "Hap´isaykin, mikhusaykin kunanqa", nispansi
nin. Chaymantas puriyuchkan, puriyuchkan. Chaysi chaykamas puriyuchkan riki. Manas mayuta pasayta atiyuchkanchu condenadu. Chaykama chaypis pampa manañas kanchu, imapas. Ichullawanña, chir-
illawan, wayrallawanñas puriyuchkan.
   Chaypis rikusqa nata, huk runakuna piara-piara, mulakunantin ha-
muchkaranku, askha peonnintin (*piara es*, piaraqa, pachaq mula).
Chaynintinsi tawa pichqa kasqa piara mula. Chaypis samachkasqaku.
Chaysi warmiqa achhuyun. "¡Ay, condenadun qatimuwachkan!"
   Khayna niqtinsi, lliwta chay q´ipinkunawan tapayunku warmita riki.
Hinaspansi. "¿Mayqinchá kaypi qhari? Chaymi kunan churanakunqa
kaywan." Hinaqtinsi phawayunsi condenaduqa riki, Chay (hasp´iq na)
udrikunas kasqa. Trago apananku. Chayman chaytas, chaywansinyá
p´anaparusqaku, warmita mana mikhunanpaq. Chaysi hasp´in Chaymansi qhariqa, qhari hina dalinkus. Kutipakamunsi qaqayniraqta. Ay-
chansi akna aknamansi partiyunkuraq surriaguwan waqtaspanku. "Kay

cook our meals for us. She can be of some service to us. That's why we'll save her," they said, and fought the condemned soul.

By then, he was only a pile of flesh, but still moving. They thrashed it out near the woman. The condemned soul was winning against the men. But then what did they do? They said "He's still alive. We can't kill him. So they tied him to the back legs of a mule. When they tied him to that mean, wild mule she said "Whey, whey, whey," and kicked the condemned soul. She kicked him to pieces. The mule-drivers said "Now we've broken him to pieces. Let's gather him, and with the dried horse-dung and mule-dung, we'll burn him."

So they burned his pieces, and out of that there flew a white dove. The dove said "Thank you all. I was a condemned soul. I made a promise to Emilia. 'If you die, then I'll carry you off. If I die, you carry me off.' But God sent me back here. Now you've saved me," said the white dove, and flew away.

warmitaqa salvasunchikyá, siquiera mikhuna wayk´unallanpaqpis. Serviciun kanqa, kay nuqanchikpaq. Chayraykuchá riki salvasunchik", nispansi daliyunkus.

Chaysi chay aycha muntunpas puriyuchkansi. Aknata quspayuchkan nallamantaq, chay chicap, p´asñap ladunman. "¡Ay, khaynaniraqtas!" Chaysi na runataqa vincichkanña condenadu. Chayqa, ¿imatas ruwanku? "Kachkanraqtaq. Kay mana tukukuyta atinchu." Chasyi na, chúcara mulaman watarusqaku chakinman. Chaysi chakinman wataqtinkus, chúcara mulaqa, "Whi, whi, whi!" qatinkus chay mulataqa. Hayt´ansiyá chay condenaduta. Chay ñut´uta ruwayusqa riki. Chaypiñas riki nisqa, "Kunanqa ñut´unchik, ruwanchikña; huñusunchik. Hinaspa kay mulap hip´ayninkunawan, caballup hisp´ayninkunawan muntuspa kanasunchik."

Chayqa kanayunkus riki. Chaymantas yuraq paloma lluqsimusqa. Hinaspa nisqa: "!Ay, gracias qamkunallataqchá! Condenadun karani. Juramentotan ruwarani Emiliawan. 'Qam wañunki, chayqa pusapuwanki. Nuqa wañusaq, pusapusayki.' Chaymantan Dios kutichimuwan. Kunanqa salvawankin", nispansi yuraq paloma phawaripusqa. Chayllan chay.

The River Siren

This little legend, clearly European in inspiration (a woodcutter is its protago-nist), finds its local habitation in the Willkamayu ("sacred river") that runs through the Sacred Valley of the Incas, its current sometimes mellow, sometimes wild. Seventy-two-year-old Miguel clearly had a crush on my girlish wife, and lost no opportunity to bring her up in conversation, and even to give her cameos in his stories. Here, she makes her most sustained appearance, as a mermaid who tests the honesty of a wood-cutter. Among the various attractions mentioned is her braided hair. The women in Cusco would often touch her hair, sometimes without asking. Since they themselves sported thick black braids, of which they were justifiably proud, almost vain, it was a feminine trait in my wife with which they could identify, thus making her into a familiar. Yet the strangeness of her braid's honey-blond color lent it a special fascination, and lent Miriam enough of an aura to rate incorporation into a folk tale. Her husband, on the other hand, could only be recognized, in Miguel's stories, as either "The Stupid Gringo" or the gringo who poisoned himself by mistaking inedible toads for frogs.

The River Siren

Told by Miguel Wamán

Once there was a worker with a big family. He provided for his family by cutting and gathering wood, cutting and gathering. That worker had rich relatives. They saw him, poor, but didn't help him out in any way. So he stayed that way, poor. In those conditions he had to provide for his children and his wife. Only with what he earned cutting wood. One day when he was cutting wood on the banks of the Vilcanota River, his little axe fell out of his hands, and into the Vilcanota. Oh, the poor man walked up and down crying. "Oh, father, oh mother! How will I take care of my children? Oh, my little axe, my little axe!," he cried out like a madman.

At that moment, a mermaid, a water nymph, a beautiful damsel, good-looking, with a face like your wife's, with braids, like her, came to the surface of the Vilcanota River. "My child, why are you crying?"

"Because of my axe, little siren." When he saw the damsel come out of the water, he thought that she was God. She came to the surface, beautiful and with braids, like your wife. "For no reason, little siren. Because of my axe."

The damsel disappeared into the water and by gosh, she brought out an axe of gold. "Is this your axe?"

"No, that's not my axe."

She went down in the water again and brought out an axe of silver. "Is this your axe?"

"No, that's not my axe either," he answered, crying.

Willkamayu Ninfa

Huk trabajadorsi kasqa, familla sapa. Hinaspas famillanta mantieneq llat´akusqallanwan. Hinaspas ay, famillankunapas qapaqkuna. Hinaspas wakchata rikuspas, mana proveeqkuchu, ni imawanpas. Hinalla payqa wakchakayninpi askha wawasapa mantinichkan llak´akusqallanwan wawakunata, warminta. Hinaspas llank´achkasqa riki, willkamayup patanpi llant´achata. ¿Hinaspas hachachan. . . chhulquyrukun i? Willkamayuman pasayrapun; chinkayrapun willkamayuman. ¡Ay pobre qhari wichay, uray waqyuspa purin! "¡Ay papacha, ay mamacha!, ¿imaywan wawayta mantinisaq? ¡Ay hachachalláy hachacha, ay hachacha!", waqayuspa, lucu hinaraq.

Chaysi chay sirenata, ninfa de las aguas sumaq, buenamoza dama, warmichayki hina uyayuq, anchhayna simp´ayuq; kaychallamanta lluqsiramun, marmanta, chay willkamayupi. "Hijo, ¿imamanta waqachkanki?"

"Hachaytan, mamitáy." Creesqa payqa diospaq, chay niñata lluqsiramuqtin. Warmiyki hina buenamoza, chhayna trensayuq lluqsiramuqtin. "Mamá mamitáy, mamacita. Hachachamanta."

Chinkayurunsi unuman chay dama. Hinaspas urquramun hinan karay, quri hachata. "¿Kaychu hachayki?"

"Maman hachaychu."

Kutiyurunsi. Hinaspas huk qullqi hachatañataq hinata urquramun. "¿Kaychu hachayki?"

"Manapunin hachaychu", waqayuchkallan.

One more time she went down into the water, and brought out the axe of the woodcutter. "Is this your axe?"

Oh, the woodcutter almost fell down dead dancing for joy! "My little axe, my little axe, river siren!"

"This is your reward for not being avaricious. I'm giving you this gold axe, this silver axe, and your own axe." That river siren, who looks like your wife, handed all three axes over to him.

So, he was a happy man. He returned to his house, and called his wife to him. "This is what happened to me. Don't cry any more."

One day, the hacienda owner came to him with a proposal. "What do you say?"

"My lord, sir."

"What I'm trying to say is I want to sell my hacienda."

"My lord, all I have is my gold and silver."

"Okay. So we'll trade," he said. They traded, the axe of gold for the hacienda. And so the woodcutter came to be a hacienda owner, after having been so poor.

The woodcutter had brothers, rich hacienda owners. When the woodcutter was poor, his brothers didn't give him any support and his own parents treated him like a dog. That's why he got along in such a sad way. But when he came to be a hacienda owner, his brothers said to him, "How wonderful! My brother owns a hacienda!" They went to visit him. His nephews too, started calling him "Uncle, uncle." When he was poor they hadn't called him uncle. Now that he was rich, they called him their uncle.

So, what did they do? Those boys were now young men. "What shall we do? Should we play a trick on our uncle? We won't hit him. We won't do anything to him. We'll cut off the heads of our three dogs." They killed their dogs, and brought them for his birthday. And they served him roasted dog. His brothers, to win him over, went to his birthday celebration. The brothers by now were getting along well. The boys brought the heads, paws, skin, and all to their uncle. "This is what we gave you to eat," they said. And they ran away as fast as they could, to one of the men who didn't get along with his brother. They had given their uncle dog meat to eat.

Qipata kutiyuruspas, urquramun chay huch´uy hachachanta, pay-
pata. "¿Kaychu hachayki?"

¡Ay, tususpa yaqaraq wañurun! "Hachachaymi, hachachaymi mamita."

"Kayqa respondesunki, mana ambisiosochu kasqanki. Respondesunki
kay quri hachapuwan, kay qullqi hachapuwan, kay hachachaykipuwan."
Quyqapun chay ninfa de las aguas, warmiyki anchhayna. Niña al-
cansaykanpun hachata kimsantinta.

Chayqa, hinaspa contentunña kapun. Hampun riki nata, wasinta.
Warminman willan riki. "Khayna hija pasan. Amaña waqaychu."

"¿Imatataq ruwasun?" nispa huk haciendayuq nin riki.

"Wiraqucha, papáy." Compradenraqtaq kasqa.

"Haciendaytan vendepusaq nichkani", nispas nin.

"Papáy, qurillaymi kachkan; qullqillaymi."

"Chayqa bueno, cambiasun", nispas nin. Quri hachawan cambiarunku
haciendata. Chayqa haciendayuq kapun, wakcha kachkasqanmanta,
qaqayniraq pobre kasqanmanta.

Hinaspas chay wawqinkuna kasqa, qapaqkuna, haciendayuq. Hinaspa wakcha kachkaqtin mana imatapas sostienesqakuchu; rikusqakuchu
imawanpas taytamaman. Manapuni imawanpas. Allquta hina rikusqaku.
Hinaspa khuyaylla riki mantienen. Chayqa haciendayuq kaqtinñataqsi
riki. "Añañaw, wawqichayqa haciendayuq." Watukuq rinku ah, sobri-
nonkunapas, "Tío, tío." Wakcha kachkaqtintaq mana "Tío" niranku-
chu. Kunan qapaq kaqtintaq "Tío" ninku.

Bueno, ¿imatas ruwanku? Wawankuna (chay leñadorpa) waynaku-
naña kasqa. "Imatan ruwasun? ¿Tiota joderusunchu?" nispa. "Ama
maqasunchu. Ama imanasunpaschu. Allqunchikta ñak´arusun, kimsantinta", nispas. Allquta ñak´arunku. Fiestanpaq apanku. Chayqa haciendayuq mikhuykun kankata. Chayqa hanpun wawqinqa, amistad.
Wawqintinpi sumaqta kawsachkanku qipatañataq riki. Wawakuna
apanku umanninkunata, kimsantinta, patasninta, qaranta ima. "Kaytan mikhuchirayki", nispa. Tira kutiripunku anchaynata wawqinta
sumaqta, mana allin rikuqta. Allqu aychata mikhuchinku.

An Apparition

Sara Vargas, in the way she ends this anecdote, separates herself from the "superstition" it describes. The girl's attribution of the belief to "the little Indian man" shows the ambivalence of a middle-class mestizo whose parents or grandparents might have told this same anecdote with little or no self-consciousness, let alone embarrassment. Unlike what happens in some of the other stories of apparitions in this anthology, the girl's straight-ahead Christianity tames the unknown threat of the undead, divesting it of all the linguistic ambiguity that would give it power. The attitude of some tellers makes their stories into virtual talismans.

An Apparition

Told by Sara Vargas de Mayorga

Once upon a time, a woman sent her hired girl out from town on an errand. She said, "Run out and bring me back the horse." And the girl ran off to do it. The girl was a tomboy, not at all like a girl, didn't even have the features of a girl. Nothing scared her. She flew off. Then her mistress said to her, "Okay, hustle up to the mountain field. I want you to take the horse and bring me back a bunch of ears of corn, unshucked, in the stalk. Bring it back so that tomorrow the horse will have something to eat."

"Yes, ma'am," the girl said, and hurried off to do it. She gathered fifty or sixty ears, and was bringing them back down to the village. So she was bringing them back on the horse, coming along, coming along. She hadn't used a rope to bundle the corn. Instead, she'd used fruit vines. And she was going through a gloomy pass. She got that far. All of a sudden, the horse threw all the corn to one side and down to the ground. She hadn't distributed the weight evenly. And when it fell for want of a counterweight, she said, "Oh, no! Now what am I going to do? Who's going to help me in a place like this? Whatever am I going to do?" By herself, she tied the horse to some brushy trees. "I'll fix this back," she said. So she gathered the load up, and gathered it up. As she was working, all of a sudden a woman appeared. And the girl said to the woman, "Oh, ma'am, little dove, dear heart, could you help me with this?"

When she said that, the woman answered, "What? Are you asking me

Phiru Sitiopi Rikhuriy

Huk kutinñataq huk chicachata chhaynata, namanta, huk llaqtamanta kachanchu. Hinaspa, "Phaway, aparamuy caballuta", nispa. Niqtinkuqa, chicachaqa phawaylla tiran. Qhari hinayá karan, mana warmi, warmi rasguyuqchu. Mana imatapas manchakuqchu. Tiran. Hinaspas patronanqa nin: "Phaway yaw. Qam kunan aparamunki caballuta, chuqlluyuqta, nantintawan, llapan chhalnantawan, imalla apamunki. Cargayamunki por cuanto de que paqarin caballuq mikhunanpaq", nispa.

Niqtinqa: "Bueno, mantáy", nispa, phawaylla payqa tiran. Hinaspa cargayamusqa, yaqa pichqa chunkata, u suqta chunkata. Hinas cargayamuran riki naman, caballuman. Hinas hamuchkan, hamuchkan. Manas nawanchu, lazuwanchu cargamusqa, sino tintinllawan cargamusqa. Hinas ay, na huk sitiuman phirus. Chayqa chaymansi chayan. Chaysi qunqaylla caballumanta chuqllukunaqa ladeakuyta pampaman urmamuyta. Waqllin riki. Waqlliqtinsi nin. "¡Ay!, ¿imanasaqtaq? ¿Pitaq yanapawanqa kaypiri? ¿Imatataq ruwasaqri?" nispa. Sapallan watarun nataqa ch´aphrakunaman caballutaqa. Hinaspansi. "Allchasaq", nin. Allchachkansi, allchachkansi. Hinaspas qunqaylla huk señora rikhuriramun. Hinaspa kay señorataqa, "¡Ay, señora, urpicha, corazón, yanapayuway kayta!" nispa.

Niqtinsi, señoraqa nin: "¡Ah! Nuqatataq niwanaykipaq. ¿Tiempuyuqchu kani? Nikuwaqchá riki mayupi sirenakunatapas. Paychá yanapasunkiman, paychá. ¿Imatataq nuqatari nawanki?"

"Hinatayá mamitáy, urpicha corazón. Tardiyaramuwanqa; ripunayta",

to help? Do you think I have time for this? Why don't you ask the river sirens instead? Maybe they'd help you, yes, maybe them. Whatever do you want with me?"

"Please ma'am, little dove, dear heart. It's getting late; I need to be going." At that moment, in that deep, low place, the sun began to shine brightly. The sun became blindingly bright. The sun was really shining.

"There you go," the woman said. "So, now you don't have to go ask the river sirens, since I'm helping you." Next, she made a gesture, and the load flew up on her shoulder. It flew up, and she fixed it back on the horse. She bundled it up neatly.

The girl said to herself, "What is this woman? She fixed it in an instant, without even touching it." But the girl wasn't afraid. "How could she have done that?" She said to the woman, "Thank you, ma'am, little dove, dear heart." And she went on her way. Then she looked back. She looked all around on the ground, but the woman wasn't walking. Instead, she was flying in the air. And her head was ugly, like a hag's, her hair like that of a crazy person. That's how she was.

The girl said, "Oh! What's this? Father, Son, Holy Ghost," and made the sign of the cross. "Oh! They always told me that evil spirits present themselves to bad women. To bad, evil women, to those kinds. But I don't think about those things. That's why Our Father has sent me a good spirit. And look, I wasn't even afraid. I didn't vomit up foam, get sick, or anything like that." She hurried home. But she didn't look back behind her. She was a little unsettled, and in that state she arrived at her house, see. She hastened right back. And she told her mistress all about it, saying "Listen to what happened to me."

"Oh, that's foolishness. How could a surprise like that happen? How? What are you saying?"

"Don't you remember, ma'am, what that little Indian man told us? Good spirits appear to women who have been good, ones who haven't been bad or indecent, who haven't stolen, who haven't acted wrong, who haven't lied. And this spirit turned into a good one. Yes, it seems like it turned into a good one. I think it was a demon spirit." That's what she told her. She thought she'd seen a little demon. "That demon turned into a good one," she said to the woman.

nispa nin. Chaysi actualsi, chay sitiupi chay horapi inti lliphllirichkan riki munaychata. Inti k´ancha k´ancha lliphllirichkan. Intipiqa k´anchay. "Hinatayá", nispa.

"Bueno, manataq ninkichu mayupi sirenakunata, chayqa nuqayá yanapasayki", nispa nin. Huktas nallawan, hombrollanwan, aknayun. Aknayaruqtinsi naqa, iman cargaqa listo. Munaychata cargarakapun. Hinaspa: "¡Ay!, ¿imataq kay señoraqa? Ratuchalla, ni llamiyunpaschu", nispa. Manas, manas mancharikunchu. "¿Imanaqtintaq khaynata ruwarun?" Hinaspas: "Gracias mamitáy, urpíy sunqucháy", nispas nisqa. Hinaspa pasamun. Hinamansi qhawarun. Urayta qhawaruqtin, qhawayrukurin, manas chay señoraqa purinchu; sinoqa (este, ima), altullantas phawachkan. Hinaspas millay umanpas, t´ampa, millay, locakunap hinas, chukchampas. Haqayna kasqa.

Chayraqsi, "¡Ay!, ¿imataq kayri? Padre, hijo, espíritu santo", nispa cruzchayukun. Hinaspa nin: "¡Ay¡, nirantaq, willawankutaq, espírito malignukunaqa presentakun millay warmikunapaq. Millay khuchikunapaq, chaykunallapaqmi. Mana nuqaqa chaypi pinsanichu. Chaymi nuqaqa mana mancharikullanipaschu", nispa. "Ni maytaq aqtupakuchkanichu, ni imatapas, ni phusuqutapas, ni imatapas", nispas. Phawaylla pasan. Pero manañas ni qipantapas qhawarikunñachu. Mancharisqa hinas, rezaspallas, llaqtamanqa chayaramun, ¿ih? Chayaramunsi apuraysi. Hinas. "Mantáy, kaymi pasawan", nispa willakun.

"¡Ah, sonceras! ¿imataq chaykunari kanman, chay maytaq manchana? ¿Imataq? ¿Imanasunki?", nispas nin.

"Manan, mantáy. Willawaranchiktaq chay indiuchaqa. Espíritu buenokunaqa presentakun allin, mana ima millay khuchi, mana imapi, mana suwapaq, mana chay millay, mana llullakunapaq. Lliw allinmanmi tukupun. Niranku. Chayqa allinmanchá riki tukurapun. Saqrachá riki karan", nispas willakun, ¿ih? Chayqa, saqrallapi payqa pensayuchkan. "Chay saqraqa allinmanmi tukupun", niqpuni riki, nispayá willakun riki. Chayllapi tukupun.

Child Jesus, Yarn Spinner

The pun in this title is intended. Spinning yarn to make wool, and telling tales, are two primary activities for those Quechua-speakers still somewhat based in agrarian ways. Maria Laura Ugarte learned this story from her grandmother when she used to visit her often in Ollantaytambo. I find this narrative especially appealing since so much of the copious Christ-focused iconography in Cusco lugubriously emphasizes his crucifixion and martyrish qualities: a bleeding head pierced with the crown of thorns, the stigmata. "Child Jesus, Yarn Spinner," though it has its distressing moments once the parents are on the scene, shows us not only the Jesus who said "Suffer the little children to come unto me," but Jesus himself as a child. He is irreverent and playful, offering a child-like "miracle" not easy to forget.

Child Jesus, Yarn Spinner

Told by María Laura Ugarte

I'm going to tell you a story about something that happened in the town of Ollantaytambo. This story is from the days of the Child Jesus.

A little boy named Kasimiro lived in Ollantaytambo, with his parents. Every day, at sunrise, he went to a pasture to graze the sheep and the cattle. And every day his mother gave him wool to spin, for ponchos, so she could weave ponchos. And every day, at sunset, the boy returned to the house with his dog.

One day, the boy was doing his work, by himself, when a child wearing a beautiful embroidered poncho appeared. "Little Kasimiro, Little Kasimiro," he said. "Don't you want to come play?"

The boy answered, "I can't play, child. My mother would hit me for sure. I have a lot to do. I have to spin this yarn, and stretch it."

"Please, come play with me. Later, in the afternoon, I'll help you so you can go back to your house."

"No, child, I can't. I can't play with you. My mother will beat me. When I don't do my work well, you can't believe how she beats me."

"Please, play with me." At last, the boy let himself be persuaded, and went to play with the child. They began to play. They began to run among the sheep, and played all sorts of games. The boy forgot about his work.

At sunset, around about five or six in the afternoon, the boy remembered his work, and said, "Oh, little child! Now what will I do? My mother is going to hit me plenty. I'll run away somewhere. I can't go

Niño Jesus, Puchkaq

Willasayki huk cuentuta. Ollantaytambo llaqtapi pasasqanta; kay willakuyqa kachkan niño Jesuspa p´unchawninkuna willakuypi.

Huk chicucha Casimiro sutiyuq tiyaran Ollamtaytambopi, hinaspa taytamamanwan. Pero chay chicuchaqa sapa punchaw, sapa inti paqariq punchaw naq, riq uywa michiq; uvijan wakankuna michiq, q´achu pampaman. Mamitantaqmi sapa púnchaw quq ruwananpaq millma (t´isananpaq utaq) puchkanapaq pumchukunapaq; pumchu mamita awananpaq. Hinaspa sapa inti yaykuytataq kutiyapuq chicucha allquchakunantin. Sapa púnchaw chayta ruwaq.

Hinaspa huk p´unchaw kay chicucha (pukllachkaran sapallan na) ruwachkaran ruwanankunta sapallan. Chayñataq huk munay pallay pumchuchayuq niñucha rikhurin chaypi. Hinaspa nin: "Casimirocha, Casimirocha. ¿Hakuchu pukllachkasun?"

Chicuchaqa nin: "Manan niñucha pukllaymanchu. Mamitaychá waqtawanman. Ruwanaymi askha kachkan. Khaynata puchkanay; chaymanta millma t´isanay."

"Ama hina pukllachkasun. Hinaspa nuqa tardiman inti yaykuyta pasapunaykipaq yanapasayki."

"Mana niñucha, manakaw manapunin pukllaymanchu qamwanqa. Sasachá mamaypas maqakuwanman. Khuyayta maqawan mamitáy, manan allinta ruwanayta ruwaqtiy."

"Ama hinata pukllakusun." Chayqa niñuchaqa rinsis niñuchata, kasuspataqsi chicuchaqa pukllan. Pukllayta qallarinku. Imaynapi,

back to my house, because then my mother will beat me. My mother might even kill me for not having done my work. Look, I haven't done anything."

"Don't fret. I'll help you."

"How could you help me, child? What do you know how to do? It isn't as if you knew how to smooth out yarn, or spin it. How are we, in so little time, going to do what I should have done the whole day long?"

"Don't fret. I'll help you." The child said to the boy, "I'm going to feed the wool to one of the sheep. Then you'll pull it out of her behind and roll it into a ball."

"What makes you think a sheep would eat wool, child? Never. They only eat grass."

"I know what I'm doing. Just do what I say." So the child caught hold of a sheep, and began to feed it wool. The boy pulled spun wool from its behind, as fast as he could, and rolled it into a ball. In that way, they finished it all, to the last little piece.

When they'd finished the task, the boy returned content to his house and said to his mother, "I'm back, mama."

"And you shut all the animals in their pens?"

"Yes, mama, I shut all the animals in their pens."

"And you finished your work?"

"Yes, mama."

"Let's see. Show me." The boy showed her.

"Wow, you've done very well today. You've never spun it like this. You've never spun such beautiful wool. Who helped you do this?"

"Nobody helped me, mama. I did it by myself."

"You didn't do this. I know, because every other day you show me what you did. This isn't your work. I know somebody else did this, while you played. You gave it to somebody else, to do it for you. And I'll bet you paid him a sheep for the help you asked for."

"No, mama. I did it." Another day, the boy went back to the same place. Every day, the two children played with the same zeal.

One day, the mother of the boy was conversing with her husband, and said to him, "It isn't possible that the boy is doing this himself. This is difficult work. I believe another person is doing it for him. And for all we know, he's giving sheep to someone for the help he asks. Because this wool is gorgeous. He couldn't stretch it and spin it so well."

Her husband answered, "Yeah, I think you may be right. That must be what the boy is doing. What do you say we spy on him to see what's

phawakachayta qallarinku uvijakunawan kuska. Chayqa chicuchaqa qunqarapusqa ruwanantaqa.

Inti yaykuyta chay, las cincuchu, las seis horasta, ña chay yuyarinsi ruwananta. Chaysis nin: "¡Ay!, ¿niñucha imanaykusaqtaq kunanri? Mamaychá kunanqa suq´aywanqa. Maytapas ripusaq. Manan kunan kutiymanñachu wasiytaqa, porque mamaymi nisyuta maqawanman. Sipirullawanqañachá mamáy mana ruwasqaymanta. Khaynata mana imatapas ruwanichu."

"Ama llakikuychu. Nuqa yanapasqayki."

"¿Imaynatataq qamri niñucha yanapawankiman? ¿Ima ruway yachasqaykita? ¿Qamri yachawaqchus millma t´isayta utaq puchkaytapas? Imatapas kay ratuchallapichus puchkayurusunman p´unchawnintin ruwanayta."

"Ama llakikuychu. Nuqa yanapasayki. Chaysis niñuchaqa nin chicuchata. "Nuqa mikhuchimusaq millmata uvijaman. Qamtaqmi sikinmanta kururamunki."

Chaysis, chicuchaqa, "¿Imaynataq mikhunmanri uvijari millmata niñucha? Manan hayk´aqpis, q´achullatamá payqa, paykunaqa mikhun."

"Manan, nuqan yachani ruwasqayta. Qamqa kasukullay, nisqayta." Chaysi, niñuchaqa mikhuyta qallarichin, uvijata hap´ispa mikhurachin. Chicuchataqsi sikinmanta kururayuchkan apuraylla. Chaysi, tukurunsi llapantaqa, llapanta.

Chay llapanta, chay chicuchaqa kusisqa siqayapun wasinta. Chasis mamitanman nin, "Ñan kutimuniña mamá."

"¿Ñachu allintaña wisq´amunki uywakunata?"

"Arí mamitáy, ñan uywakunata."

"¿Chay ruwanaykita tukumurankichu?"

"Arí mamitáy."

"A ver, qhawachimuway." Chaysi chicuchaqa qhawachin. "Yaw allintamá ruwaramusqanki kunanqa. ¿Hayk´aqmanta hinataq khaynatari ruwaramuranki? Manataq hayk´aqpas khayna sumaqtaqa puchkamurankichu. ¿Piwanchá qamqa yanapachikamuchkanki?"

"Mana mamitáy piwanpas yanapachikamunichu. Sapallaymi ruwami."

"Manan kayqa ruwasqaykichu. Qam a ver qhawachisqayki qaynin p´unchawkuna ruwasqaykita. Manan kayqa qampa ruwasqaykichu. Huk pipunichá kaytaqa ruwamuchkan. Qamchá pukllayuchkanki. Chayllamantaq hukwan ruwachimuchkanki. Uvijata imapaschá quchkanki ruwachinayki rayku."

"Manan mamáy. Nuqan ruwani." Chaysis, chicuchaqa hukkaq p´un-

up?" So they followed behind the boy. They went to spy on him at midday. The boy was there playing with a child. "You see? Look at them playing. But I wonder who's doing the spinning for him. Anyway, now I know I'm going to kill that boy. I'm going to beat him silly. I'm going to hang him up," said the husband.

The boy realized that they were looking at him, and said, "Oh, my mama, my mother has been looking at me from over there!" But the mother went off, as if she had been passing by and hadn't seen.

"Your mama is going away. Let's go on playing." So they played. When the sun began to set, they went to work. Again they gave the sheep wool to eat.

But his mother was spying on him from one extreme of the pasture. She said to her husband, "Look what they're doing. How do they do it? How can they give a sheep wool to eat? Then they pull the spun wool out of its behind and roll it into a ball. How can that be?" The two remained watching, astonished.

The boy said, "They've seen. Oh, my mama was over there spying on me! Now what will we do?" The parents ran to grab hold of Kasimiro and the other boy. But the child, at that instant, disappeared. He wasn't there anymore. He'd turned to nothing.

The parents said, "What is this? What can it be? He's not here anymore. The child was right here, running around and playing, and from one minute to the next, he disappeared. How? And where has he escaped to? There are no mountains around here, or anything. There's nothing but a pasture here." Another day the parents followed their son. "Sooner or later we're going to get hold of that child. And whose is he? We've never seen anyone like that child. He has such a beautiful face."

One day they made ready to catch him. And at last, they caught the child. They locked him up in the church of Ollantaytambo. But one afternoon the child escaped. Today the child is in Ollantaytambo, tied down by one little foot, shining like gold. There you'll find the child, in the church of the town of Ollantaytambo.

chawmanqa yapamanta kutillantaq. Sapa p´unchawsi chay afan pukl-lanankupaq.

Chayqa huk p´unchaw maman nisqa "Manan kay warmachaqa", qu-santa nisqa rimapayasqa, "Manan kay warmachaqa paychu ruwanman karqan. Kaytaqa sasan. Hukwanchá ruwachimuchkan. Uvijatachá pi-manpas regalachkan ruwachinanrayku. Porque khayna sumaq-tañataqchus. Pay millmata t´isaspa puchkanman."

Chaysis papanqa taytanqa nin: "Arí yaw, chiqaqpas; kay warmachaqa chaytapunin ruwamuchkan. ¿Hakuchu qatiparusunsi?" Chaysis qati-panku chicuchataqa. Chicuchataqa qatipaqtinkus, chay chawpi p´un-chawta imas qatipanku. Chayqa chicuchaqa pukllayuchkansis chaypi huk warmachawan. "¿Rikunkichu? A ver chhaynata pukllayuchkan-chayá riki. ¿Piwanchá kunan pichá puchkayachichkan? Khunanqa sipirullachkaqña, kay warmachataqa. Q´asuyusaqchá; warkullasaqña-chá", nin qusanqa.

Chaysis chicuchaqa rikurakamun. Rikuramuspa nin: "¡Ay, mamáy mamaymi haqaypi qhawamuwachkasqa!" nispa. Chaysis pasaq hina ma-manqa, mana rikuq hina pasakapullan.

Chayqá, "Pasapuchkanña mamitaykiqa. Haku pukllachkallasun", niñuchaqa nin.

Chaysis "¿May mamáy yapamanta kutiramunqa chayrí?"

"Manan kutimunqañachu. Haku pukllachkallasun." Chayqa pu-kllankus. Chay inti yaykuy horastaqa yastá. Yapamanta mikhuyachichka-llankutaq uvijata millmata.

Chay mamanqa huk ladumanta ñataq qhawamuchkasqa. Chaysis "Qhawariy haqay ruwasqankuta. ¿Imaynata haqayta ruwanku? ¿Imay-natan uvijaman millmata mikhuchichkanku? Chaymantataq sikin-mantataqmá riki millmataqa kururamuchkanku. ¿Imaynataq chayri kanman?" nispa, mancharikuspa paykunaqa qhawallanku riki.

Chaysis nin chicuchaqa: "Rikurakamun. ¡Ay, mamitáy qhawayamu-wachkasqa ¿Imanasuntaq kunanri?" Mama-taytasis phawamun chicucha Casimirucha hap´inankupaq. Pero niñuchaqa chinkarapusqa chay rat-ullapi. Mana karapusqachu. Ch´usaqman tukurapusqa.

Chaysis "¿Imantaqri, imataq kayri kanman? Manatáq karapunchu. Kayllapitáq muyuchkaran pukllachkaran niñuchaqa. Manatáq kara-punchuqá. ¿Imaynapitaq, maytatq siqayrapunmanri? Manatáq urqupas ni imapas kanchú. Pampallatáq kayqa kachkan." Chaysis yapamanta qati-pallankutaq huk p´unchawmanqa. "Niñuchata, hap´irusunpuni kay niñuchataqa. ¿Pipunin kanman? ¿Piqpachá? Manan kayqa manan hayk´aqpas rikuranchikchu, khayna niñuchata haqay hinataq. Sumaq uy-

achantin kachkan." Chaypis huk p´unchawqa hap´inankupaq alis-
takusqaku. Chaysis hap´irapusqakupuni niñuchataqa. Chayqa hap´irus-
paqa wisq´arapusqaku Ollantaytambo iglesiapi. Chay yapamantas tardinta
hukaq kaq p´unchawman escapamusqataq niñuchaqa. Chhayna yapamanta yapa-yapamanta escapamusqa. Kunanqa chay niñuchaqa Ollantaytambopi kachkan; huk quri grilluswan chakichanmanta watasqa.
Chaypi kachkan chay niñucha Ollantaytambopi llaqtapi, iglesiapi.